Compliments of the

Fort Worth Star-Telegram

DATE DUE	BORROWER'S NAME	ROOM NUMBER

STARS & STRIFE

Inside The Dallas Cowboys' Reemergence as America's Team

STARS & STRIFE

Inside The Dallas Cowboys' Reemergence as America's Team

MIKE FISHER

THE SUMMIT GROUP
FORT WORTH, TEXAS

Published by The Summit Group
1227 West Magnolia
Fort Worth, Texas 76104

Copyright 1993 by The Summit Group

Publisher's Cataloging in Publication
(Prepared by Quality Books Inc.)

Fisher, Mike, 1959-
    Stars and strife : inside the Dallas Cowboys'
reemergence as America's team / by Mike Fisher.
        p. cm.
        ISBN   1-56530-064-5

        1. Dallas Cowboys (Football team)--History.
I. Title. II. Title: Inside the Dallas Cowboys'
reemergence as America's Team.

GV956.D3F47 1993   796.332'64097642821
                     QBI93-677

Jacket design by Becky Flanders/Cheryl Corbitt
Page design by Troy B. Reese

— For Kelli, my love
everlasting

CONTENTS

★

FOREWORD

There are few stories more compelling in the world of sports than this one about how the Dallas Cowboys went from 1-15 in 1989 to Super Bowl XXVII champions four years later. This is true in part because so much about the Dallas Cowboys has always been so compelling.

The Cowboys are to football what the New York Yankees are to baseball. Because of people like Tom Landry, Tex Schramm, Bob Lilly, Don Meredith, Don Perkins, Chuck Howley, Mel Renfro, Roger Staubach, Lee Roy Jordan and many others, there is a rich tradition of greatness here. I am proud the Cowboys have returned to the pinnacle of football, where they have always belonged.

I am also pleased that the challenge of recording the climb of the Cowboys was taken on by Mike Fisher. He knows how things work around Valley Ranch, and he knows how to write about it.

With this book, Mike has done something akin to what we've done with the Dallas Cowboys: he's built a champion.

Jerry Jones
Owner/General Manager, Dallas Cowboys

ACKNOWLEDGMENTS

This book is by no means an "authorized account" of the building of the 1992 world champion Dallas Cowboys. Which means, to the chagrin of some of its subjects, it is not a sanitized account. But it nevertheless was written with the cooperation and contributions of many people inside the Cowboys organization.

My thanks to Jerry Jones and Jimmy Johnson, two flesh-and-blood characters more intriguing than any fiction writer could dream up; to so many present and former Cowboys players, coaches and staffers, for allowing me insight into how they do their work and live their lives;

To the people at the Summit Group, for their support, and the people at the *Fort Worth Star-Telegram*, who have always been generous concerning any project I've involved myself in;

To my co-worker, Richie Whitt, who helps make covering the Cowboys an enjoyable experience;

And most of all, to Kelli, Nathan and Anthony, who help make life a wonderful experience.

1   AIKMANIA   ★

Here lies the Almighty Aikman.

Hours removed from what he calls "the greatest moment in my life," two blocks away from a Dallas Cowboys' post-Super Bowl XXVII victory party, seemingly a phone call away from his parents or his teammates or a president or a king or anyone else he'd like to befriend now that he is A Football Hero, Troy Aikman was alone in Room 226 of the Loews Santa Monica Hotel, reclining on his bed, punching the phone number for room service.

"A twelve-pack of beer to Room 226, please," said the Super Bowl Most Valuable Player, destined to spend this night of all nights feeling as empty as those beer cans ended up being.

Earlier, a few minutes before midnight on January 31, 1993, Aikman decided against spending much time across the street at the Santa Monica Civic Center, where team owner Jerry Jones was hosting a lavish party. Though Aikman's family and friends and many of his Cowboys teammates were over there, a lengthy stay would have meant being confined in a suit, and it would have meant being confined by autograph-demanders. "I kind of wanted to be with people I knew," he says. "There

1

were a bunch of strangers there, and it got to be a big ol' free-for-all." Instead, Aikman placed a handful of phone calls to other extensions in the hotel. No answers.

He recognized the voice of backup quarterback Steve Beuerlein three doors down, and figured that might be the place for a quiet celebration. It was one of Aikman's few postseason miscalculations.

Aikman walked in. Beuerlein was slapping on some cologne. A few other people he didn't know were watching television. And a very attractive young woman was staging a solo performance, playfully bouncing up and down on the bed. The trampoline lady looked familiar. It was Tanya Tucker, the singer and a friend of Aikman's, who was in the mood to party till (Delta) Dawn.

Something about the atmosphere suggested Tucker was destined to be Beuerlein's escort for the night. But Tucker jokingly suggested Aikman owed her one for not agreeing to be her escort five nights before.

Tanya, berating Aikman for not loaning her his arm at the American Music Awards in Los Angeles, became unrelenting. Beuerlein, concerned this Country-and-Western beauty might decide to not stand by her man, became unhappy. Aikman, who, God bless him, just wanted to share some of his half-case of beers with somebody, became uncomfortable. And with thoughts of a *National Enquirer* headline forming in his mind — "TWO COWBOY QBs JOIN TANYA TUCKER IN A REAL COUNTRY SWING!" or "AIKMAN AND BEUERLEIN BRAWL OVER BABE" — Aikman escaped back to the loneliness of Room 226.

"Here's the weird thing," Aikman says. "I had tons of friends out there to watch the game. But the problem was I had so many people in town, everybody thought I'd already be busy. So nobody wanted to bother me. They all made plans of their own. What's that they say about it being lonely at the top?"

Aikman acquaintances had tried to prepare him for bitter-sweet moments like these, for the times when triumph would be trying. On the one hand, he had much to savor. He had just been the ultimate player in the ultimate game. His Cowboys had just beaten the Buffalo Bills 52-17. The Cowboys, who only four years ago staged a tragicomedy every Sunday under what at the time was judged the misguided leadership of a buffoon-ish back-water rookie owner, an arrogant pop-psychologist rookie coach and a poorly prepared, self-doubting rookie quarterback, had needed only four years to become an over-night success.

"We can all look back now and swear we knew someday we'd win," Aikman says. "But realistically, think of how bad we were in 1989. You had to go through it to understand what hell that was. And I don't just mean our 1-15 record. I mean everything about our entire organization: the players, the coaches, everything. To predict the 1992 Cowboys were des-tined to be the Super Bowl champions would have sounded really stupid."

"Destiny" is the wrong word. It cheats the winner and cheapens the feat. It makes the Cowboys' rise sound as simple as their Super Bowl victory looked. Aikman, playing in the Rose Bowl where he'd starred at UCLA, threw four touchdown passes. It all happened with such ease that coach Jimmy Johnson — who only a few months before had finally settled on a symbiotic relationship with his quarterback — actually found time to make a request of the assistants in the press box.

"What's the record?" Johnson asked into his headset, try-ing to confirm that Joe Montana's five TD throws in a Super Bowl is the top mark. "Let's get Troy the record."

Aikman completed 22 of 30 passes for 273 yards and the four scores while being complemented by the excellence of his offensive mates. Running back Emmitt Smith, often guided by rest-in-pieces blocks from fullback Daryl Johnston, darted 22 times for 108 yards and added a 10-yard touchdown run. Receivers Michael Irvin, Jay Novacek and Alvin Harper took turns shining, combining for 14 receptions and 231 yards. Irvin caught two TD throws, Novacek scored once, and Harper snared a deep pass from Aikman and punctuated the offense's day by dunking the ball, basketball-style, over the crossbar. The offensive line manhandled the front-seven standouts of the Bills defense; end Bruce Smith and linebackers Cornelius Bennett, Shane Conlan and Darryl Talley. The line permitted one meaningless sack of Aikman, who retired with his touchdown passes of 23, 19, 18 and 45 yards in favor of Beuerlein.

"You never in a million years think about scoring 52 points in a Super Bowl," offensive coordinator Norv Turner said.

Unless your defense manufactures a Super Bowl-record nine turnovers, that is. The Cowboys defense, building all season long for the chance to prove its No. 1 statistical ranking was no fluke, forced what Johnson called "a feeding frenzy." Three of the steals set up offensive touchdowns. Two others were returned for touchdowns. Still another, a fumble scooped up by six-foot-six, 295-pound defensive tackle Leon Lett, should have been good for a score. But Lett traveled 64 yards with the ball before allowing it to be slapped away by Buffalo's Don Beebe at the three-yard line. Lett's problem? By trying to showboat his way into the end zone, he prematurely joined the celebration being led by Aikman on the sideline.

About the time Lett was becoming blooper-reel history, Aikman tried to savor the historic implications of his own accomplishments. In play-off victories over the Philadelphia Eagles, San Francisco 49ers and now the Bills, his team had scored 34, 30 and 52 points. He'd attempted 89 postseason passes, completing 61 for 795 yards. Eight of those throws went for touchdowns. None of those throws went for interceptions. As a rookie in 1989, Aikman's quarterback rating was 55.7. His 1992 postseason rating of 116.7 is the finest in NFL history.

"As good as a quarterback gets," Turner says.

Aikman donned his white Logo Athletics cap — the National Football League (NFL) hates that, because the suits in the New York office believe their endorsement contract with him supersedes his deal with Logo Athletics — and he tried to add up his numbers. But his math was interrupted by the crew from Disney Productions, who reminded him that he was contractually obligated to do a few seconds of performing in exchange for the $50,000 they were prepared to pay him.

"I'm going to Disneyland!" he screamed on cue, thus earning $7,142.85 per syllable.

"I'm going to Disney World!" he screamed on another take, willing to work the unpaid overtime because he hadn't decided if he'd rather squeeze a trip to Anaheim or Orlando into his off-season itinerary.

Aikmania.

All of this was The Dream, he reminded himself. This is what he always wanted. Blossom into a big-time athlete, into a world of million-dollar contracts, of television commercials, of being secure enough to turn down dates with starlets like Tucker and Janine Turner, the headliner on TV's "Northern Exposure." Before the age of twelve, when his family moved from southern California to Henryetta, Oklahoma (population 6,000), Aikman practiced crossing the T's and A's of an autograph he thought might be a baseball collectible. In fact, he might be a New York Mets catcher today had he not guilelessly turned off the Mets scout who wanted to draft him out of Henryetta High by casually suggesting he'd want a $200,000 signing bonus. "I didn't know if that was high or low," says Aikman, the old Henryetta Fighting Hen. "I had no concept."

Once Aikman moved to Henryetta, it was clear football would be an option. For one thing, that's the game the region adored. (When he decided to attend the University of Oklahoma, where he started his college career before transferring to UCLA and away from coach Barry Switzer, "It was like a state holiday had been declared there," a friend says.) For another thing, it's the game his jerky-tough father, Ken, adored. And Troy Kenneth Aikman, loathe as he is to admit it, undergoes many of his occupational hazards to impress his pipeline-laying, Marlboro Man-looking dad.

"I liked football, too," Troy says. "But my father signed me up for it. He liked the roughness of it all."

Like father, like son. Troy Aikman also enjoys the ruggedness of the sport that before 1992, caused him to miss starting twelve of his team's fifty games. At times in his four years in Dallas, Aikman's stubborn insistence on proving himself was a masochistic fault. His desire to demonstrate he was worth his six-year, $11.037 million contract, his passion for making the big play and his willingness to recklessly subject his six-foot-four, 225-pound frame to abuse combined to create flaws that suddenly disappeared when his supporting cast became passable. Still, there is that indelible 1989 image of the unsightly collision with the Phoenix Cardinals' Anthony Bell. Aikman was a rookie, so he was already wet enough behind both ears when the Bell blast left him with blood squirting from one of them. And there is that 1990 image of Aikman's season, and the Cowboys' play-off prospects, being crushed when the Philadelphia Eagles' Clyde Simmons separated Aikman's shoulder. And that 1991 image of two Washington Redskins transforming his right leg into an accordion, thereby effectively killing his chances to contribute when Dallas did qualify for the play-offs.

"There were times," says Aikman's mom, Charlyn, "when I looked back there just to make sure he was still alive. And there were other times when I didn't look back there at all."

Looking back. The 1989 roster featured bigger holes than the one in the Texas Stadium ceiling. "We were a joke from top to bottom," says tackle Mark Tuinei. That first new-regime team did one thing consistently, losing fifteen times in sixteen tries. In opening the season with eight straight losses, Dallas allowed the opponent twenty-seven points or more seven times. The Cowboys scored ten points or fewer seven times. Paul Palmer was the rushing leader. Their points leader, Roger Ruzek, didn't score often enough to be ranked against his NFL kicking contemporaries. Dubious club records were established: an average of 12.7 points per game; most first downs allowed in a season; the franchise had been shut out twice in its first twenty-nine years, but was blanked three times in 1989.

Johnson installed in this wobbly, nascent structure "the revolving door," and tried lineups that produced forty-one starting players, but precious few starting-caliber players. "You'd look up in the huddle," says offensive lineman Kevin Gogan, "and almost use up the time just introducing yourself to all the new faces."

"We shouldn't have even bothered to take a team picture," defensive coordinator Dave Wannstedt says.

Those Cowboys had nothing better to do than clash — with the opponents, and one another. In his first spring mini-camp, Johnson launched into one player, free agent kicker Massimo Manca, because of his failure to run wind sprints. Manca explained to the coach that he suffered from asthma. "Asthma my ass!" screamed Johnson. "The asthma field is over there." Linebacker Steve DeOssie didn't hang around long after he engaged defensive coordinator Dave Wannstedt in a screaming match. Cornerback Everson Walls sealed his fate when he did the same with Johnson. "People got sick of getting beat on by other teams," Wannstedt says. "They had to lash out at somebody once in a while."

On Thanksgiving Day 1989, Aikman was a centerpiece of "The Bounty Bowl," when Johnson accused Philadelphia Eagles coach Buddy Ryan of putting a price on the heads of some Cowboys. Eliminating Aikman from the game would draw $500. Kicker Luis Zendejas was worth $200. There was a melee or five on the field. And there was a catty conflict that still simmers today between Johnson (labeled "High School Charlie" by Ryan) and Ryan ("senile" to Johnson). Cowboys haters were delighted by it all. Even ex-coach Tom Landry, always available when the media asked him to second-guess a boneheaded move made by country-come-to-city bumpkins Jones and Johnson, might have cracked a detectable smile or two.

"We were the punch line of every joke," says defensive end Jim Jeffcoat.

Despite the fact that he arrived in Dallas as one of the Cowboys' few marquee players, Aikman has always thought of himself as one of the "grunts," an offensive lineman who's mistakenly been issued a single-digit jersey. He attempts to perceive himself as being no different than Mark Stepnoski, Kevin Gogan or Dale Hellestrae, the linemen he hangs out with. He likes to prop a foot on a rail of the fence that surrounds the 400-acre Aikman family ranch north of Dallas and talk live-stock with his father and former Cowboys defensive tackle Randy White, who owns the property next door. "A can of beer and a fence between 'em, and those men solve the problems of the world," says Aikman's personal manager and family friend, Verna Riddles.

But this is no grunt. This is no ranch hand. This is a silver-and-blue-chip superstar who was destined to be just that long before Super Bowl XXVII. "Troy came to Dallas at a time when it needed a hero," Johnson says. "And along comes this good-looking, single, All-American quarterback with a bit of Southern gentleman in him. He fit the mold."

April 20, 1989, when Aikman signed as the first overall player taken in the college draft, was just his christening. It was back on November 21, 1966, when Aikman was born to be America's Quarterback. "He has charisma," says Roger Staubach, the former Cowboys quarterback whose legend Aikman is pursuing.

Says Dallas receiver Michael Irvin: "He's only a baby, and he's already got it all. I laugh my ass off when I hear people criticize him. Every time I heard someone rip Troy, I marked that person off my list as far as thinking they knew anything about football. I wouldn't trade Troy for any quarterback in the game."

In 1989, when Jerry Jones could be counted on to verbally stumble into laughable trouble, he tried to explain Aikman's appeal to ABC-TV's Sam Donaldson in a nationally televised news interview. "Troy looks good in the shower," Jones said. The remark resulted in a great deal of embarrassment for Jones. And a bit for Aikman, too. "I've still never seen that interview," Aikman says. "I wasn't bothered by what Jerry said. But the guys on the team gave me a hard time, and of course, the media ran with it because they were looking to pounce on everything he said. But anyone who was watching that show objectively knew what he meant."

Which was that, homophobia aside, Aikman does look good in the shower.

"He is perfect," said Aikman's agent, Leigh Steinberg, "in the sense that every man wants to be like him and every woman wants to be with him."

Within hours of the end of Super Bowl XXVII, the world became aware of the fact that Aikman had "It." "Good Morning

9

America" knew. They wanted him on at 3:30 a.m., which meant Aikman might as well not even sleep. He had another beer. "Today" knew, and they needed him on at 4:09 a.m. No time for sleep. He had another beer. Aikman did the Most Valuable Player (MVP) press conference once the sun rose, did radio interviews by phone all day long and did "The Tonight Show" with Jay Leno once the sun set.

In March, *People* magazine came to Dallas for a photo shoot and an interview. Aikman was one of their choices for "50 Most Beautiful People."

The Super Bowl acts as cosmetic surgery. This was The Dream.

"Troy always played football like he had something to prove to somebody," Ken Aikman says. And now he'd proven plenty. There was a time when criticism was like a garbage man in reverse, pulling up the Aikman driveway to dump off fresh trash on a weekly basis. What he accomplished as an all-American at UCLA (a 20-4 record in his junior and senior years, wins in the Aloha Bowl and the Cotton Bowl, the third-best passing numbers in NCAA history) wasn't near enough for a public that craved nothing less than Staubach, Jr. Was Aikman a deep thrower? Was he a deep thinker? Was he mobile enough? Or did he take off and run too often? Did he lack leadership skills? Or did he yell at his teammates too much?

"I laugh at the criticism now," Aikman says.

Back in Henryetta, folks were joining in the last laugh. Kids were stealing the street signs that designated Aikman Avenue. Folks were polishing up the "Home of Troy Aikman" markings positioned at the city limits. Workers were putting the finishing touches on an athletic facility funded by the quarterback. The city fathers were preparing to honor Aikman as the Henryettan of the Year in a March 6, 1993, ceremony and parade he made sure to sandwich into a two-week period that included business trips to Germany, Oklahoma City, San Francisco and Washington.

"Henryetta is poor," Aikman says. "There are people there who think that just because they're from a small town, they can't accomplish things. Henryetta is in desperate need of something."

Now it had something. And any other Cowboys fan in the world who thought Dallas had forever run out of America's Steam had something. Something that Aikman and most of the Cowboys didn't even dare try to envision four years ago.

Even once these young Cowboys had pushed that 1-15 season behind them, they were reluctant to bother trying to envision a Super Bowl appearance. Johnson's annual preseason predictions of prosperity were considered by many players to be motivational mumbo-jumbo.

Before the start of the 1990 season, Johnson announced, "I don't think it's wise to put it in numbers. But I'd be severely disappointed if we didn't win more than we lost. I don't judge if it's realistic. I just know how I am." Dallas finished 7-9, and might have fulfilled Johnson's prophecy had Aikman not been erased from the picture in Week Fifteen in Philadelphia.

On the opening day of 1991 training camp, Johnson said, "Our expectations are to not only be in the play-offs this year, but to have some success in the play-offs." Then the Cowboys went on to compile an 11-5 record, and beat the Chicago Bears in the opening round before a loss to the Detroit Lions left them one game short of the National Conference Championship Game.

And before 1992, Johnson made noise about "taking it to the next level," about making it to the NFC Championship Game, "and then seeing what happens from there."

Upon hearing that proclamation in training camp, many players thought the Austin heat had fried Johnson's sun-worshipping brain. The NFC Championship Game? The Cowboys were the NFL's youngest team, and therefore had few proven commodities. Emmitt Smith was clearly the real deal, having won the 1991 rushing title with 1,563 yards. Aikman had been a Pro Bowler, along with Irvin and Novacek. But the offensive line seemed to be in disarray, as it always had been under Johnson, because of his relentless tinkering. Second-year lineman Erik Williams, a raw six-foot-six, 320-pounder, was ready to start at right tackle, the Cowboys announced with their fingers crossed. Additionally, center Mark Stepnoski was unsigned and absent, and considering sitting out the season. Guard Nate Newton had just returned from a diet center, where he'd melted 100 pounds from his rotund 400-pound body, and there were doubts he could be effective after such a drastic and rapid change.

There were also problems in the defensive line, where undersized tackle Russell Maryland, the top overall pick in the 1990 NFL draft, was struggling, where no pass-rush threat was emerging, and where defensive end Tony Tolbert was without a contract. Linebackers Ken Norton and Vinson Smith were also home from camp because of salary disputes. And even when they did finally sign, their track record suggested an inability to be "playmakers." How ably were they going to carry the load while flanking the starting middle linebacker, sometimes clueless first-round rookie Robert Jones?

Things looked worse in the secondary, where the featured players had been the goats of the previous year's 38-6 play-off loss to the Lions. Johnson promised changes. But incumbents James Washington and Ray Horton, castoffs from other clubs, were preparing to again start the season as the safeties. Larry

Brown, whose flaws are revealed by the fact he was a twelfth-round pick in 1991, and Issiac Holt, whose flaws are topped by a countenance his coaches find disagreeable, were positioned to do the same as the cornerbacks. Changes? Yes, the Cowboys had botched their handling of reliable kicker Ken Willis, letting him escape via Plan B, and now had to decide between scattershooting Brad Daluiso or undrafted rookie Lin Elliott as their kicker. There was your change.

Combined with the fact that Dallas's 1992 schedule was the league's toughest (based on opponents' 1991 records), thinking this team that had been a surprising 11-5 in 1991 was automatically assured of leaping to the next level was absurd. But then, seven months later, came that leap in the heart of Texas. This was the best team in football, one big happy family, living its collective dream.

"No matter what happens from here on out, they'll never be able to take what we've accomplished away from us," Aikman says. "I can fall off the face of the earth tomorrow and I'll still be part of a Super Bowl champion."

What Aikman began to learn in the hours after the title game is that if he fell off the face of the earth now, "Entertainment Tonight" would send a rescue team. Maybe he used to be just a grunt, a guy his linemen buddies call "Roy" because Troy sounded too regal. Maybe he used to be just another good ol' Wranglers-wearin' boy from Henryetta who idolizes his mom and fears his dad. Maybe he used to be able to get away with the "aw, shucks" answers that seem to satisfy journalists convinced he's been spliced into the world from a John Wayne flick. But all that was over now.

"Here's what sucks," says Aikman buddy Doug Kline. "People who once wouldn't give him the time of day, now want a piece of him, so they kiss up to him."

Aikman thought it was wise but outlandish a few months before when his family looked for ranch land without telling Realtors of the family surname for fear the price would be jacked up. He felt bad about being reluctant to talk about his mom as "being like a best friend" for fear someone would twist his words and make him sound like a mama's boy.

"You might want to be Troy for a day, to see what all that attention is like," fullback Daryl Johnston says. "But forever? No thanks."

"It's fun being the glamour boy," Aikman says. "But that's also the pain in the ass of it all. You know how careful I am about the way I conduct myself in Dallas. I don't go out and get rowdy. I don't make a scene. A guy might come up to me and challenge me to a fight. I just leave."

Well, not always. There was that time at the east Dallas dance bar Cowboys when Aikman grabbed an unrelenting heckler and slid him head-first across a table and into a collection of bottles and glasses, like a bowling ball into pins.

"I never try to throw my weight around," Aikman says. "A couple of times I've gone out with people, and maybe somebody in the group will go up to the manager of the restaurant and tell him, 'This is Troy Aikman's party,' to try and get us to the front of the line. I hate that. And I can stop that kind of thing in Dallas. But this off-season made me realize something. I thought it was as difficult as it was going to get just being around town in Dallas. But now I have a hell of a lot tougher time keeping a rein on what goes on everywhere else."

Aikman can be naive. His buddies still laugh about him being duped into an appearance on "The Oprah Winfrey Show" in spring of 1991, when Oprah was staging a celebrity "Dating Game" program that would pair actresses with male jocks. "Just dress casual," the producers told him. Aikman obeyed, wearing jeans, boots and a golf shirt. The other athletes were in double-breasted, Italian-cut suits. Oprah, wanting Aikman to portray the hick — maybe she'd read the magazine article that described him as being "right out of a Skeeter Haglar photograph" — all but shoved a stick of hay in his mouth.

Aikman's naivete created a furor at the Pro Bowl in Honolulu a week after the Super Bowl when he departed Aloha Stadium while the game was still going on. This is a no-no. It made the league look bad and unimportant. It made Aikman look spoiled and self-important. It might have gone undetected had, say, some backup free safety skipped out toward the end of the third quarter. But the Super Bowl MVP?

"Yeah, I guess," Aikman says. "But what is this? Like, 'Ladies and gentlemen, Elvis has left the building'? C'mon."

Before the game, Aikman did tell two NFL officials about having an 8:00 p.m. flight to catch back to Dallas/Fort Worth International Airport. And it bugs him still that those officials didn't speak up when commissioner Paul Tagliabue nailed Aikman with a $10,000 fine for his "quarterback sneak."

But why didn't Aikman anticipate this trouble and avoid it simply by telling NFC coach George Seifert of the San Francisco 49ers of his plans to bid the islands an early "Aloha"?

"I did ask (49ers quarterback) Steve Young about it," Aikman says with a shrug. "He didn't see any problem with it, either."

Why wasn't he able to see all of this coming a few weeks before the Super Bowl, when Steinberg sat him down for a strategy session on how Aikman would handle himself with the media should Dallas make the title game?

"Which face will you put on for the press?" Steinberg asked.

"I didn't know I had more than one," Aikman answered.

Trapped? You bet. But Aikman hadn't noticed how extensively the cage of stardom had surrounded him until a few days before the January 7 Pro Bowl. He figured he could use an escape from the hassles of celebrity, and he figured he could use a haircut, so he found a little barber shop. A quiet place. No fans. No customers.

Aikman plopped down in the chair and leafed through a *GQ* magazine. Finally, he thought, a moment of peace. He did a double-take after thumbing past one full-page clothing advertisement. In the photo, a muscular, blond, handsome model with a crooked grin drapes himself seductively over a diving board.

"It was me," says Aikman, dumbfounded.

Aikman looked worn out on "Good Morning America" and "Today," and at the press conference and even on "The Tonight Show." Someone commented that his bleary-eyed appearance must have been the result of not enough sleep and too much celebrating, of acting the part of the glamour boy.

But Troy Aikman wasn't as tired as he was intoxicated. By his thoughts of where the Cowboys had been. By where they were going. And by the dozen beers he drank alone in his private Super Bowl victory party in Room 226.

2   THE POWERS THAT BE   ★

"To hell with it!" Dallas coach Jimmy Johnson yelled. "If I'm not running things, maybe I should take my whole staff and we'll move to Tampa Bay!"

Before the play-off game against the Detroit Lions that would kill the Cowboys's 1991 season, Jones intuitively and correctly sensed that injured Troy Aikman's confidence was as torn up as his knee because fill-in Steve Beuerlein had played so well. Aikman suspected Johnson was toying with him by not announcing that Aikman would resume playing when the quarterback decided he was ready.

Jones therefore took it upon himself to make Aikman's status as the No. 1 guy clear in a January 2, 1992, *Fort Worth Star-Telegram* story headlined "Aikman Won't Be Dealt Or Benched, Jones says."

Johnson was livid.

"Who is running the football team?" he said to one of his assistants, waving a Xeroxed copy of the story in the air. "Is Jerry the coach? Or am I the coach?"

Johnson and Jones confronted each other. There were volcanic rumblings from both men. Says Johnson: "I told Jerry that it was my job to get Beuerlein ready to play against Detroit, and that if he's reading in the paper that he's a short-termer, then I don't know if he'll be fully ready. So in those areas, we've got to be on the same page when it comes to what statements we're giving out."

Since then, there has been speculation that before Johnson and Jones are finally moved to wring one another's neck, the coach might some day take his staff and move to any NFL franchise that will let Johnson live on the beach. Probably, both men have levels of intelligence to match their levels of ego and will therefore not let their few conflicts override their many successes. But both prudently preface most responses to queries about their relationship by using the word "sensitive." And neither is very forthcoming when the subject is their interpersonal dealings.

"Jerry and I have an understanding," Johnson says. "We don't always agree. Everything's not always hunky-dory. But even when that's the case, our situation is a lot better than most of the situations I know of."

That acknowledgment is enough to prevent Johnson from pitching his umbrella on a Tampa Bay beach any time soon. But clearly, that "Who is running this team?" incident was the beginning of the end of the pretense that Jones and Johnson are anything more than business partners who roll up their sleeves. Or, on their worst days, employer and employee who roll their eyes behind the other's back.

"One thing Jimmy gets away with that I don't," Jones says, "is he can be public with his anger. He can pound his fists and rant and rave. CEOs of major companies can't do that. They have stockholders to answer to. I get just as mad as Jimmy does. But I don't pound my fists. I have to have the bigger picture in mind."

There was a time when the big picture seemed to need some fine tuning. The man on the street didn't sense the Cowboys's direction. Nor did the lady in the limousine. After the 1990 season, a couple of high rollers named Jones and Johnson hit Tampa to be a part of the Super Bowl XXV festivities. Their limo driver was a woman who couldn't quite comprehend what she had seen and heard from the two guys who'd spent the week riding in the back.

"That was Jerry Jones and Jimmy Johnson, right?" she asked after she let the pair out.

Right.

"No offense," she said. "But how the hell did those two guys come to be in charge of America's Team?"

Funny she should ask. The football world had been scratching its collective head over that very issue starting in February 1989, when Jones and Johnson rewrote the old chestnut about there being trouble when one bull enters a china shop. The Dallas Cowboys were a china shop. And through the glass double doors at One Cowboys Parkway stampeded two bulls.

Johnson might have charged onto the NFL scene — and might have even succeeded Tom Landry as the Cowboys coach — without Jones. The Cowboys are one of four teams that contacted Johnson in his University of Miami days to gauge his interest in jumping to the NFL. The San Francisco 49ers were considering him as a replacement for Bill Walsh in 1989. The Philadelphia Eagles thought about Johnson in 1987 when Buddy Ryan directed the Eagles to a 1-4 start. It was rumors of their interest that first prompted a call to Johnson from Cowboys president Tex Schramm, who wanted to beat the Eagles to the punch. That same year, Johnson was one of two candidates for the Tampa Bay Buccaneers job — except that he never knew it. The Bucs, being as sharp as a bowling ball, immediately decided to hire their first interviewee, Ray Perkins.

"(Tampa Bay owner) Hugh Culverhouse says Ray was so pushy for the job that he got it done right there, and they never got around to interviewing me," Johnson says. "But Hugh jokes that while Ray cost me the job then, I cost him the job by beating the Buccaneers twice in 1990."

Schramm says, "What got me going is that Jimmy told me his goal in life was to someday become coach of the Dallas Cowboys."

Says Johnson: "I had my thoughts toward the NFL, which is one reason I was visiting training camps and studying how pro coaches conducted things. I was going to end up in the NFL."

Jones has always insisted he would not have purchased the team and the lease on Texas Stadium (for $65 million and $75 million, respectively) from H.R. "Bum" Bright had Johnson been unable to join him in Dallas. "A package deal," Jones says. It made for a digestible legend back in that first year, when the actual football team was so impossible to stomach. Jones and Johnson, in desperate need of something to take the public's mind off the actual on-field product, allowed outsiders to believe the myth that they were "best friends and college roommates back at Arkansas." Roommates? Both were married while in college. Their roommates were Gene (Jerry's wife) and Linda Kay (Jimmy's wife).

"Our names began with "J' so we shared a room for road games," Johnson says.

The suggestion of Jimmy and Jerry as a lifelong, unified team is difficult to believe today, especially when one considers how often these two powerful, driven bulls in a china shop have quietly seethed at something the other has done. Associates of both say their relationship today is deeper and richer than ever. Their Super Bowl-related labors make it deeper. The raise to a salary of $1 million annually Jones gave Johnson after winning the title makes it richer. (When the Cowboys visited President Clinton in the White House on March 5, 1993, Clinton, Jones and Johnson revisited their Arkansas ties for a time before Johnson finally said, "Here Jerry gave me this nice raise and now I might as well turn it straight over to you.")

But through it all, the joined-at-the-hip act is debunked when one sees how both these powerful, driven men shift it into reverse when asked to define their precise roles within the organization.

Johnson fidgets and says, "We don't worry about titles, 'general manager,' that sort of thing."

Jones fidgets and says, "There's enough credit to go around for everyone. I've always believed that if you're willing to give someone else the credit, you can conquer the world."

In 1991, President George Bush sent a letter to the Cowboys owner. It was addressed to "Jerry Jones, Coach, Dallas Cowboys." Why was Jimmy laughing harder at the faux pas than Jerry was? Simply, the Dallas Cowboys's boss likes to think of himself as a coach, and how their coach likes to think of himself as the boss.

Take Johnson's contract. There is a clause in the ten-year pact negotiated by Jones and Johnson's lawyer friend, Nick Christin, stipulating that Johnson has "the final say" on all personnel matters. So no trade, no roster move, no promotion or demotion, can be made without his approval. Does this give Johnson supreme authority? On paper, yes. But in reality, doesn't the owner of the club, the man who signs the checks, actually have the final say?

Who calls what shots? Jones and Johnson even ask themselves that question on occasion. Twice in 1992, one man finalized a swap without going through what the other man considered to be proper channels. On draft day in April, Johnson completed a minor deal with the Cleveland Browns, irritating Jones, who hadn't been fully consulted. "If one of us made a deal without checking with the other, would that be right or wrong?" Jones said to his coach in a patronizing tone. In October, when receiver Alexander Wright was shipped to the Los Angeles Raiders, Jones made the deal and told reporters of it before informing an angered Johnson.

Jones and Johnson confer and collaborate far less frequently than the hyperbole suggests. As hectic as the Dallas "War Room" is on draft day, the organization makes time to consider an odd sort of choreography that promotes the all-for-one angle. The cable television network ESPN broadcasts the draft, and in its quest to appear to be "on the inside," asks the Cowboys to allow them to mount a camera behind closed doors. For the last few years, when the red light on ESPN's cameras is about to go on, some of the Cowboys principals in the War Room make certain they're carefully positioned in a busy pose.

Johnson is telling the truth when he says, "Jerry does his things, and I do my things."

Jones is also telling the truth when he says, "We arrive at the same conclusions once we get to geein' and hawin'."

And sometimes, yellin' and screamin'.

Jimmy Johnson admits to being selfish, to being egotistical, to being a "control freak." He says that before his 1989 divorce, he'd "never even changed a light bulb" because he sees his job as a football coach to run his fiefdom, not to run a household. "I've put myself in a position where I have very few things that are important to me," he says.

At Miami, he did television commercials and spoke frequently at what he sourly calls "functions." He hopes it doesn't sound too arrogant when he says he skips those events now because he doesn't need them. There is no doubt the children's charity organization he set up in February 1992, the Jimmy

Johnson Foundation, is more a product of Johnson wanting to do "the right thing" than it is an outlet for some burning, heart-felt altruistic need to do community service.

Says Johnson: "What I really want to be is just a football coach. My idea of torture is going to some banquet and sitting next to some little old lady with blue hair who wants to know what I do for a living. I hate small talk. I hate jokes. I like funny stories, I like cuttin' up with the guys in our circle. I laugh hardest when they have something to do with football."

Because of Johnson's increasingly high profile, the world wants to know his motivational and organizational secrets of success. Brenda Bushell, who coordinates the Johnson Founda-tion, says Johnson has been overwhelmed by requests to speak before major corporations. He is so disinterested in spending much time outside of the football arena that his appearance fee is "off the charts," Bushell says. Johnson does appear free for some organizations, does charge a nominal fee for others, but if he's asked to explain the Johnson Way to a Fortune 500 company that wants to learn how to win their version of the Super Bowl, that'll be $50,000, please. That fee is double the standard celebrity coach's rate.

But the world also wants to know Johnson's secrets, pe-riod. You know, the scandals. The dirt. The juice. True, Johnson is viewed as an architect of one of the greatest turnarounds in sports history, and that is notable enough. But he is also photogenic, interesting and colorful. With the firing of Chicago Bears coach Mike Ditka after the 1992 season, Johnson is neck-and-neck (cheek-and-jaw?) with Miami Dolphins coach Don Shula for the league lead in television sideline shots. TV direc-tors often instruct a cameraman to stick with Jimmy, knowing he can illuminate a seventeen-inch screen as brightly as any gorgeous touchdown catch or vicious quarterback sack.

All of this magnetism and success makes Johnson fair game for the tabloids, or for the inevitable "unauthorized biographies" that will re-cycle the tales of his days charging kids twenty-five cents to sneak peeks inside a Port Arthur whorehouse. After winning the Super Bowl, he was flooded with offers to write his autobiography, to write of his management techniques, to write about X's and O's. Hundreds of thousands of dollars were waved at him. He finally accepted a $400,000 advance from Hyperion to spend a few moments being interviewed by *Sports Illustrated*'s Ed Hinton, who will then craft Johnson's memoirs under the tentative title *Turning the Thing Around: Pulling America's Team Out of the Doldrums and Myself Out of the Doghouse.*

"I agreed to do it so somebody else doesn't have any success selling an unauthorized version full of things that either aren't true or things that will piss me off," he says.

Some of the stuff now being thrown against the wall to see if it sticks is fabricated. But because of his fast-lane lifestyle in some of his years as a college coach, because of his interludes with celebrities while gambling in Monaco or watching a prizefight in Las Vegas, because of the admittedly selfish manner in which he bulldozes through life, some stuff is true.

"As far as what people want to say about me or write about me, I don't see that it's different than it's always been," Johnson says. "Let 'em gossip. Let 'em take shots at me. Hey, not everybody is going to like you. And I think a lot of people are jealous of who they think I am. But nobody really knows me. And that's the way I like it."

If Johnson is the worm in his cocoon, Jones is the (social) butterfly. Jones has made a living of being able to make small talk. He pursues friends the way he's pursued dollars. And who wouldn't want an estimated 500 million friends?

Naturally, Jones is comfortable when in his "Life Styles of the Rich and Famous" mode. Celebrities? The list is almost without an end and almost without a pattern. Here's Liz Taylor! There's Supreme Court Justice Clarence Thomas! Hi, Robin Leach! Should we get Charlie Pride to sing, or Hank Williams, Jr.? Bow to Prince Bandar of Saudi Arabia! Good evening, Donald Trump and Marla Maples, and thanks for telling ESPN that you wouldn't be presenters at their March 4, 1993, ESPY Awards for achievements in sports unless you were allowed to present one of their trophies to Jerry Jones!

Before the presidential election of 1992, Jones did not dissuade any corner of the political world from convincing itself he supported their candidate. What other NFL owner had talked sports with George Bush, talked finances with Ross Perot and talked over whose turn it was to make the next trip to the bar with another of Arkansas' favorite sons, Bill Clinton?

But Jones's network includes those from all walks. In July 1990, a janitor at the Cowboys's Valley Ranch headquarters named Ruben Rodriguez was driving the family van in Mexico when his young daughter was killed in an accident. Mexican authorities made it difficult for Rodriguez to bring the body home. Jones quietly simplified matters by greasing the palms of authorities with the thousands of dollars they demanded to release the body.

Jones's commitment to being ubiquitous is awesome. He will shake any hand, will speak at any banquet, will agree to any request, as long as he is allowed a moment to peddle his product. "Cah-*boys*," he calls them, heavy on the "*boys*." Other public figures tell reporters "no comment." Jones says "no comment, but..." He has held court in a room of fifty media people, half of whom he'd never seen before, and askeed that his following comments be "off the record, just between us girls."

The pace, the handshaking, the ninety minutes of sleep per night, has worn on Jones. He developed an arrhythmia, an irregular heartbeat. He has back problems that once threatened to require surgery. "Oh, that's just from too many years knocking my head against things," jokes Jones, the old Razorback. Says his daughter, Cowboys executive Charlotte Anderson: "We can't even get him to take one day off. If he has surgery and they tell him he has to spend a month in bed, forget it. He won't have the surgery. Can you see him missing a game?"

What Jones needs is a doctor. Dr. No.

"He has a difficult time turning people down," says his wife, Gene.

Sometimes, Jones's "yes" means "no." Some of the fired employees who view themselves as victims of a machete-swinging owner are still bitter over being told "no" when they asked if Jones's "cutting the fat" meant they had jobs. But that might be easier to take than being told both "yes" and "no." On May 21, 1992, Bob Ackles, for six years the Cowboys's director of player personnel, walked into Jones's office for an "organizational meeting." He walked out no longer part of the organization.

Jones emerged from the session unwilling to announce what everyone could sense: Ackles had been fired. It was the same trigger Jones had been unwilling to pull for the previous nine months. Since the beginning of the 1991 season, Jones had suggested to Ackles that he might want to explore other job opportunities, that his duties in Dallas would some day be absorbed by Jones's son, Stephen. But Jones frequently followed up those statements by reversing his field. One day, Jones hugged Ackles' wife. "Kay," Jones said, "I just want you to know how important Bob is to the future of the Cowboys."

When you consider that a few months later, Ackles, now a college scouting director with the Phoenix Cardinals, had no future at all with the Cowboys, it's little wonder Jones has made enemies of former employees who consider him mean-spirited and deceptive. Was Jones ruthless? Heartless? Cheap? From a business perspective, there were alterations that had to be made. Jones and Johnson were reviewing some employee-related documents one day when they were stunned to learn of the number of complimentary season passes and complimentary automobiles that were in the hands of people who were actually former employees who hadn't worked for the Cowboys for years.

Still, in cleaning up the mess, Jones fired so many of Schramm's Valley Ranch staffers — "My people," Tex calls them — at such an apparently reckless pace you wondered if one day, this Arkansas-crude Jones would be spotted out front of the facility in overalls, mowing the vast Valley Ranch lawn himself.

"I'm not exactly sure how this idea got started that I was going around Valley Ranch lopping employees' heads off," Jones says. "In all my years in business, I don't know that I've ever fired anyone. But changes were necessary, even if the public perception of how those changes were handled didn't come off right."

Mean-spirited and deceptive? No. A more apt explanation for such incidents is that Jones flies by the seat of his pants, that he thinks with his tongue, that he makes commitments to people that he can't possibly keep. Marry his loose personal style with his tight professional schedule and you sometimes get The Absent-Minded Professor. This man, entrusted with so much responsibility, often leaves his keys in the ignition of his Cadillac. In a pants pocket where most people carry a wallet, he carries a money clip and a three-inch-by-three-inch sheet of crumpled paper on which is written the basics of the organization's financial structure. Two Christmases ago, his family stuffed his stocking with prescription eyeglasses. Ten pairs. "I guess Santa knew I'd forget where I left them," Jones says.

After he altered Cowboys tradition by selling the broadcast rights to KVIL-FM Radio in 1991, Jones could be heard doing a commercial for KRLD-AM Radio, the former flagship station. "Nobody knows the Cah-*boys* like KRLD," Jones proclaimed, in an announcement that must have come as a shock to the KVIL-FM people who'd just paid $3.5 million over five years to be "The Cowboys Station."

Jones's aim-to-please nature is hereditary. Born on October 13, 1942, in Los Angeles to Arminta and J.W. "Pat" Jones, there is reason to believe that when the doctor reached out to slap Jerral Wayne on his pink behind, the infant entrepreneur reached up, pumped the doc's hand and tried to sell him something.

"Both my parents taught me early on the value of treating people like they were something special," Jones says. "They were wonderful teachers."

In 1950, Pat Jones purchased a new automobile and left it at a service station to be checked over. When Pat and some members of his family, including little Jerry, returned, they were horrified to discover the service-station owner had accidentally ripped one of the car's doors from its hinges. "No one feels worse about it than he does," Pat told his family. "Here's a situation where we can have a friend for life or an enemy for life."

Pat Jones left his family for a moment and quietly had a word with the service-station owner. "Don't you worry about it," Pat Jones said. "Now c'mon over to my store and let's have a cup of coffee."

Says Jerry: "That man patronized my father's businesses, first by buying groceries from him, then buying insurance from him, for the rest of his life."

Jones can come across as a sort of Elmer Gantry, a twangy fire-and-brimstone snake oil (and gas) salesman. "Some of the vernacular and expressions that were the tools of my trade. ... the humor, the colorful expressions. ... that is simply the way I talk," says Jones, who after the 1989 season employed a firm called Fairchild-LeMaster to coach him in techniques to soften his rough public edges. "I've never wanted to put on airs. I might say, 'Boy, you look like your heinie's draggin.' I don't say, 'My, you appear exhausted.' But when you see what I say in print, it doesn't always come across the way it was intended. People twisted it all around a little bit. The way I was attacked when I first bought the team hurt. It hurt a lot. I don't think anything the media did with me was vindictive. But I think the media took advantage of a part of my personality."

There was a "Bury Jerry" mentality. Jones received two death threats. He was interviewed by reporters aiming to do what he calls "gut cuts" on him. He was investigated by private eyes who lurked from L.A. to Little Rock mining for dirt. A Jones friend suspects some of the old-regime Cowboys employees were behind the hiring of one investigator who contacted a grade-school teacher of Jones's to ask if little Jerry "ever had his hand caught in a cash register."

"I was gone over with a fine-toothed comb, like not even a presidential candidate had been," Jones says.

But while those who came in contact with Jones might once have been "shill-shocked," he's worn most of them down with that omnipresent grin, and with a genuine level of kindness and understanding. On rare occasions, he has privately reacted almost violently to a newspaper story. "That (reporter) has painted himself into a corner with me now, by God," Jones will bellow, vowing to cut off contact with the offender. He never has. Nothing — not the possibility of a newspaper digging into a ticket-scalping story on the eve of Super Bowl week, not potentially libelous stories about his finances, not personal attacks on his looks or lifestyle — has forced him to forget that grudges are bad for business.

Instead, he makes sure writers from around the country receive one-on-one audiences with the owner, a privilege all but unheard of elsewhere. You can tell when an out-of-town scribe is making his virgin trip to Valley Ranch by whether or not he pumps quarters into the Cokes machine outside the team locker room. Anyone who has been around the place for long knows Jones has left the machines rigged. The Cokes, a small price to pay for "a friend for life," are free.

Once Jones learns your first name, you are forever "Mister Joe" or "Mister Rick" or "Mister Mike." There is the feeling the owner, president and general manager of the Dallas Cowboys, this celebrity with his own TV show and two radio shows, this influential member of the NFL's Competition Committee and confidante of movie stars and politicians, has his very own pet name for little ol' you. Jones's habit of beginning sentences with "frankly" or "candidly" is a sales technique that takes some time to dissect; eventually, listeners relax from the edge of their seats when they discover that rarely after introducing a statement with "frankly" or "candidly" does Jones follow it with anything the least bit frank or candid. But he's got his "customer" — "Mister Bob" or "Mister Jack" — hanging on every frank, candid word.

"He's sly and smart and charming," says Cowboys receiver Michael Irvin. "He's a snake with a smile."

Both of Jones's parents were high school valedictorians. In his first couple of years in Dallas, while critics suggested he should have moved not to Dallas, but to Beverly Hills like TV sitcom character Jed Clampett before him, Jones resisted the temptation to boast of his successful efforts to match his parents' accomplishments, academic and otherwise.

By 1964, Jones had romanced and married Miss USA Arkansas, was a father, was a 200-pound starting guard on a national championship team and was months away from being named executive vice-president of Pat's insurance business. In 1965, after deciding against law school, Jerry got the promotion at Modern Security Life soon after being handed his undergraduate degree and his master's degree in the same graduation line. In 1970, the company was sold and Jones took his $500,000 profit and took a stab at the oil-and-gas exploration business. To those who have watched Jones's cost-cutting methods and the success of his Cowboys product help the team's revenues to double, up to almost $70 million after the Super Bowl, it comes as no surprise that as a rookie oil man Jones struck it big on his first thirteen wells.

Jones, a former North Little Rock High School fullback, is self-effacing about his limitations as an athlete. In 1990, when ABC-TV wanted to do a Monday Night Football halftime feature on him, the network dug up reels of old film from his playing days as a University of Arkansas guard. "The reason they had to go through all that film," Jones says, "was to find a play of me actually putting a successful block on someone."

Johnson likes to poke fun at Jones's athletic shortcomings, too. "Jerry," he says, winking, "was a try-hard player."

He is also a try-hard owner. You can take Jerry Jones out of his dad's Kwik Check Superettes, off his Modern Security Life sales route, out of the oil fields and out of the loop of high finance. But you cannot take the grocery aisles and the sales routes and the oil fields and the high finance out of Jerry Jones. He wants the world to know he's a family man and what NFL people call "a football man." He loves to tell the story about the

1975 Little Rock YMCA football team that starred Stephen Jones and was coached by Jerry Jones, how he somehow never missed a practice or a game despite his daily supervision of an oil site a state away, in Kansas.

Clearly, the anecdote reveals his passion for family. And maybe it says something about Jones and football. But his incredibly quick assimilation of the inner workings of the NFL aside, Jones is more businessman than football man.

Besides, in Johnson, the Cowboys have their football man. Johnson, 52-9 at the University of Miami, where he won the 1987 national championship, also serves as a partner for Jones in what sometimes seems like a "Good Cop, Bad Cop" act. Every Metroplex reporter has Jones's home phone number. Johnson's "home" number is listed on the in-house employees phone list as (214) 556-9930. Dial it. You'll get Johnson's secretary, Barbara Goodman, at Valley Ranch.

"I let reporters do stories about me in the last couple of years that I regret now," Johnson says. "I wish I hadn't opened up my private life as much as what I did. It was probably inevitable that people would eventually want to find out who this guy was who coached the Cowboys. But there are some things about me I want private. I like to be in control. Sometimes, in interviews, that control gets taken away."

Johnson's house is hardly a home. He has the swimming pool, the satellite dish, and a fridge stocked with Diet Coke, Mexican food leftovers, Heineken beer and Blue Bell ice cream. But it's not lived-in enough to prevent Johnson from going berserk when one of his visiting sons leaves a McDonald's wrapper on the floor. There are no loose ends. Freedom of movement in the place is allowed to only his saltwater fish; the shrimp and lion fish and coral bandits can go wherever they wish within the confines of his four aquariums. The handsome, immaculate two-story house's most critical feature is, as the real-estate people would say, location, location, location. It is 1.1 miles away from his Valley Ranch office, where there are stashed more Diet Coke, more Heineken, more ice cream and pillowcase-sized bags of nacho chips.

"I like things a certain way," says Johnson, as good an explanation as any for his 1989 divorce from Linda Kay. "Not that my way is the right way, or the way everyone should do it. But I like to do things my own way."

The divorce, Johnson says, is typical of how the media tries to frame events inside of image. Numerous times, he says, it's been written that his desire to focus on his new job with the Cowboys, his workaholism, caused him to "put Linda Kay on waivers," as writers cleverly but indelicately phrase it. "There were a lot of things that went into it. Things were at a different stage with my wife, but it just so happened the Cowboys thing happened to be at that same time. I was moving away from one city, to a new city, a lot of people didn't know us personally, so we didn't have our old circle of friends keeping us together. ... It was something I had thought about for quite some time, and I felt like it was the right time to do it.

"She and I have talked about how it might have been different had we stayed in Miami," he says. "The big thing is, I really just wanted to live alone."

Most every Monday, Johnson orders ten servings of a Mexican, Italian or Cajun dish. "I eat two," he says, "then microwave the rest of them for dinner as the week goes on." This sort of meticulous planning was part of the Johnson profile even back at Port Arthur High School. He was born in Port Arthur, Texas, on July 16, 1943, a year after his parents, C.W. and Allene, moved from Clarksville, Arkansas, so C.W. could take a job as a supervisor at a local dairy. At age nine, James William Johnson drew up a schedule of household chores to be followed by him and his two siblings. As a teenager, Jimmy worked at the dairy — the ice cream was plentiful — and decided against being a multiple-sport star. Playing shortstop on the Jefferson High baseball team was out, he figured, because it wouldn't aid his football career as a five-foot-eleven, 195-pound nose guard. Sometimes, maybe because his 160 IQ allowed him to get away with it, he decided against attending classes, too.

"When he was in the eleventh grade, a teacher made a big fuss about Jimmy not turning in an assignment," says C.W. "So Jimmy tells the teacher, "I don't need this class. I'm going to be a football coach.""

First, he was a football player. He possessed a sunny attitude (the guys called him "Smiley), and he had great quickness, but not much size, characteristics that would be embodied a generation later by the defensive players on his Super Bowl-champion Cowboys. He quickly and easily absorbed the philosophies of Arkansas coach Frank Broyles, who sometimes allowed Johnson to go to the chalkboard at clinics. But as in high school, Johnson did what he could to avoid dealings with the teachings of his professors.

"I had it all figured out," says Johnson, who at one time planned on majoring in vertebrate zoology. "I'd go take the tests on the last day of class and get good enough grades to stay eligible for football. The rest of the time before football practice, I'd set up shop over at the student union and play bridge. Bridge is a lot like football." Only when he found out poor attendance would affect his grades did he dump the bridge idea.

Without coaching, Johnson might have gone into "industrial psychology." What does an industrial psychologist do, exactly? "I never found out," says Johnson, who used his psychology degree to dive into the profession that would be his calling, first as a defensive line coach at Louisiana Tech, then at

Picayune (Mississippi) High School, and eventually back to help run the defense at Arkansas, where his reputation as a players coach was born. "I was a character," says Jimmy, who presented his toddlers, Brent and Chad, with a pet boa constrictor. Linda Kay didn't like it; but the Arkansas football players invited over to feed the snake mice and hamsters thought it was neat.

The idea that Jimmy Johnson might invite some of his Cowboys players over to the house to play with his boa constrictor no longer computes. But Johnson was a different man, and a different coach, then. "The pro game changes you," he says. "I can't get as close to my players now as I did in college. In college, relationships don't have to end. Players graduate, but they still have ties to the university. In the National Football League, those days when I have to make cuts, to tell a player he's not good enough to make my team, those are the most difficult days I go through. I may not show it. But I have compassion for those players."

Hugh Green, who still calls Linda Kay "Ma," knows all about this side of the man. The former NFL linebacker, who played for Johnson when he was the defensive coordinator at the University of Pittsburgh, has all but begged Johnson to bring him to the Cowboys. Green thought it would be natural. After all, they got along well enough when they were at Pitt that Green lived with the Johnsons for a time. He was part of the family.

Which is exactly why Johnson never brought him to Dallas. "Imagine what we'd all go through on the day I had to cut Hugh Green?" Johnson asks.

Alonzo Highsmith should know that side, but doesn't. Highsmith played for and looked up to Johnson while at the University of Miami, and was reunited with him when Dallas acquired the fullback from the Houston Oilers on September 3, 1990. The cost was high: No. 2 and No. 5 picks. The payoff was low: knee problems prevented Highsmith from contributing anything more than his 48 yards on 19 carries in 1990. In late September of 1991, Johnson laid out the facts for Highsmith. Other teams' doctors believed he suffered from a degenerative joint problem, a belief that precluded anyone from trading for him. The Cowboys were secure with Daryl Johnston as their starter at fullback, which meant little chance for playing time for Highsmith.

"The Cowboys said to hell with me, so I said to hell with them," said Highsmith upon his October 1 release. "Now they have their team the way they want it, and I don't have to be humiliated by standing around doing nothing on the sidelines."

What Highsmith didn't say — or maybe in his anger didn't see — was that Johnson had offered him a chance to stay on the roster. Highsmith wasn't going to be allowed to play much, but he could have continued collecting his weekly $30,000 paycheck. Instead, he ignored Johnson's generous gesture and demanded to be released.

There is this perception of Johnson as some unfeeling ogre who would designate his mother Allene as "the player to be named later" if it would make a trade go. Isn't Johnson some one-dimensional idiot savant who understands the intricacies of the new collective bargaining agreement but who doesn't know what MTV is? Isn't he some atheist cretin who doesn't observe holidays, doesn't attend church, doesn't love his sons?

None of these perceptions are completely accurate. But all of them are completely Johnson's own fault.

"People tend to take a grain of truth, or one isolated incident, and build that into a whole picture of what they think of somebody," Johnson says. "Down in Port Arthur, the minister moved back the Sunday night service so my parents wouldn't miss the start of the Super Bowl on TV. You see, Mother and Daddy go to church three times a week. I was raised a Christian and I am a Christian.

"But I disagree with a lot of individuals who want to go tell the world, 'Look at me, I'm a Christian.' They're not ministers or preachers or priests, yet they want to push their religion off on everybody else."

Johnson, on the other hand, has quietly missed only three team chapel services in the last ten years. As a head coach, he's taken charge of making chapel available — but not mandatory — to his team.

"But I don't go around telling everyone I do it," Johnson says. "I just sit in the back of the room and participate. I worship my way."

There is a part of Johnson that wants him to be perceived as a tireless hustler happy only when he's sticking it to every other coach in the NFL. But, counters Dave Wannstedt, one of Johnson's best friends and his defensive coordinator before taking over the Chicago Bears after the Super Bowl: "Jimmy's different than what you think. But what you think he is is pretty much what he wants you to think." Adds Jimmy's mother, Allene: "He is tender-hearted. He just doesn't want you to know it."

Of course, a man can't help but be saddled with a Faustian image when he lists the two priorities in his life, in order, as 1) "Winning football games" and 2) "My two sons." Or by saying he doesn't give out presents to his grown offspring just because it is Christmas, or just because it is some loved one's birthday. "We know he loves us," says Brent, twenty-eight. "He shows us that all the time. He does give presents. He just gives them when the mood strikes him, instead of when the calendar says it's time." Johnson does give expensive gifts. His annual invitations to his assistants and their wives to join him for all-expense-paid trips to luxurious travel spots are typical of Johnson. "I'm not tight with my own money," he says. "Now company money, I'm tight with. I might not recommend a raise for a guy when that raise is the same amount we just spent on a vacation."

Money, Johnson says, is not the object of his life. Back at Miami, where Johnson coached from 1984-88, he once got into an argument with a university administrator over some spending involving the football program. Johnson won the dispute by removing a Rolex watch from his wrist and tossing it across the table. It bounced off a place mat and landed in the lap of the administrator.

"You don't understand," Johnson calmly informed the man. "Money isn't the issue. Winning is the issue."

Meanwhile, Jones admits his life revolves around a number of issues, including family, winning and money. Before he purchased the franchise, he hired a highly regarded financial consultant to predict the Cowboys's future viability. "In 1994, the Cowboys will lose $25 million," the consultant reported to Jones, who then fired the man and refused to pay his bill.

"I did not buy the Dallas Cowboys to get my head amputated financially," Jones says. "My purpose in buying the team wasn't to make money — I didn't buy the team so I could someday sell it at a profit — but I couldn't look myself in the mirror as a businessman knowing we were losing money when we didn't have to be."

Jones instructs his secretary, Marylyn Love, to let him know how much she's spending for coffee filters, pencils and staples. "Knowing where the pennies are going is how rich men keep from going poor," Jones says.

But how do you keep a smart man from looking stupid? On February 25, 1989, Jones couldn't.

Bum Bright knew it was time. So did Schramm. Even Landry will now admit that while Jones botched the way he fired him, there was nothing wrong with the timing. "By that point, I was starting to look at a change myself," Landry says, in an indication that four years of martyrdom might be growing burdensome.

Jones traveled with Schramm to an Austin golf course and faced off with Landry. This twenty-nine-year monument of Cowboys football, this possessor of 250 wins that placed him third on the NFL's all-time list, this icon with thirteen division championships and five NFC championships and two Super Bowl championships and twenty consecutive winning seasons from 1966 to 1985, was out of a job. The Plastic Man, as former Dallas running back Duane Thomas once called Landry, had been canned by the Spastic Man.

Even with Jones's promise to Landry that the old coach would get the $1 million due him for the 1989 season, the move lacked grace. "That conversation made me feel more awkward and inadequate than I've ever felt in my life," Jones says. But what do bulls in a china shop know from grace?

"We did three major things in one fell swoop," Jones says. "The change in ownership. The management and coaching change. And the hiring of Jimmy Johnson. Each of those was a huge sports story by itself. But we lumped them together, and that was a mistake, because it gave the appearance that I lacked sensitivity, that I lacked an appreciation of the past. Bum Bright offered to handle the firing of coach Landry. He said I could 'come in with a clean slate.' But I felt I had to stand up like a man and do it.

"If I had it to do over again, I would have spread out those events. I would have purchased the team in one separate action. Then I would have done some of the other things — things that people knew needed to be done — at a later time. Then I would have hired Jimmy. Each of those events could have been given their due then. Instead, there was the one big press conference, which I didn't handle very well, and what happened happened."

At a later time? Jones has many attributes. But patience is not one of them. Three months after the purchase of the franchise had been announced, Jones made dozens of changes in the organization's structure. This created a bit of the problem at the NFL's spring meetings. Jones had made all these moves before the league had even approved him as an owner.

"Jerry didn't know all the rules," says close friend and team vice-president Mike McCoy. "He just kind of adjusted as he went along."

They were The Man Who Fired Coach Landry and The Man Who Replaced Coach Landry. But no one knew then that they were also The Men Who Saved The Cowboys. Saved them from Landry. Saved them from Schramm. Saved them from the fat-cat, country-club atmosphere that prevailed at Valley Ranch. Saved them from traditional operating procedures and philosophies that worked well enough when Dallas qualified for five Super Bowls between 1970 and 1978, but weren't dynamic enough to pull the Cowboys from the disturbing depths they'd reached by the late 1980s.

"It tore my heart out to see Tom and Tex had become totally different people when I came back to the Cowboys," says former Dallas scouting director Dick Mansperger, who left for a time in the late 1970s, then was nudged out by Jones and Johnson in May 1992. "It was a terrible thing to see people you idolized, respected and admired not have the same means to do what they'd done once before.

"To be once again around definite, positive, clear, bright, decisive people like Jimmy and Jerry, it was an awesome thing to see."

Jones and Johnson are as close as they are because they work together on the Cowboys. They don't work together on the Cowboys because they're close. They do not socialize, except at Cowboys-related gatherings. They do share a bond from having survived the University of Arkansas together, from having survived a 1983 twin-engine plane crash in Oklahoma City, and from having survived their hostile takeover of the Cowboys.

But all the mythical aspects of their relationship aside, their living legend is this: Jones and Johnson saved the Dallas Cowboys from other would-be owners and coaches who couldn't have been counted on to so completely pour themselves into this insane project of adding substance to what by February 1989 had become a franchise that had nothing bigger to boast about than its cheerleaders' breasts.

3   HERSCHEL TO HALEY   ★

Charles Haley, who has been clinically diagnosed as a manic depressive, relies on medication to control his mood swings.

The rest of the 1992 Dallas Cowboys relied on each other.

It took until halftime of the December 6 game against the Denver Broncos before Jimmy Johnson considered Haley a problem worth addressing. From the outside, it looked as if the Cowboys defensive end had undergone some magical intermission transformation between the first half (in which he jogged around the field while allowing pedestrian Broncos tackle Russell Freeman to maul him) and the second half (when he electrified his teammates by recording a sack and helping them to two others).

The magical transformation took place inside a bathroom stall under the north stands of Mile High Stadium. What an appropriate location for Johnson to attack a player he believed was going into the toilet on him.

"Ever since that one major session Charles and I had, I couldn't ask for anything more from him," says Johnson, who at the time was wondering if the only way to resolve the Haley problem might be to put the Haley problem on waivers. "After that, he was a model citizen, believe it or not. But it was in that Denver game when I saw he needed a little attitude adjustment. As much as anything else, he wanted to push me. He wanted to see how far he could go and how much he could get away with.

"As most players who've been around me for any period of time understand, that's not a smart thing to do."

Two weeks earlier, one day after the Cowboys' 16-10 win in Phoenix on November 22, a reporter approached defensive end Haley — ostensibly a "team leader" who stayed home from the Cardinals game to nurse a sore groin — seeking an injury update. Haley flashed the exact sort of antisocial attitude that concerned Johnson.

Reporter: "Mr. Haley, I've got three questions for you, if you've got a minute. First of all, how's the groin?"

Haley: "Who are you?"

Reporter: "A reporter. With three questions."

Haley: "You know my schedule. You know when I talk to reporters." (Haley had been persuaded by public relations staffers to occasionally grant token interviews on Sundays after games.)

Reporter: "Charles, we have a little problem with your schedule. You see, you weren't available for questions on Sunday because you didn't go to Phoenix because of your groin. So that's my first question. How's your groin? Also, do you plan on playing Thursday? (the Cowboys played host to the Giants that week in a Thanksgiving Day game). And finally, can you talk about how difficult it might have been to be home watching a game I'm sure you wanted to be playing in?"

Haley: "Get the f— out of my face."

Reporter: "I'll make a deal with you. At this point, if you say the magic words — 'no comment' — I'll give up. You say no comment, that's what I'll write down on the old notepad. Whatever you say, I'll write it down and that will be the Charles Haley quote of the day." (Boy, was it.)

Haley: "You're mistaking me for someone who gives a shit. I don't have to answer your f—ing questions. Who the f— do you think you are, you piece of shit?"

Reporter: "I already told you. I'm a reporter. Now is that your final word on your groin?"

Haley: "I just came up with a new resolution. I'm going back to the way it was (not talking to most reporters at all). I'm not f—ing talking. You can't make me. You don't run the f—ing world. So f— you."

Of course, Charles didn't cease conversation with all reporters. Just white reporters. Scott West of KVIL-FM Radio maintained a civil relationship with him all year long. So did Chris Arnold of KKDA-FM Radio and WFAA-TV Channel 8. When Thomas George of the *New York Times* came to town, he visited Haley's apartment to conduct an interview. Jarrett Bell of the Marin (Calif.) *Independent Journal* also did a one-on-one. Charles Haley is black. So are West, Arnold, George and Bell.

"I think I'll try and pull that," says a Cowboys player who is white. "I'm only going to talk to you, and the other white reporters. How long would that last before Jimmy, the NAACP and the commissioner all showed up to straighten my racist ass out?"

The National Association for the Advancement of Colored People and commissioner Paul Tagliabue might swoop down. But Johnson would not necessarily rush in to correct that hypothetical situation. Johnson has little tolerance for players who buck his system, as Charles Haley found out in the bathroom stall that day in Denver. But the better they are at playing football, the less likely it is that Johnson will bother noticing their human frailties.

And, Johnson is proud to admit, blacks sometimes are treated differently according to the Johnson Way, which includes "favoritism" as Rule One.

"All the time, I show favoritism," Johnson says.

In every NFL locker room, there are barriers unintentionally built on the basis of age, economics, regional origin, position, status and color. Defensive players tend to socialize with other defensive players. Skill-position players tend to socialize with other skill-position players. Veterans befriend veterans. Floridians bond with other Floridians. So it was with the Cowboys.

Early in 1992, black players whispered among themselves about the adulation given veteran safety Bill Bates, a white man who is extremely popular with fans. White players bemoaned the off-season Plan B losses of tight end Rob Awalt and linebacker Jack Del Rio, who are white.

"You have to address the racial thing early on if you ever expect to do something like win a Super Bowl," says tight end Alfredo Roberts. "For a team as young as we are, differences in ages and salaries aren't a big deal because we have a lot of guys who are at the point in their careers where they're just happy to have such a good job. Race is never spoken about. But it is a subconscious issue. You can't help but notice all the blacks sometimes getting on one bus and all the whites getting on the other. What we did was try to cross over. Get along. Make it a Rainbow Coalition."

There are going to be gaps. On March 5, 1992, as one of the Cowboys' buses pulled up to the White House when the team visited Washington D.C., one of the black players commented on the building's resemblance to a plantation. This triggered a playful, soulful chorus of the old hit, "Chain Gang."

An example of using humor to deal with racial differences was born in "Cell Block 6," the offensive line's meeting room.

Some of the white offensive linemen, especially Mark Tuinei, Kevin Gogan and Mark Stepnoski, possess caustic wits. Cultural differences being what they are, the white linemen sometimes failed to laugh at the jokes of the three black offensive linemen, Nate Newton, Erik Williams and Frank Cornish. So the three blacks formed a tongue-in-cheek fraternity called "The Committee." Newton purchased expensive leather ballcaps with "The Committee" stitched proudly across the front, and the three kidded their white mates about the African-American's inately superior gifts — including sense of humor.

The Cowboys dealt with racial obstacles better than most clubs in part because of the color-conscious management style of Johnson, who makes no bones about his varied handling of players, sometimes based on race. Johnson actually has a stronger following among his black players than he does among whites. Some of the white players have nicknamed Johnson "Spanky," after the moon-faced kid in the old "Our Gang" film shorts. Meanwhile, many black players are almost reverent toward their coach.

Says Irvin: "You know how many homes of black folks he's been in? What, maybe hundreds? He goes in there to recruit that black kid, and he ends up recruiting that black kid's mama and his daddy, too."

Johnson explains further:

"I've always had a good relationship with black players because I have some feeling for what they had to go through. I don't mean to push myself off as one of those white guys who thinks he understands the black man's problems. I'm not saying that I'm anything special. But, maybe from growing up in Port Arthur (where as a youth many of his playmates were lower-class black kids), I do have feelings for what some of them have had to go through.

"Don't get me wrong. A bunch of black players are complete bums, just like a bunch of white players are bums. But when I decided to get my degree in psychology, it was because I enjoyed the courses and because I enjoyed studying people. Trying to understand some individuals I've worked with probably allowed me a closer feeling for them."

Johnson says his bond with black kids when he was a college coach grew deeper than his bond with whites because "most of the whites came from good homes, had both parents, the family had a decent car, there was money every month. They didn't need me. They didn't need for me to understand. So I was one thing to some blacks, and with some whites, I simply coached them."

The blacks' respect for Johnson — and their desire to be recruited by his wildly successful Miami program — increased when they saw him bending his rules for them.

"When I would give a black player a break, a second chance, because I felt I understood why he might get into a scrape, some of the black players respected that," Johnson says. "They appreciated that. See, if one player from certain environment reacts in a certain way, it might mean something completely different than the same reaction from someone from a different environment. Take language. A (profane) word thrown my way by an inner-city black player would mean a heck of a lot different thing than it would from an upper-middle class white kid from a good home with two parents. If that upper-class white kid says the same word, there is some meaning there. The inner-city kid might not even mean it as a negative."

The subject of profanity brings us back to Exhibit A, Charles Haley, a card-carrying misanthrope who, fortunately for society, funnels most of his rage onto the football field.

Acquired by the Cowboys from the San Francisco 49ers on August 26, 1992, for second- and third-round picks, Haley arrived with an unusual amount of malevolent baggage. In his six years with the 49ers, a time he played in three Pro Bowls and won two Super Bowls, he engaged in off-field fistfights with teammates at least five times. He profanely ridiculed 49ers coach George Seifert to his face. He periodically waved his penis at both male and female reporters in the locker room, then loudly accused them of "staring at him." He urinated on teammate Tim Harris's car. He privately bemoaned the fact that as a 49ers outside linebacker, he was teamed with Bill Romanowski, Keith DeLong and Mike Walter, three white guys. "We need a Soul Patrol," he told friends.

As a rookie in 1986, he was wary enough of whites to fall for an elaborate prank perpetrated by teammates. Tired of Haley's sometimes cruel sense of humor, they set him up by informing him that the area just south of San Francisco where he lived was crawling with racist cops. Then they put the fear of God in Haley by hiring a cop to "arrest" Haley. The incident did nothing to curb either Haley's relentless assault on prank victims or his anger toward "rednecks."

Sources say Haley's manic-depressive state is what caused the 49ers to employ one man to coach only him (Dwaine Board), one man to counsel him (Dr. Harry Edwards) and a medical staff aware of the necessary medication.

People who meet Haley outside the arena swear they find him charming and intelligent. And former 49ers teammates whose opinions demand respect, such as safety Ronnie Lott and running back Harry Sydney, likewise stress Haley's positive qualities. They tell stories of his brilliant wit and his burning passion for winning. They claim he's misunderstood. That is probably true of many blacks who speak their minds in a predominantly white environment. It is best left to sociologists to debate whether being "misunderstood" is justification enough to create such miscreant behavior.

It is left to a 49ers source to say, "Charles was our psycho."

Says Cowboys guard Nate Newton: "Charles is very opinionated, and his opinion isn't usually the same as other people's opinions. He has a very short fuse, and he can be hard to deal with. I've seen people ask him for autographs, and he always asks them, 'Why do you want it?' If they have a clever answer, or a very sincere answer, he gives it to them. I've seen him walk into a bar and buy every person a drink. I've seen him treat his teammates like brothers one day, and like hell the next day. He's not your model citizen."

Haley acknowledges his reputation as a "problem player and a troublemaker." But he offers an alibi. "Maybe sometimes in life, you are like a kid, you do things that are wrong, you make a wrong decision," Haley says. "People remember the bad things. You have to take me for who I am. If that doesn't work for you, then I'm sorry."

During a postgame party in his first month in Dallas, Haley horrified a number of teammates with a virulent outburst in public at the Humperdink's restaurant in Irving. From that point on, he was treated like a curiosity. His teammates respected him for his football skills, and were surprised at how comfortably he sometimes fit into their lunch-time dominoes games in the locker room. But they otherwise either avoided him ("Charles is a neat guy," says linemate Tony Casillas, "but there are times when you learn to keep your distance") or ridiculed him. Because of Haley's Neanderthal nature, he found bananas hanging in his locker, courtesy of the same teammates who teased him with the line, "Charles, why don't you go off somewhere and evolve?"

Network broadcasters fell all over themselves explaining that Haley's modest 1992 numbers (39 tackles, six sacks) were the result of "double- and triple-teaming." Motivated by their desire to identify an individual star on a defense that truly didn't have one, they raved about Haley's 42 hurries, a rather arbitrary figure that his own teammates admit seems bloated. Management is certainly convinced Haley was a major difference between Dallas's "bend-but-don't-break" approach to defense in 1991 and 1992's attacking style. After both Johnson's psychological evaluation of Haley and a review of the season's game film, he got with Jerry Jones and persuaded him to give Haley a three-year contract worth $5.25 million, lucrative enough to prevent him from entering the free agent market. Haley's value, all said, "is that he makes everyone around him better."

Better? Or bitter? Says the other defensive end, Tony Tolbert: "There's this notion that because Charles has a big reputation, the rest of us without big reputations suck. I'm not sure we needed any one player to 'put us over the hump.' We were going to be a good team without any one guy."

"Half the time around here," notes safety James Washington, "all anyone wanted to talk about was how Charles was our one-man team."

Perhaps Haley's greatest contribution was in expanding the off-field boundaries that had confined earlier editions of Johnson's teams. As recently as late 1991, Johnson said his itinerary for the team on the road was structured to avoid any "Cowboys will be boys" misbehavior. "A lot of players go to their hometowns and want to visit family and friends," Johnson said then. "Visiting family and friends is what the off-season is for."

Yet during the week before the Super Bowl, Johnson did not place a nighttime curfew on the team until Wednesday. From Sunday through Tuesday, dozens of party-weary players wobbled into the team's Super Bowl headquarters around

4:00 a.m., shaking their heads and grinning at their coach's sudden flexibility. But how could he not bend his rules when they were being stretched so by Exhibit A?

Two weeks before the Super Bowl, upon the team's arrival in San Francisco for the NFC Championship Game, Haley deplaned and exited to the right. A few of his teammates who'd been instructed to board full-sized buses to the left thought he was lost (or maybe, again lacking proper medication). But Charles knew exactly where he was going: he became the lone passenger on an American Airlines minivan, which whisked him away from the drudgery of team meetings to allow him to visit family and friends in San Francisco.

Haley also took a mini-vacation for a couple of days following the NFC title game. Just minutes after the victory, Haley whispered into Johnson's ear his request to be excused from the charter home. Haley got away with the same privileged treatment in December, when the Cowboys traveled to Washington to play the Redskins and Haley managed a side trip to his hometown of Gladys, Virginia.

"I looked into Charles' background," Johnson says. "I investigated the concerns. But the things I look for, he's got. He's a special, special player."

Only in the Jones-Johnson regime would someone with Charles Haley's reputation be deemed "special" while someone with Herschel Walker's reputation be deemed "expendable."

New-regime lore will always underline the date October 12, 1989. It was the day Walker was officially traded. But in reality, the day the biggest trade in NFL history was essentially made came sometime in July 1989, in Thousand Oaks, California, when agent Peter Johnson told Jerry Jones of Walker's upcoming salary demands.

"I'm proposing a contract extension," Jones said, knowing that Walker's contract was up after the 1990 season.

"No thanks," Johnson said. "When the time is right, we'll be looking for 'quarterback money.'"

Jones's sky-gray eyes almost popped out of his head. Walker's existing contract was guaranteed — in this league a highly unusual arrangement that required the Cowboys to send a huge chunk of money to the NFL's New York offices to be held on account. The financial arrangement was very difficult on Bum Bright at times; all by himself, Walker created a cash-flow problem. And now Herschel wanted "quarterback money," guaranteed? What was that, Jones wondered to himself, ten or twelve million bucks?

"I'd just committed $140 million to buying a whole company," Jones says. "Now they're telling me I have to guarantee ten or twelve million dollars to one employee of that company? As a businessman, I wouldn't have been able to look at myself in the mirror."

And right there, under a shade tree at training camp in Thousand Oaks, the wheels started turning on what in retrospect may be the most significant trade in football history.

Later came the celebrated brainstorming coaches jog, when Johnson suggested to his assistants the idea of dealing Walker, twenty-seven, a two-time Pro Bowler and the Cowboys' only marketable veteran. "That's when the subject of whether or not Herschel still had his heart in football first came up," says Tony Wise, the Dallas line coach now with the Chicago Bears.

Says Johnson: "I decided to trade Herschel Walker, and it was a difficult decision. I knew it was going to be controversial. It was controversial among my staff. The offensive coaches were not at all pleased. They weren't happy with the prospect of trading the only player we had who could score touchdowns."

Cowboys officials decided that Walker's public profile as a team-oriented do-gooder was a facade. His heart, they thought, was elsewhere. For any reasonable offer, they were prepared to have this Texas lone star elsewhere, too.

Later still came the involvement of Cleveland Browns owner Art Modell, whose belief that his team was a Walker away from a Super Bowl beefed up Dallas's already ridiculous asking price. And finally came October 12, 1989, the Great Minnesota Vikings Robbery. Vikings general manager Mike Lynn agreed to hand Dallas five players, a No. 1 pick and six conditional picks. The windfall helped net the Cowboys (in part through a dizzying web of subsequent transactions that involved fifty-five players and seventeen trades and fifteen teams) running back Emmitt Smith, defensive tackle Russell Maryland, cornerback Kevin Smith and five others who were still Dallas property at the end of 1992.

Walker was heading north. And the Cowboys, eventually, were heading to the Super Bowl.

Says ex-Bears coach Mike Ditka of Jones and Johnson: "They're just ol' country boys. But they came into the league. ... and hoodwinked several of the so-called geniuses. They went right to the geniuses and pulled the wool over their eyes. They whacked a few people around. ... The greatest hoodwink in history is what they did to Minnesota."

Walker leads the list of "white hats" who were shown the door by Johnson. "We knew we needed to build a team that had chemistry," Johnson says. "A team's ability to play together is just as important as its talent." Haley, a "black hat," somehow became part of the chemistry. So did just enough of the principals in the forty-six trades and assortment of signings the Cowboys engineered in the first four years of the Jones-Johnson era.

"We have no fear," Jones says. "We don't say, 'What if he doesn't work out?' Especially in the early going, we brought new players in here based on the belief that they couldn't be worse than the old players. If that meant looking at somebody with a supposedly bad attitude, we didn't run scared. It just became a matter of researching that player's background."

Says Johnson: "I like the guy who can walk into a pool room and sink the eight ball. Some people, when the game's on the line, it's very tough for them. I eliminate them from our program. The people I want around me are the ones who want to play in the big games. That's what matters. I can handle people who are a little out of the ordinary. I can't handle people who don't know how to win."

Once these diverse newcomers from diverse backgrounds had been assembled in Dallas, it was left to Johnson to pour them into the mold of a team.

The rookies, Johnson figured, would not be the challenge. He has never had a problem selling his program to fresh-faced recruits. Besides, on top of his always persuasive talents, he now was backed by Jones's rallying cry to push to the kids. "With the Cowboys, success doesn't just mean you might end up on the cover of *Sports Illustrated*," goes Jones's alluring line to players on the outside looking in. "You might end up on the cover of *Time*."

The veteran holdovers wouldn't cause the problems, either. First of all, Johnson had established who was the boss with them by quickly dethroning team heroes such as Walker and cornerback Everson Walls. "I never knew if I'd be gone the next day," says ten-year fixture Bill Bates. "None of us did."

The native Cowboys might have gotten restless, but they never dared get rebellious. In the spring of 1991, a group of six unsigned veterans talked of banding together to boycott one of Johnson's "voluntary" mini-camps, which in fact are as mandatory as a voluntary event can be. The boycott withered when they considered the Johnsonian ramifications.

"He'll cut our nuts off," said one, whose diagnosis was an "attitude adjustment," about wanting to see how far the coach could be pushed? "As most players who've been around me for any period of time understand, that's not a smart thing to do." That is Johnson's message.

Besides, by the end of 1992, only ten players remained from the Landry years. So most of those who might have been tempted to buck the system had already been bucked themselves. Says Bates: "Not everybody liked the way coach Johnson did things at first. But everybody learned he wasn't running a democracy around here."

Johnson's job is made easier by his able reading of the personalities of his three highest-profile stars, Troy Aikman, Michael Irvin and Emmitt Smith. "I feel like it's my job to know who the players are looking up to and who they respect," Johnson says. "Then I get to those players, especially, to get an indication of how the players feel, and to let them all know how I feel."

Johnson displayed his understanding of the dangers of misdirected leadership in his first year, when he decided to rid his team of Walls. By 1989, Walls had spent eight glorious years as a leader of the team in his native Dallas. A former free-agent success story, the cornerback swiped a team-record 11 interceptions in his rookie season of 1981. He'd played in three Pro Bowls, led the team in picks five times and had established himself as a locker-room cornerstone. But in a November 12, 1989, loss to Phoenix, Johnson decided Walls had to be torn down.

Walls and safety Vince Albritton seemed to deserve the blame for the Cowboys' collapse in the loss. Troy Aikman's 80-yard touchdown pass to James Dixon put Dallas up 20-17 with 1:43 left in the game. But Cardinals quarterback Tom Tupa and receiver Ernie Jones teamed up to beat Walls and Albritton, as they had earlier in the game, for a long touchdown that gave Phoenix a 24-20 victory.

On both Cardinals scores, Walls was supposed to chuck Jones at the line before releasing him to Albritton. Walls failed to do so. It also appeared Albritton goofed up his assignment: both plays were made possible by Albritton's decision to go for interceptions rather than tackles. But after the game, Johnson made Walls the sole scapegoat, and even accused him of "fraternizing" with the opponent. And the next day, Johnson not only demoted Walls from the first team, but shifted him from cornerback to safety.

On Monday night, the media asked Walls to comment on his future. "You'll have to ask the man with the chubby cheeks," said Walls, who exited the west end of a Valley Ranch hallway just before Johnson — his body wrapped in a towel and his usually shellacked hair dripping wet — darted through an entrance at the hallway's east end.

Johnson was aware Walls wielded enough wave-making authority in the locker room to possibly undermine the coach. He needed to be kept abreast of what this team leader was saying. So he interrupted his shower to find out, and asked the reporters who'd talked to Walls to relay his comments.

Said *Arkansas Democrat* writer Bob Holt: "It was like seeing the Pope in his underwear."

But Johnson didn't want to expose his team to dissension. Better that he expose himself, at least until he'd established his own lieutenants. By 1992, they were entrenched.

Irvin, the team's top pick in 1988, arrived in Dallas the year before Johnson did. But Irvin had performed for Johnson at the University of Miami, and the coach knew the receiver would lend him bridge-gapping assistance. Irvin's outlandish, flamboyant style often sets the tone for the Cowboys, sometimes by brightening their moods, sometimes by taking the heat of the media, fans or opponent upon himself.

Aikman, the top pick in 1989, had carefully cultivated a placid public demeanor that was adapted by the Cowboys when appropriate. It is less likely that supporting-cast members will lose composure when their top-billed quarterback is seen conducting press conferences in that intentionally monotone-voiced, sleepy-eyed delivery.

And sometimes, aloofness and arrogance are the necessary emotions. Sometimes, the Cowboys need a chip on their collective shoulder. Enter running back Emmitt Smith, the top pick in 1990, who so frequently butts helmets with imaginary obstacles and imaginary critics he's conjured up that he ought to sign an endorsement deal with a company that manufactures shoulder chips.

Irvin, Aikman and Smith are fantastic athletes. No NFL team has had a 3,500-yard passer, a 1,500-yard rusher and a 1,500-yard receiver in one season. In 1992, the Cowboys' troika came closer to that than anyone ever has. But in the community and in the locker room, Irvin, Aikman and Smith transcend their places as jocks. They are the thermostats; people around them go hot and cold when they do.

"The best setup is when your top players set the example for everyone else," says Newton, along with linebacker Ken Norton and Bates, another controller of the Cowboys' spirits. "Emmitt, Michael and Troy would be respected even if they weren't great players. But because they are, they're like E. F. Hutton: They talk, people listen."

Adds tight end Alfredo Roberts: "Emmitt is so much younger than the other two guys, so he's not your classic vocal leader. But he's been put in that position by Jimmy because if you're going to have people lead by production, you designate as leaders your most productive people."

The Cowboys' Big Three certainly have some of the most God-given reasons to devolve into egomaniacal nightmares. Indeed, there was a time in his rookie year when Smith teetered on doing just that. In 1990, Smith complained to friends that no Dallas-area auto dealer had approached him about free use of a car. And Smith still has this befuddling habit of alternately begging for 30 carries a game, then angrily announcing he's been overworked. Still, by 1992, even after capturing back-to-back NFL rushing titles, Smith understood the potentially implosive side effects of caste-system greed and was slapping down any suggestion that he be given special treatment. One of Smith's few concessions to his status comes annually in training camp, when he gladly rests on the sidelines while lesser backs take the pounding in brutal drills.

Smith is five-foot-nine, 200 pounds. He's relatively slow afoot (he runs a 4.5 40). And he was decidedly slow to sign (his 48-day contract dispute is what caused him to fall 63 yards short of 1,000 as a rookie). But as Johnson knows, he is gifted, in more ways than as a runner.

Says Smith: "Leadership doesn't have to be talking. If my teammates need me to be the strong, silent type, I try to be that. Some of them might think I'm being arrogant. But I'm just trying to set a tone. Sometimes leadership is never talking."

And sometimes, as in the case of Irvin, leadership is never shutting up.

"People might say I'm a hot dog," Irvin says. "But in a league — and a world — where so many people are trying to be something they're not, I'll go to my grave being Michael Irvin.

And Michael Irvin is a talker."

Being Michael Irvin means spending more time in the light than a lamp shade. It means getting suspended from one high school back in Fort Lauderdale and missing his junior year before surfacing at another school. It means getting in trouble for allegedly throwing a punch at a referee in a charity basketball game. It means the mother of his young daughter suing for child support. It means being chastised by members of the Philadelphia Eagles for not showing more respect to the memory of the late Jerome Brown, the former Eagle and a close friend of Irvin from their Miami days. It means missing the Cowboys' team flight to Detroit for the November 8, 1992, game with the Lions. And with Johnson as his coach, it means being let almost completely off the hook for that gaffe.

Unquestionably, there are players who would have been cut for the same violation. Irvin was benched. For one series.

Being Michael Irvin means being a lightning rod for negatives and positives. Some teammates do view him as a teacher's pet, as a beneficiary of the Johnson Way. "Michael is one of my favorites," says Johnson, putting up no argument.

But Irvin is impossible not to like.

"Michael is the Pied Piper," says the other starting receiver, Alvin Harper. "You want to follow him. It's tough to have a bad outlook on things when he's bouncing around here, strutting and bustin' on you and laughing at you. So you do what he says."

Aikman says it his position more than his personality that places him in a leadership role. "I'm the guy who's doing the talking in the huddle, that's all," he says. "Now, sometimes I raise my voice in the huddle. Sometimes I get in somebody's face if I don't think somebody is doing everything they can to help us win. I've always done that. You know how they say the quarterback gets too much credit if you win and too much blame if you lose? Well, if the quarterback is going to have all that much responsibility, he might as well do something constructive with it."

Once Johnson had Aikman, Smith, Irvin and a few others plugged in, he had his emotional backbone. Johnson's test as a chemist/coach would be the stirring in of veterans from other teams. Couldn't one spoiled ingredient ruin the delicate mix?

Not all of the Cowboys' trades for veterans are laudable. Fullback Alonzo Highsmith cost the Cowboys two high draft picks, but he was damaged goods when he arrived in the fall of 1990 from the Houston Oilers and in worse shape when he departed a year later. Running back Terrence Flagler and Stubbs, acquired from San Francisco in April 1990, were billed as building blocks. But Flagler was released in training camp. And Stubbs, one of Johnson's University of Miami pets who compounded that mini-camp absence by receiving so many fines for avoiding the weight room that he suggested the weekly penalties just be subtracted from his paycheck, lasted just more than a year.

These were the sort of failures that sent the previous regime running scared from trades. In 1987, tackle Ron Essink came to Dallas from Seattle for a fifth-round pick then immediately retired. The Cowboys suspected a conspiracy. Says former team executive Bob Ackles: "We were so concerned about getting screwed after that, that we became too careful."

Johnson does not trade carelessly. But like all home-run hitters, he isn't troubled by the occasional swing-and-miss. Actually, he almost denies their existence. "They weren't busts," he'll say of ill-fated moves. "They were disappointments."

And Jones has seen too many business deals backfire to lose sleep over a stinkbomb of a trade or two. He was almost the owner of the San Diego Chargers back in 1966, when Jones, then twenty-three, labored to scrape together $5.8 million to buy into that franchise. "People now think I was buying an expensive toy," Jones says. "But it wasn't just to have a hand in something different. I don't have an "acquire things" mindset. And it wasn't an ego thing, like I know a lot of people think the Cowboys is for me. I could sit and watch from 50-yard-line suites, and rub elbows with football heroes, without spending $140 million, believe me."

Pat Jones talked his son out of the Chargers deal. Unfortunately, sixty days later, that $5.8 million interest was sold for $11 million. But as Jones says, "If you can say you've never been tackled then it's because you've never carried that ball."

A few years later came the opportunity to purchase southern Missouri rights to one of three fast food chains.

McDonald's? Jerry Jones said no.

Kentucky Fried Chicken. He said no.

Shakey's Pizza Parlors? Jones said yes, and cost himself millions.

The Cowboys' football version of that sort of regrettable decision was the sloppy Jesse Solomon mess, featuring a truly gifted linebacker who was only a bar exam away from qualifying as one of the sport's best clubhouse lawyers. He came to the Cowboys from Minnesota as part of the Walker trade. On August 24, 1990, Jones announced he and Solomon (who acted as his own agent) had agreed to a new contract. On August 26, Jones announced, "I do not think Jesse Solomon will be a Dallas Cowboy in 1990." The deal had fallen through, largely because agent Solomon had a fool for a client.

When Solomon finally signed on October 18, Jones tossed some of his own foolishness into the equation. Solomon was near the Cowboys' Valley Ranch practice field, holding court with the media, expounding on the subject of how slavery was alive and thriving in the National Football League. Meanwhile,

Jones strolled into the area to guide a tour of the facility for some business big-wheels. Jones spotted the reporters and the TV cameras. He saw Solomon. And he found himself magnetically drawn to an opportunity to prove just how in synch his 1990 Cowboys would be.

"Should I go over?" Jones asked team vice-president Mike McCoy, who admits now he should have responded, "Jones, are you out of your mind?"

"Um, tough call," McCoy mumbled.

"I believe I'll try it," said Jones as he bounded boldly into Jesse's Inferno.

Jones extended a hand. Solomon refused to accept it. There probably weren't too many TV stations in the land that didn't run this juicy footage of a man who claimed to be a slave figuratively spitting in the face of the man who moments ago had been portrayed as a slave owner.

Jones closed the impromptu press briefing as congenially as he could. "I hope you take that good, hostile attitude with you out there on the field," Jones told Solomon, who eventually took his attitude on a journey that would land him with five different teams in four seasons.

But despite the errors, the Cowboys front office had erected a reputation. Jones and Johnson were so much more active on the trade front than other teams that there was suddenly an assumption that they must know something all the other teams were oblivious to. This edge, whether real or imagined, often works to the Cowboys' advantage. "When teams want to make a deal, they know who to call first and last," Johnson says. Of course, some clubs find the Cowboys' image intimidating. In 1992, the image actually prevented the Cincinnati Bengals from acquiring Cowboys cornerback Brian Mitchell in exchange for a bottle of Heineken.

Toward the end of the 1992 training camp, Johnson called Bengals head coach David Shula, a former Dallas assistant, and offered to do him a favor.

"David, you guys need a defensive back, correct?" Johnson asked.

"Yes, we do," Shula responded carefully.

"Okay, I'll give one to you," said Johnson. "His name is Brian Mitchell. He's played in the league with the Falcons, a pretty good special-team guy. In return, you just buy me a beer sometime down the road."

Shula didn't get it. He wanted more specifics. Exactly what were the terms of this trade? How would the paperwork read? And what did you really want in exchange for Mitchell?

Johnson explained that the official terms of the deal would detail a trade of Mitchell in exchange for "future considerations." And those future considerations would be a Heineken, courtesy of Shula.

Jimmy would have to buy his own beer. Shula would have to make do with his existing defensive backs. The Bengals coach, lacking the authority to do a deal by himself, and wary of what Johnson was trying to pull, simply couldn't bring himself to trust his old boss.

"My reputation is such that no one believes I'm a nice enough guy to just want to do a friend a favor," Johnson says.

Johnson does, however, have a way of winning the trust and cooperation of trade acquisitions, of veterans indoctrinated in the ways of other organizations.

"Don't think Jimmy doesn't have different rules for different players," a Cowboys veteran says. "He makes sure every veteran who comes in here looks at it like it is this great opportunity. For some of the guys who had troubles elsewhere, that was easy to convince them of. So that made them happy. Then he bent some rules here and there to fit them, to keep them happy. Maybe a Thomas Everett didn't need different rules. But Charles Haley did, so he got different rules. Jimmy knows who to cross and who not to cross."

Johnson sees it differently. "Favoritism," remember?

"I always said I fully plan to treat everybody differently," Johnson says. "They do not have different rules. Each of them knows what I expect of him. I might deal with a problem differently depending on the different individuals."

The texture of the champion Cowboys is a cross-stitch of the obvious and dominant personalities — Jones and Johnson and Haley and Aikman and Irvin and Smith — with some other personalities who uncannily and unselfishly supressed their egos for the greater good. Yes, Johnson has an undeniable gift for massaging psyches. "Sometimes it's rah-rah, or stroking, or motivating through fear, or respect, or positive reinforcement, or one-on-one counseling, or a kick in the rear," Johnson says. "I try to do a little bit of all of it."

But also, Johnson's veteran additions to the Cowboys responded by displaying an invaluable gift by being able to wait patiently in the wings before making their sometimes unheralded offerings to Dallas's Super season.

The veterans reared in other organizations who pitched in during Dallas's 1992 run ranged from the high-profile to the no-profile. Quarterback Steve Beuerlein. Safety Ray Horton. Tight end Jay Novacek. Defensive tackle Tony Casillas. Linebacker Vinson Smith. Guard John Gesek. Linebacker Mickey Pruitt. Tight end Alfredo Roberts. Safety James Washington. Offensive lineman Frank Cornish. Fullback Tommie Agee. Offensive lineman Alan Veingrad. Safety Thomas Everett. Cornerback Issiac Holt. Running back Derrick Gainer. Tight end Derek Tennell. Offensive lineman Dale Hellestrae.

Meld them with Aikman, Irvin and Smith. And with old-timers Bill Bates, Jim Jeffcoat, Mark Tuinei, Mike Saxon, Nate

Newton, Kevin Gogan, Kelvin Martin, Robert Williams and Ken Norton. And with Daryl Johnston, Mark Stepnoski, Tony Tolbert, Jimmie Jones, Kenny Gant, Russell Maryland, Alvin Harper, Dixon Edwards, Godfrey Myles, Erik Williams, Leon Lett, Larry Brown, Kevin Smith, Robert Jones, Jimmy Smith, Darren Woodson, Clayton Holmes and Lin Elliott.

They blended.

"Chemistry matters," says Aikman, who met with Johnson while he was making final cuts in preparation for the 1992 season to petition the coach to remember the subtle, sometimes intangible contributions made by the Hellestraes and the Agees. "Everyone has a role. Some players motivate. Some tell jokes. It all adds up."

It seems like an oxymoron to say subtleties are huge. But it is true in the case of the Cowboys. Everett, for instance, has aspirations that serve as inspiration. Numerous young players say he has, in passing, related to them the story about hearing Chicago Bears legend Mike Singletary, like Everett a Baylor product, talk of "still waiting to play the perfect game."

"That's what you strive for," Everett preaches. "The perfect game."

The Cowboys haven't played the perfect game. They haven't assembled the perfect team. But in 1992, by sidestepping strife while assembling talent, the organization came closer to both goals than any other in football.

"We've got players nobody wanted," Washington says. "We've got guys who were supposed to be head cases. We've got guys who other teams thought were too slow or two small or too stupid. We're a melting pot."

The 1992 Cowboys were a melting pot that never boiled over.

The racial chasm was no more of a hurdle than the status gap, and there were times when it caused the chemistry to nearly go sour. In December, Newton made public his plans to star in a music video along the lines of the Chicago Bears' 1985 "Super Bowl Shuffle." But the project was officially cancelled when Johnson wisely ruled that a celebratory song was not appropriate in December, when the Cowboys didn't yet have anything to celebrate. But petty jealousy might have caused the project to bog down, anyway.

Players who had tentatively agreed to participate balked when they learned the video would be called "Nate and the 'Boys." The idea that quarterbacks and running backs and wide receivers would make up the supporting cast while an offensive guard took center stage was not well-received by (you guessed it) the quarterbacks, running backs and wide receivers.

Marquee names Aikman and Haley found themselves in the middle of an early-season "conflict" that drew national attention. On September 9, ESPN gossip Fred Edelstein reported that Haley had confronted Aikman to inform the quarterback that "he couldn't carry Joe Montana's jock."

In the segment, Edelstein said: "It didn't take long for Haley to ruffle feathers in Dallas. The word out of the Cowboys locker room is that last week, out of nowhere, Haley went up to Troy Aikman and told him he couldn't carry Joe Montana's jock. Aikman did not bother to debate the subject."

As is frequently the case with Edelstein and his "In the End Zone" reports, he wasn't even in the stadium.

Aikman and Haley did in fact have a one-on-one conversation on the sidelines during the Cowboys' preseason finale against the Chicago Bears. Aikman heard Haley grousing about the media. The two had met months earlier at the Pro Bowl, and again at a charity basketball game in Sacramento, and Aikman felt comfortable stepping in as a favor to offer some advice as to how the newcomer might best handle report-ers in the Metroplex.

A few days later, 49ers owner Eddie DeBartolo, interested in how the just-traded Haley was doing in Dallas, found out about the Aikman-Haley exchange. He told Dr. Harry Edwards, a team advisor who had been close to Haley. Predicted Edwards: "Charles will address the top Cowboys. He'll tell Aikman he's no Montana. He'll tell Irvin he's no (Jerry) Rice. He'll get in Emmitt Smith's face. That's just Charles' way."

DeBartolo is one of the few NFL officials Edelstein actually interviews. Their discussion of Edwards' remarks, possibly meshed with remarks made by Channel 8 sports anchor Dale Hansen at the Cowboys Kickoff Luncheon that week (Hansen joked that Haley might suggest Aikman "is no Montana") triggered Edelstein's erroneous report. "Edelstein never called me," Aikman says. "He never called Jimmy or Jerry or Charles. He hears something, makes it a little juicier than he heard it, and puts it on ESPN. Can you do that? Doesn't he have to answer to somebody for that?"

Aikman proved he could carry Montana's jock a day after the news was all over the country. Worried that he'd somehow created a controversy by doing absolutely nothing, Aikman returned to his Las Colinas home looking to escape questions about Haley and Montana. Hanging from his doorknob was an athletic supporter. Someone used a black magic marker to write "MONTANA" on the band. Montana's jock strap, get it? Aikman carried it to the trash can, laughing his head off, suddenly assured Edelstein's misinformation would fade with-out triggering trouble for a team that couldn't afford it.

"I knew Charles coming here would spice things up a little bit, because I knew Charles was sort of an odd man," Irvin says. "But I also knew that if Charles is a little bit off the wall, he'd come to the right team."

4 DEALING WITH
   THE DEVILS   ★

Pick an envelope. The Cowboys push it. All the way up to the Pentagon, they push it.

Some paperwork detailing the possibility of Air Force pilot/defensive lineman Chad Hennings joining the Cowboys once actually crossed the desk of United States Secretary of Defense Dick Cheney. The request was denied. Dallas would have to wait until the spring of 1992 before Hennings, fresh off flying missions over northern Iraq during the Persian Gulf War, would be released from his commitment because of overstaffing in the military.

But the Pentagon had learned first-hand that if the Cowboys didn't have omnipotent pull — "Since when is America's Team a branch of the military?" Cheney must have asked himself — they at least had no shortage of testosterone.

Ian Fleming and Tom Clancy might have become sportswriters had they the chance to cover these Cowboys. The people who run this franchise delight in espionage (which follows the tradition of their Dallas predecessors who, according to an old-regime source, occasionally ordered wire taps installed in the Valley Ranch phones). These Cowboys invent.

They innovate. They stretch loopholes into caverns. They force the National Football League to investigate. They ignite complaints from competing organizations that have been twiddling their thumbs for too many years to understand why the Cowboys can't politely twiddle right along.

Hennings serves as a lesson in the Cowboys' attempts at string-pulling. Hennings was drafted by the old regime in 1988's eleventh round. Jerry Jones had been trying to "have him transferred to the Cowboys" before his stint was up. As early as 1989, Jones asked Robert Strauss, a Dallas native who at the time was a high-powered Washington attorney (and future ambassador to the Soviet Union) to see what he could do. Strauss, a Cowboys fan, made the request of Cheney.

"We talked about how the visibility of Chad joining the Cowboys might help the Air Force just as Roger Staubach coming to the Cowboys years earlier probably helped the visibility of the Navy," Jones says. "We just wondered if there would be a value to both parties there."

Pushing the envelope.

More than ever in 1992, the Cowboys obviously took that approach in the most easily-chronicled area, play-calling. How else to explain the decision to throw out of their own end zone in the December 13 game at Washington, when Redskins lineman Jason Buck barreled into Troy Aikman, causing a bizarre scramble for the football that directly resulted in Dallas's 20-17 loss?

"Everyone was comfortable with us throwing the ball in that situation," Aikman says. "The fact that it didn't work does nothing to change that."

How else to explain the decision to skip a chip-shot field goal in the NFC Championship Game in San Francisco and go for it on fourth-and-goal from the one-yard line? The 49ers stopped the run attempt and used it as a springboard to threaten what ended up being a 30-20 Dallas win. But at the time, the Cowboys were up 24-13. It was the fourth quarter. Wouldn't a field goal have been more prudent? Had the decision led to a loss, "I could have been the goat," said coach Jimmy Johnson, who fought off offensive coordinator Norv Turner's attempts to persuade him to kick it. "But, well, I'm not the goat."

"You've got to admire Jimmy's aggressiveness," Turner said later.

How else to explain another exhibit of attack-dog mentality against Buffalo in Super Bowl XXVII, a high-stakes point at which even the most wide-open NFL teams nervously fold their cards of creativity? Ahead 31-10 with two minutes to go in the third quarter, the Cowboys passed on fourth-and-three from the Bills' 38. Aikman's throw to Jay Novacek was knocked down. Five plays later, the Bills had cut the lead to 31-17. A nervous moment? "Nah," Aikman says. "Our style is our style. We don't do it any differently in a preseason game than we do in a Super Bowl."

Pushing the envelope. Indefatigably. On the field and off the field, too.

In February of 1993, the NFL finally etched in stone most of its guidelines for free agency. There were, however, still some gray areas. Jones was not disappointed. "We seem to thrive around here when there is a little 'vagueness' or a little 'give' in the rules," he says.

"When new ideas come along, the National Football League is like lining up the wagons for the Oklahoma land rush," says superagent Leigh Steinberg. "Some pioneers had plans and concepts, and their wagons shot out ahead of everyone else. Other wagons never left. My sense is that Dallas will always shoot out there."

Bob Ackles, the former Cowboys executive, says it is Jimmy Johnson's intellect and attitude that makes it so. "When you sit in the draft room with Jimmy, you see what he has that so few other people do," Ackles says. "Most of us are trying to think one step ahead. Jimmy is talking with four different teams on four different lines, considering trading up, considering trading down, considering the merits of the available players. And all the time the rest of us are trying to think one step ahead, Jimmy is literally thinking four or five steps ahead."

The Cowboys stride where other teams fear the ice is thin or the dirt is quicksand. Maybe it takes devious to recognize devious, but just four years after coming to Dallas, the people who run the Cowboys seem to know where the league's bodies are buried. They dig under rocks, search in closets, force open closed doors. They're aware of the NFL's dirty little secrets.

This is the organization, for instance, that finally thought to ask the Los Angeles Raiders whatever happened to Derrick Gainer. Gainer, a 250-pound running back and special-teams standout known by the Cowboys staff from his days as a Florida prep star, was not on the Raiders' active roster in the early part of 1992. Nor was he on injured reserve, or the practice squad or any other NFL-sanctioned list. He was technically a free agent, yet indications were he was in the employ of the Raiders. A shady deal.

"It's odd how one week there's some former Raiders player working at a 7-Eleven, and the next week (Raiders boss) Al Davis has him in his starting lineup," says Dallas running backs coach Joe Brodsky.

"I was being stashed," Gainer says.

The Raiders freed Gainer (who says he was living off a lump-sum payment the club gave him when he was released with a preseason injury) to Dallas on October 12, 1992. That was the same day L.A. acquired receiver Alexander Wright from the Cowboys. The timing was no coincidence. Gainer and others say he was in essence an unofficial throw-in with the Wright trade.

Clearly, by 1992, the Cowboys — who had once been criticized for leaving such an important job to neophytes such as Jones and Johnson — had learned how to play the sometimes underhanded game of operating an NFL team.

The week before the Cowboys were to play in Super Bowl XXVII, Dallas college scouting director Larry Lacewell was asked by a coaching acquaintance to list the names of the executives in charge of the team's various departments.

"Here's the names," Lacewell said. "Jones and Johnson."

"But an organization can't work that way," the acquaintance argued.

"The hell it can't," Lacewell said. "We're in the Super Bowl, aren't we?"

Says Jones, "I never saw the need for a middle man, for someone with NFL experience. Everyone kept saying, 'But you need a general manager. You need someone who knows the ropes.' But Jimmy Johnson is no dummy. I'm no dummy. I knew we'd get things done faster if it was just the two of us making decisions. I knew eventually, the decisions we'd make would be the right ones. And I knew we were both fast learners.

"Certainly there was a time when the other people in this league saw the two of us and thought, 'Boy, are we going to take these guys to the cleaners.' But we ended up soliciting opinions and ideas from a lot of those people. We found ways to learn things from our critics."

When the Cowboys agreed to a deal with San Diego Chargers Plan B offensive lineman Frank Cornish weeks before announcing it on April 1, 1992, was that fair to their veteran linemen who knew nothing about this newcomer who might steal their jobs? Had the veterans on Plan B known Cornish had been signed, some of them might have departed. Is this fair? Maybe not. But nothing in the NFL bylaws prohibits this.

On February 1, 1992, the Cowboys offered stay-home bonuses to Plan B players. The payments were advances on their 1992 salaries. Is this legal? All the Cowboys knew is that there was no NFL rule that specifically outlaws it. Which was legal enough to them.

At the start of the 1991 training camp, the Cowboys brought draft picks to Austin before they'd signed. This is definitely against the spirit of NFL rules, and the league did investigate. Its findings: the team brought players in on a Sunday. The Cowboys golf tournament was Monday. Practice didn't actually begin until Tuesday, the day Cowboys management said camp officially kicked off. Hence, no violation.

"You've got to hand it to the Cowboys," agent Ted Updike says. "The kid's already flown in. He's already eating dinner across the table from his coach. And he's expected to listen to his agent when his agent tells him to be patient, to wait a few more days for a few more dollars? That's unreal pressure." The unreal pressure worked. Each of those rookies who arrived on Sunday without contracts were in uniform with agreements by Tuesday.

Can you bypass agents and directly contact your unsigned players? Agent Richard Howell called it "despicable" when Jerry Jones did exactly that in the summer of 1990, when negotiations with top picks Emmitt Smith and Alexander Wright were going nowhere. Risking similarly venomous reactions from other agents two years later, Jones sidestepped "professional courtesy" and again went directly at two of his unsigned veterans, center Mark Stepnoski and defensive end Tony Tolbert. In Stepnoski's case, Jones marched out to the practice field one day to corral fullback Daryl Johnston, hoping to persuade Johnston to give him the number in Pennsylvania where Stepnoski could be reached. In Tolbert's case, Jones phoned his home and attempted to negotiate a contract on the spot, without the knowledge of Tolbert's agents, Jean Fugett and Abner Haynes.

"Mr. Jones, do my agents know you're calling me? Because I'd prefer you dealt directly with them," Tolbert said.

"Tony, I don't know that your agents are dealing with you as straight as I'm going to deal with you," said Jones, who was completely sincere.

Can you negotiate contracts with players before you draft them? No. But the Cowboys determined that it is permissible to "explore contract parameters" with potential draftees to "assess signability." So starting in 1991, the Cowboys explored and assessed their tails off.

Motivated by their frustration over the previous year's summer-long holdouts of Smith and Wright, the Cowboys hoped to create a way to guarantee that their picks would be in camp. "Alexander Wright in particular wasted a year of his career for a little more money," Johnson says. "It was foolish." The NFL had always allowed the team with the first pick in the selection process to negotiate before the start of the draft; Dallas did it successfully in 1989, when Troy Aikman was the top overall pick. In 1990, the Chicago Bears took it a step farther by presenting USC safety Mark Carrier a take-it-or-leave-it offer. The Bears had the No. 6 pick; Carrier was projected to be chosen about ten slots later. Carrier accepted less money than a standard No. 6 would get, but more than he would have received had he fallen to No. 16 or so.

When Carrier was one of the rookie stars of the 1990 season, it alerted the Cowboys to the realization that they could add some sense to this retarded system that resulted in most high-round picks waiting until August before reaching agreements. Not only would they make take-it-or-leave-it offers to their targeted player in the first round, as the Bears had done; they'd do it with virtually every potential pick in almost every round. They'd hire trusted friends from around the country to station themselves near the homes of possible picks, with blank contracts in hand.

And then they'd negotiate "on the clock," during the fifteen minutes allowed by the league to turn in their choice. And they'd put the kids in the frying pan. If you wanted to be a high pick of the Cowboys, do it at this lesser price, they'd say, or turn down our deal and end up a lower pick of some other team at that same lesser price.

University of Tennessee wide receiver Alvin Harper was pinpointed by the Cowboys, who had the No. 12 pick in the 1990 draft. The Pittsburgh Steelers were also interested. They held the No. 15 pick. The problem for Harper was that while Dallas was willing to commit, Pittsburgh was not. Should he take a risk and turn down Dallas's deal, then hope he doesn't slip beyond the Steelers and into less-monied territory? "You're sitting there with the Dallas Cowboys talking about millions of dollars, and none of the other teams are willing to talk about anything," says Harper. "Man, it's a persuasive way of doing business."

"It's simply common sense," Jones says. "If the player wants to be signed in time to fulfill his potential, and if the Cowboys want to sign him, then why goof around? Let's get it done."

"It works," Cowboys vice-president Mike McCoy says. "We haven't lost a player we've wanted yet."

The Cowboys finagled their way to seventeen picks in the 1991 draft. All seventeen of the rookies were under contract in Austin in time to show their wares. Other teams who entered camp not having signed their rookies were still leafing through the NFL rules on early signings, still calling the league office in protest of what the Cowboys had done. How do you agree with so many players so quickly without breaking the rules? "We got on the phone," Jones says. "Other teams shouldn't be complaining about it. They should be trying it."

Adds Johnson: "Other teams are starting to see that Jerry has some smart ways of conducting business. Other teams are doing some of what he does."

Is it possible? The owner who once seemed to have just fallen off the turnip truck is now spawning Jones's Clones?

In part because Jones's quick deals made them training campers from Day One, at least seven of the names taken in that 1991 draft now form an important part of the Cowboys' foundation. With the first overall pick, acquired from the New England Patriots in a complex swap, Dallas took from the University of Miami defensive tackle Russell Maryland, a six-foot-one, 275-pound pet player of ex-Hurricanes coach Johnson and who was seen as a certain solid contributor, if not a superstar pro. With the other first-round pick came a six-foot-three, 200-pound Harper, a high-jumper who, like Maryland, became a starter in his rookie season and began to blossom into a standout by 1992. The Cowboys traded down three times, from the fourteenth spot to the thirty-seventh, and still got the linebacker they'd coveted, Michigan State's Dixon Edwards, with a second-round choice. Florida linebacker Godfrey Myles was a third-rounder, as was Central (Ohio) State offensive tackle Erik Williams. Williams might be the steal of that draft. Or maybe the steal will prove to be the man-child chosen in the seventh round, Leon Lett, the defensive lineman from Emporia (Kansas) State taken almost on a whim. In the twelfth and final round came Texas Christian University's Larry Brown.

"Every championship team needs that one great draft to put them over the top," says Butch Davis, the defensive line coach elevated to coordinator after the Super Bowl. "That one might have been ours."

Maryland, Harper, Williams and Brown are now starters. Myles and Lett are contending to be.

For a time, it seemed the most notable aspect of the 1991 draft was the player the Cowboys did not select. On April 19, they gave New England a No. 1 pick, a No. 2 pick and three players, cornerback Ron Francis and linebackers David Howard and Eugene Lockhart, for the Patriots' top overall spot. It was assumed that top pick would be used to select wide receiver/kick returner Raghib "Rocket" Ismail, the Heisman Trophy winner from Notre Dame.

"We knew exactly what we wanted to happen," said Johnson, dismissing the idea that Ismail was ever on his wish list. And it was true that by Saturday, the day before the draft, Maryland was the Cowboys' man. His qualities as a person and as a player had been evaluated into the night by Jones, Johnson and staff. And his "signability had been assessed." Still, its doubtful the Cowboys were completely certain Maryland, and not Ismail, would be their man until they received the Rocket's salary proposal from agent Ed Abram. He wanted a five-year, $17 million contract, a deal that would make him the NFL's highest-paid player.

"That was money no team in the NFL was going to pay him," Jones says. "I took one look at the fax, and threw it in the trash can."

Ismail signed with the Toronto Argonauts of the Canadian Football League. (His NFL rights belong to the Raiders, who took him in the fourth round. The Cowboys admit they goofed in not spending a similar pick on Ismail). Maryland signed a five-year, $6.8 million deal to come to Dallas. The Cowboys had beaten the NFL system again. Had they been able to beat the D/FW Airport security system, their 1991 draft would have come off without a hitch. But the car that was to transport Maryland from the airport to his draft-day press conference at Valley Ranch was illegally parked and towed away.

In 1992, the Cowboys didn't know which college player would be their first-round pick in the April 27 draft. But the coaches who had flown all over the country on scouting trips in Jerry Jones's Lear jet 35, the plane with the Cowboys helmet insignia on the tail, knew it would be a defensive back. Florida State cornerback Terrell Buckley joined Pitt defensive lineman Sean Gilbert atop Dallas's draft board. Was there a way to trade up from Dallas's Round 1 spots at No. 13 and No. 24 to get Buckley? "Buckley might have been the ideal, but it was a pipe dream when we realized the price it would take to get him," Jones says.

Johnson, who played a frenetic game of Checkers with first-round picks and ended up using the No. 17 selection on Texas A&M cornerback Kevin Smith, pretended Smith was always the target. Did Johnson mean to suggest that Buckley was not more highly regarded than Smith? "I'll bet you my annual salary that we did not try to trade for Buckley," responded Johnson, shifting into a game of semantics.

During the draft, Johnson has lots of games going. In the 1992 draft, different factions were petitioning for different DBs. Smith, the five-foot-ten, 173-pound cover man, was a playmaker. He holds A&M's school record with 20 career interceptions. That made him a desirable addition to a Cowboys team that totaled 12 interceptions in all of 1991. But Buckley, eventually taken by the Green Bay Packers in the No. 5 slot, was judged to be the better player. And what of Dale Carter, the spectacular Tennessee defensive back? In 1992, he was the most productive professional player of the three. But there is a belief he'll revert to being the bad actor he was reputed to be in college, thus proving the Cowboys' trust in their network of college friends to be justified.

Volunteers coach Johnny Majors insisted to Johnson that Dale Carter was "trouble." Majors and Carter had clashed frequently at Tennessee, commonly facing off in screaming bouts on the sidelines. Though others tried to persuade Johnson that the Majors-Carter problems were not solely the fault of Carter, Dallas decided to pass on him, thereby skipping an impact player who produced a Rookie-of-the-Year season with the Kansas City Chiefs.

Says Dave Wannstedt: "First of all, character is very important to Jimmy. And Kevin Smith has character. Also, at the time, we honestly didn't believe we were one great player away from being a Super Bowl team. Maybe Buckley was that one great player. But that wasn't the move we needed to make, in our view then. We figured we still needed a few more solid players, then two or three more really super players to be good enough to win it all. We had too many holes to trade a bunch of picks for one player like Buckley. Besides, as the deal with Carter proves, no matter how much homework you do, the thing sometimes ends up being a crapshoot."

Since 1936, the National Football League has distributed college standouts to its teams via the draft. "Draft Day" is the first day of the rest of these players' lives, but it is also the culmination of months of planning on the part of the clubs. It is not an exact science, but that doesn't prevent the smart organizations from attempting to make it so. Is your program in need of a linebacker who can fight off blocks? Then do as Dallas did in 1988 and draft UCLA's Ken Norton Jr., son of the former heavyweight champ. Need a fullback who can read defensive alignments? Then do as the Cowboys did in 1989 and take Syracuse's Daryl Johnston, who finished first in his

Lewiston-Porter Youngstown (N.Y.) High School class of 290 with a 4.0 grade-point average.

There is no one way to build a champion. The Washington Redskins of the late 1960s and early 1970s eschewed the draft. George Allen favored the more reliable athletes available through trades. The San Francisco 49ers of the 1980s catapulted themselves into four Super Bowl titles by hitting consistently in the draft for a decade.

"We do both," Johnson says. "You put together a championship team by using every avenue possible. But in our view, we couldn't put together a team that could win now and in the future without doing it through the draft. And because of the Herschel Walker trade and the Steve Walsh trade, we had a lot of extra picks to do it with."

While the Cowboys found ways to thicken the ranks of their draftees, the scouting department has been thinned under Jones. But he and Johnson involve the coaching staff so heavily in scouting that Dallas has plenty of manpower. There is a downside: offensive line coach Tony Wise's desire to add mammoth size to his line, and Johnson's reliance on his opinion, worked with Erik Williams. But it was what contributed to the Cowboys' failure to get production from valuable third-round picks in 1991 and 1992. (James Richards and James Brown, those respective selections, never made it through training camp.) But that Johnson web usually pays off. He not only is friendly with, say, Texas A&M coach R.C. Slocum; he also has someone on his staff who knows Slocum's secretary, who knows the Aggies athletic trainer, who knows the school's track coach, who knows the president of the booster club.

Says Butch Davis: "It's our job to know everything about everybody."

The Cowboys' 1989 draft brought them UCLA quarterback Troy Aikman in the first round, Syracuse fullback Daryl Johnston in the second, center Mark Stepnoski in the third and Texas-El Paso defensive end Tony Tolbert in the fourth. Aikman and Stepnoski are stars; Johnston and Tolbert are probably the two players on this team most deserving of additional recognition. That 1991 draft, with Maryland, Harper, Williams, Brown and others, may be judged almost as productive. And in 1992 came first-rounders Kevin Smith and East Carolina middle linebacker Robert Jones, who both became starters, as well as second-rounders Jimmy Smith (a Jackson State wide receiver who was unproductive as a rookie) and Arizona State safety Darren Woodson (projected as a future starter).

But it was in 1990 when the Cowboys cemented their image as master draftsmen with a single roll of the dice.

As always, Dallas went into the 1990 draft with a multi-armed, multi-dimensional, multi-trade plan. "Some people think I trade just for the sake of trading," Johnson says. "I've never done that. I get no kick out of the wheeling-dealing thing. I trade only to get in the best position to get the best players. That's all." The way the Cowboys plotted to get in the best position in 1990 was to package their No. 1 pick to make a trade with the Cincinnati Bengals so Dallas could move from the No. 21 slot to No. 15, where Baylor's James Francis would be waiting. Francis would help solve the Cowboys' linebacker problems. Then in the second round, Dallas could select the University of Cincinnati's Harold Green to help solve the team's running back problems.

But the Bengals backed out, and took Francis for themselves. And the Cowboys heard rumors that Cincinnati wanted Green for themselves, and would take him in the second round before Dallas got the chance. The Cowboys moved to an alternate plan: see how far a too-small, too-slow runner from the University of Florida would slip. "Seventeen was far enough," Johnson says. The Cowboys called the Pittsburgh Steelers, who held the seventeenth pick. Would the Steelers give up that spot for the Cowboys' picks in Rounds 1 and 3? They would, and Emmitt Smith — selected behind sixteen other college players, only one of whom, San Diego Chargers linebacker Junior Seau, has had a comparably successful career — was a Dallas Cowboy.

Emmitt J. Smith III has been "the man" ever since he was a little boy. "One of our attractions to him," says Jerry Jones, "is that he's been the guy who carried the load for every team he's been on since he was eight years old." Before that, when little "Scoey" soiled his clothes while playing football in the streets, he'd turn his pants and shirt inside out upon returning home so his parents wouldn't know what he'd been up to. When he was eight, Smith pretended to be Roger Staubach and played quarterback against the twelve-year olds. At Escambia High School in Pensacola, Florida, Smith was the Homecoming King. He spoke at anti-drug rallies. He was immortalized in stories in *USA Today* and *Sports Illustrated*. The school's football team was 1-9 before his arrival, but won two state titles with him in uniform. He ran for 100 yards or more forty-five times, totalling 8,804 career rushing yards. And he goofed on the competition. He remembers darting through holes with his eyes closed. Because he was scared? "No," he says, "just for the challenge of it. Just for something different to do."

In three seasons at the University of Florida, Smith became the second freshman to finish as a finalist in the Heisman race (Herschel Walker was the other). He set fifty-eight school records, gained 100 or more yards in twenty-four of his thirty starts and would have been the Heisman favorite in 1990 had he not skipped his senior year to enter the draft.

"He'll take your breath away," Dallas running backs coach Joe Brodsky said on draft day, "and you might not get it back."

Smith has been exposed to publicity for most of his young lifetime. He has always been hungry for attention, as evidenced by the fact that as a preteen, he changed the spelling of his name from Emmit (as his father and grandfather spell it) by adding an extra T. "He always had his own style," says his mother, Mary. Smith knows money; his mom was a loan officer. He knows how to cruise; his dad was a city bus driver. Now, his family operates Emmitt Inc., a marketing and promotions firm that handles Smith's merchandising and runs Emmitt Smith's First and 10, a sports collectibles business.

But this man who makes selling himself part of his career — "If I can't market my Super Bowl title and my rushing title, I'm in the wrong business," he says — frequently stiff-arms people who come too close. Let him stray too far beyond North G Street in Pensacola, he's a loner.

"You never know which person out there might be a serial killer," he jokes.

"Emmitt is a family person," says Mary, matriarch of the three generations of Smiths who live together in two houses on one lot back home on North G. "He has three brothers, two sisters, parents and grandparents who love him. And he loves them back. I think he has a good sense of what is important."

The five-foot-nine, 200-pound Smith can make a case for himself as the league's premier running back. In 1992, he became the first NFL rushing champion to play in a Super Bowl after totalling a league-high 1,713 rushing yards. Surely he is no longer considered a third wheel behind Detroit's Barry Sanders and Buffalo's Thurman Thomas. "The problem in the NFL," Smith says, "is that teams are looking for running backs who run 40 yards in 4.2 (seconds) and who are 6-5, 250 pounds. I don't have those things. If you don't have those things, some people are always going to try and downgrade you. I'm sure Barry and Thurman, being smaller guys, went through it, too. But I can run with the football. I've proven that. I'm about as good as anybody at it."

He hadn't proven anything by September 4, 1990, because it was until then before he'd ended a bitter contract dispute. And as the Cowboys' future greatness was not yet showing itself (wasn't it a telling sign back in August when the passenger seat in Johnson's sports car was occupied by a case of extra-strength Tylenol?), Smith's greatness also took time to be revealed. He was allowed just two carries for two yards in the Cowboys' season-opener, a 17-14 win over San Diego on September 9. When the Cowboys lost to the New York Giants 28-7 the next week, Smith carried six times for 11 yards.

Smith's misuse was temporarily lost in an Aikman-Johnson conflict that centered around Aikman's being benched with 10:51 left in the Giants blowout. Aikman said a summer meeting with Johnson during which he was asked his opinion of the Dallas receivers had persuaded him the coach and quarterback "were working on the same page. I thought that showed he respected my opinion," Aikman said. And now, he complained, he'd been pulled against his will.

"Very few things around here are up for discussion," Aikman said. "I'm not trying to buck the system. But if I'm going to get pulled out every time things don't go well on offense, there might be a lot of games I don't finish."

Johnson's response was terse: "Somebody's got to make the decisions. And it isn't the players."

The Cowboys lost again in Week Three, again amid quarterback-related distractions. Before the 19-15 loss to the Washington Redskins on September 23, 1990, news broke that the New Orleans Saints were interested in acquiring Steve Walsh. That created the sidebar to a game that demonstrated how far the Cowboys had come in one season, yet how far they still had to go. Dallas was outfoxed by Washington safety Brian Davis on the game-losing play. On fourth-and-one from the Cowboys' 39-yard line with just more than a minute to play, Dallas coaches decided to throw caution — and the football — to the wind. Cowboys wide receiver Dennis McKinnon got behind Davis, who was alone in coverage. Aikman lofted the ball perfectly. "As soon as I got a step on him, I knew Troy just had to put a little air under it, and I'd run it down," McKinnon said. "I would've been gone, completely gone. I catch it, they lose the game."

But when McKinnon tried to reach up to snare what would've been a game-winning 61-yard touchdown pass, he couldn't. The desperate Davis had locked down McKinnon's arm, drawing a pass interference call. "An illegal play, but a damn smart one," McKinnon said. Aikman's next pass was intercepted by Todd Bowles, and the Cowboys were 1-2.

Two days later, they dealt Walsh to the Saints. For a team that would be in the midst of a nine-game streak during which they'd lose seven, Walsh's departure counted as a victory.

Walsh, who won a national title for Johnson at Miami, had cost Dallas a No. 1 pick in the 1989 supplemental draft. His ill-advised presence created discomfort for Aikman, whose critics were given one more reason to bash him. (These Steve-adores called for the "more intellectual" Steve Walsh to start ahead of Aikman; the same misguided folks would later call for the "more cunning" Steve Beuerlein to replace Aikman. Both contentions demonstrated such an anti-Aikman bias that one wondered if they wouldn't find Steve Pelluer or Steve DeBerg or Steve Spielberg more desirable than Aikman.)

Aikman and Walsh "weren't close buddies," says Walsh, who blames that more on the cockfight circumstances than the personalities involved. Aikman agrees. "It was an unusual deal," he says. "You had two young guys, both first-round picks, who both thought they should be starting. It was a competitive situation where we were going head-to-head every day. And Jimmy was careful not to show favoritism, so he didn't let himself get close to either one of us."

Thus, it created a problem for Johnson, who disagrees with some insiders who claim he viewed Aikman-versus-Walsh as a tough call. He says his drafting of Walsh was intended to put the Cowboys in an only temporary possession of him before they brokered the quarterback elsewhere. "The situation might have gotten unhealthy," Johnson says. "When I saw that, that's when I made the trade."

Johnson had always believed it important to develop a bond with his quarterbacks. But Walsh's presence prevented him from forging any genuine relationship with his franchise quarterback, Aikman. And it showed.

Walsh, meanwhile, told friends he liked the setup. He could move around town freely, be a sort of class clown, and not draw criticism. Aikman, Walsh noted, could never get away with those things. And best of all, Walsh got to be the underdog on the field. "A no-lose situation," Walsh called it.

But it didn't become a no-lose situation for the Cowboys until the day Walsh was dealt for Nos. 1, 2 and 3 picks. Said Babe Laufenberg, who moved from third-string to second-string with the trade: "I'm happy. Troy's happy. Steve's happy. The Cowboys are happy. The Saints are happy. It's like a big love-in. Now I'm just a heartbeat away, like Dan Quayle. I hope Troy becomes a two-packs-a-day man. I'm already planning his high-cholesterol diet with a bunch of eggs."

And how did the No. 1 like his new No. 2? Aikman lampooned the abrasive relationship he had with the old No. 2 by answering, "Babe and I are already not speaking."

Aikman followed the trade with a performance that at the time ranked as one of his best. Dallas lost to the Giants, 31-17, as Aikman completed 21 of 26 passes for 233 yards. But the Giants, who would end the year by winning Super Bowl XXV, were too muscular and too efficient for Dallas. Somehow, Jerry Jones unearthed something positive out of the loss. "I was standing out by the buses feeling better than I ever have since I've been with the Cowboys," Jones said.

Add it up. A 31-17 loss. A 1-3 record. 'Feeling better than ever?' Standing by the buses. Jerry Jones was sucking in fumes, right?

Or maybe he knew two games against the hapless Tampa Bay Buccaneers were forthcoming. For the first time in the Johnson Era, the Cowboys found a team they could handle physically. Dallas beat the Bucs 14-10 on October 8, with Emmitt Smith breaking out with 121 rushing yards, 17 more than he'd gained in his first four games as a pro. "I showed myself a little something today," Smith said. The Cowboys actually let themselves get fat and sassy off that win, and were beaten 20-3 by the Phoenix Cardinals on October 14. But then the Bucs popped up on the schedule again, and the Cowboys actually had a 3-4 record after a dramatic finish in a 17-13 win in Tampa. "I wasn't worried about catching the ball," insisted Michael Irvin, who snared Aikman's 28-yard TD pass with twenty-three seconds left for the victory. "I was just thinking how I'd celebrate."

Irvin's self-confident claim showed great prescience for a team that still had no idea how to win, as it proved the next week, in an October 28 loss to the Philadelphia Eagles at Texas Stadium. Dallas fell, 21-20, despite doing everything right for the first fifty-nine minutes of the game. Quarterback Randall Cunningham's lob into the end zone was caught by Philly's

Calvin Williams and missed by Dallas's Robert Williams, giving the Eagles a 10-yard touchdown and the win. "It's about as devastating a loss as Dallas has had," said Cowboys veteran safety Bill Bates.

But there would be others.

The Cowboys opened the second half of the 1990 season with an embarrassing 24-9 loss to the pitiful New York Jets, a debacle accented by a halftime shoving match between Dallas defensive end Jim Jeffcoat and Jets coach Bruce Coslet. The offense managed just three field goals despite five trips inside the Jets' 24-yard line. Aikman was asked his opinion of the club's offensive failure. "I'm not for it," he answered dryly.

Then came the 24-6 loss to the defending champion San Francisco 49ers on November 11. The difference between the two teams, which would be minute two years later in the NFC Championship Game, was huge yet simple. "They don't make mistakes," Jimmy Johnson said in his postmortem. "We do."

Jerry Jones tried to soft-sell the problems that were exposed in that game, noting that most teams would come up short in comparison to the 49ers. "I think I'm an average-looking guy," Jones said. "But if I was standing next to the handsomest fella in the world, I'd look pretty damned ugly." Things did get ugly, not only on the field, but in the Texas Stadium locker room, and later in the week at Valley Ranch, when fullback Tommie Agee and offensive lineman Nate Newton organized a players-only meeting.

On November 12, Aikman said he'd been instructed by coaches to "keep his mouth shut." Johnson denied any knowledge of the order. Offensive coordinator David Shula did not deny it, but downplayed it. "It was just a suggestion to be more positive, because that can help make positive things happen," Shula said. But positive things weren't happening fast enough for Aikman, or for Emmitt Smith, who on November 14 blasted Shula for his play-calling. Smith had carried six times in the San Francisco game.

"At the start of the week," Smith said, "coaches told me one of the goals was for me to rush for 100 yards. They said they needed this and needed that. But I don't see any running back gaining 100 yards on six carries. Jesus, that's asking a little too much.

"We've got a good quarterback, great receivers, a good line and we're doing nothing. We go out and play and it doesn't look like we have shit. I know potential doesn't add up to a hill of beans if you're not doing it. But I don't know the answer."

Aikman thought he'd come up with the answer to his problems: a trade.

5 AIKMAN-TURNER OVERDRIVE ★

Late in the 1992 season, Nancy and Norv Turner invited Norv's three quarterbacking pupils over to the house for a little dinner. Troy Aikman, Steve Beuerlein and practice-squadder Jason Garrett gladly accepted. "All three of us are bachelors," Beuerlein says. "It was no business, all pleasure. We kept our heads in the fridge all night. Nancy and Norv had to finally kick the three of us out."

What a contrast to the last time a Cowboys offensive coordinator tried to assemble his quarterbacks for a little "Four Musketeers" social gathering. In the spring of 1990, David Shula was the coordinator. Aikman, Steve Walsh and Babe Laufenberg were the guests of honor. Shula took the fellas to a Texas Rangers baseball game. The outing did not go well. Aikman, Walsh and Laufenberg had all had enough peanuts and Cracker Jacks before the seventh-inning stretch.

"I realized what Shula was trying to accomplish," Laufenberg says. "So did the other guys. But it was a little bit forced."

There was never a meeting of the minds between Aikman and Shula. Their strained relationship would have been tolerable for the quarterback had Aikman and Johnson meshed. Aikman was accustomed to having a friendly and frank relationship with his superiors. He had that in 1989, when he worked directly under Cowboys quarterbacks coach Jerry Rhome. But Dallas allowed Rhome to leave for a job with the Phoenix Cardinals. Aikman had it at UCLA, where coach Terry Donahue showered him with both constructive criticism and maturity-building responsibility.

"Jerry Rhome was a great teacher and a guy I really missed after 1989," Aikman says. "Terry Donahue was sometimes hard on me, even in public. But I knew he was behind me, I knew he respected me, and I knew we could talk to each other about anything."

Now Aikman had Shula, who, except for suggesting Aikman "shut his mouth," couldn't communicate with him. And Aikman had Johnson, who wouldn't communicate with him. Much of what Aikman heard from Johnson was secondhand criticism, and for most of October and November of that year the two rarely spoke at all. The most damaging secondhand comment came four days before the Cowboys' November 18 game against the Los Angeles Rams, when Johnson allegedly said Aikman was "a loser." "He was a loser. He was a loser in high school, a loser in college and he'll always be a loser."

Even if Johnson never said it, Aikman thought he did. So Aikman, the quarterback of a team with a 3-7 record in this second season of 1990 and a 4-21 record over two years, knew he didn't have enough support on the field from an underdeveloped team. And he suspected he didn't have enough support from the man on the sideline, either.

"Football wasn't fun," Aikman says. "I don't care how much money you're getting paid. I know the guy out there working construction might not sympathize with this, but the whole idea for me is to enjoy myself. Dallas was definitely the city I wanted to be in. I love the people, the attitudes, everything about it. But as far as my job, I thought I needed a change. Something needed to change."

The Cowboys were in Anaheim, California, for the game with the Rams. Aikman's stomach rumbled as he started to walk toward Johnson's hotel suite. Maybe he would calmly discuss with Johnson the direction of the club. Or maybe he would blurt out that whatever Johnson's plans were with the Cowboys, he didn't want to be a part of them.

Instead, Aikman spent some time with Babe Laufenberg, his road roommate, then ducked out of the team hotel and met with agent Leigh Steinberg. "They said some things that put my feelings on hold," Aikman says. "But I still wasn't sure this was going to work for me."

That Sunday against the Rams began in a way that seemed to verify Aikman's doubts. He threw an interception on his first pass. "It's the worst throw I've ever seen," Laufenberg says. "I knew what was going through his mind that day. I got to see him with his guard let down. I got to see his human side when the cameras are turned off. And that was the lowest point I've ever seen Troy at. People think nothing bothers him, that he has ice in his veins. But that dehumanizes him. Believe me, he saw no light at the end of the tunnel. That day against the Rams, I thought he might go 0-for-30."

But later, the outlook brightened. Johnson had obviously heard of Aikman's disgruntlement — he has ways of finding these things out — and spent considerable time during the Rams game with an arm wrapped around Aikman's shoulder.

Conferring. Consoling. Coddling. The gestures were not comfortably received by the quarterback. Nor were they comfortably offered by the coach. But they didn't hurt. Dallas won, 24-21, with Aikman throwing for 303 yards and three touchdowns.

It was the next day, Monday, when Aikman had his audience with Johnson. It was in Johnson's Valley Ranch office that Aikman told Johnson he'd heard about "the loser" remark, when he mentioned the word "trade," and when he voiced his concerns about things needing to change.

They were changing, on the field.

Four days later, the Cowboys beat the Washington Redskins, 27-17 in a Thanksgiving Day match-up highlighted by Emmitt Smith's season-high 132 yards rushing. "The victory of all victories," Michael Irvin called it. Then Dallas defeated Steve Walsh and the New Orleans Saints 17-13, for a third consecutive win.

"Some of our improvement hasn't been noticed by some people because they've been worried about controversies," said Johnson, who knew damn well that many of those "some people" wore silver and blue uniforms.

On December 16, the Cowboys won their fourth straight. By downing the Cardinals 41-10, they'd won as many games in four outings as the franchise won in 1988 and 1989 combined. Dallas was 7-7, and the mood was upbeat. Suddenly, the Cowboys' talk of making the play-offs did not seem preposterous. "I've got news for you," said offensive line coach Tony Wise. "This mood you see Jimmy and everyone else in around here, it's the normal mood. That other mood was a 1-15 mood. That year took the life out of Jimmy. This year is bringing it back."

Johnson gleefully allowed himself to become embroiled in another chapter of his riotous feud with Eagles coach Buddy

Ryan before the Week Fifteen game that figured to determine much about both teams' play-off futures. For one thing, Ryan had recently put in waiver claims on two journeyman Cowboys, wide receiver Rod Harris and offensive lineman Louis Cheek. The claims blocked Dallas's attempts to slip both through waivers and onto the roster, where they'd serve as the forty-sixth and forty-seventh men. "I think Buddy is messin' with us," Johnson said. "He enjoys needling people and getting under their skin, especially when he's got the upper hand. He'll probably put those players out on the street after the game."

Irvin watched a TV sports report that detailed Johnson's press-conference focus on Ryan and the Eagles, and worried about the direction Johnson's emotions were taking the team.

"We concentrate too much on trying to beat the Eagles," Irvin said. "Jimmy hates them. He's made us all hate them. But in a way, maybe we want to beat them too bad. I get the feeling we press, trying too hard to succeed, instead of just letting things happen. Sometimes, wanting it that bad makes things work in the opposite direction."

But the Johnson-Ryan sideshow was forgotten with The Fall of Troy. Early on in the December 16 game at Veterans Stadium, while trying to escape from the pocket, Aikman was pursued and pummeled by Eagles defensive end Clyde Simmons. Aikman's shoulder and the Cowboys' dreams of clinching a spot in the play-offs were both separated. "I'll always wonder what we might have accomplished that year," Aikman says. Dallas finished the game with Babe Laufenberg, who was not effective in the 17-3 loss. "Face it," said guard John Gesek. "Babe was thrown to the wolves."

Babe's in Troyland?

Laufenberg and the Cowboys were thrown to the Falcons next, and their task in the regular-season finale in Atlanta was uncomplicated: Win and you're in. An 8-8 record would have been good enough to qualify for a National Conference wild-card berth, and the 4-11 Falcons were bad enough to be had. The Cowboys, who hadn't been in the postseason in five years, could even make the play-offs if they lost, as long as the Rams downed the Saints on Monday Night Football twenty-four hours later. "I doubt we'll be watching," Nate Newton said. "We shouldn't even get on the plane to Atlanta if we're think-ing that way."

Newton was wrong on one count and right on another. They would be watching the Rams-Saints game. And they shouldn't have gotten on the plane to Atlanta. The Falcons thrashed the Cowboys, 26-7. "If somebody wants to put the blame on me, they are welcome to," said Laufenberg, who completed just 10 of 24 passes for 129 yards and threw two interceptions. "Whatever we did, they mauled us." Atlanta coach Jerry Glanville maliciously fabricated a story about the Cowboys stashing five cases of champagne in the Fulton County Stadium locker room in anticipation of a victory party, thus making the Cowboys look just as ridiculous as they would have looked backing into the play-offs with a 7-9 record.

A week before the Atlanta game, Jimmy Johnson joked about his habitual postseason vacation in the Bahamas or some similar tropical clime. This year, he said, ticking off NFC teams that might host play-off games, trips to "Chicago, New York or San Francisco would be nice." But Johnson knew better. The trip to Nassau, which took place on the weekend of the first-round play-off games, had already been penciled into his schedule.

On Monday, December 31, 1991, Johnson was packing for his vacation, and deciding whom he should send packing. There were dozens of decisions to be made by the 1990 NFL Coach of the Year if he expected to contend for any more meaningful honors in the upcoming season — "After each season I always try to look and say, "How can we get better?" Johnson says — and he organized each potential change in his mind.

Says Laufenberg: "One of my first memories of Jimmy Johnson is at training camp in Thousand Oaks (California) in 1989. He was all over the field. He saw everything, like a three-headed monster. I always thought he was an offensive coach, because of the style of play at the University of Miami. Turns out, he doesn't know a thing about offense. But every day, he'd come up to me and say, "Nice throw on that corner route," or something. He was too smart a guy not to teach himself how to make changes when necessary. Unfortunately, of course, one of those changes he had to make was me."

Indeed, Johnson decided he needed a new backup quarterback. He needed more active defensive linemen. He needed another receiver with enough size to fight physical coverage. But most of all, he needed to resolve his dissatisfaction with some assistant coaches, led by David Shula.

In the winter of 1988, Johnson was contacted by young Shula, who was seeking career advice. David wondered if he should consider examining coaching opportunities outside the Miami Dolphins, where he was an assistant under his legendary father, Don Shula.

Johnson didn't know David Shula well. But he knew something about rising up the coaching ladder. Johnson counseled Shula to leave the Dolphins. "I told him it would be good to get out from under his father and to make his own niche," Johnson remembers.

A few months later, Johnson made his own change, moving to the Cowboys. And in assembling a staff, he needed to act quickly. If he wanted assistants who were presently in the NFL, he had to secure them by March 1, according to league rules. That gave Johnson just a few days to find his assistants, and then only a few weeks to determine his short-term and long-term goals for the club, evaluate his existing talent and the available crop of collegians eligible for the April draft, and prepare for mini-camps in May, training camp in July and the start of the season in September. Johnson called Don Shula to ask if he could rehire Dave Wannstedt, who had left his post as the Hurricanes defensive coordinator a month before to work with Dolphins linebackers. During their conversation, it occurred to Johnson that maybe the Dolphins had another young assistant — Dave Shula — who might like a promotion to the Cowboys staff.

Contrary to speculation that festered when David Shula's critics sought ammunition against him, Don Shula did not allow Wannstedt to go on the condition Johnson also take Dave Shula. "I guarantee you the two were not connected, except that I had to ask Don permission to talk to both," says Johnson, who passed on retaining and elevating Rhome, against the wishes of his players. "It was not Don saying, 'Take one and I'll give you the other.' I thought David would give us something in terms of NFL experience that we didn't have. But the biggest factor was that deadline. I was pressed for time."

So David, not yet thirty years old, brought his famous Shula pedigree and his familiar Shula jawline to Dallas. Even for a coach who was born with a silver whistle in his mouth — or maybe because of that — the job was not an easy one. It seems Shula was used to the idea of coach as idol. "The amount of success my father had when we were growing up gave us a good idea of what it was like to be a coach," Shula says. "He was never fired. No "For Sale" signs were put on our lawn (by fans). We weren't booed at restaurants." Dave had joined his father's staff in 1982. Three years later, at twenty-six, he turned down an offer of a ten-year contract from the Philadelphia Eagles to be their head coach. He readily acknowledged that opportunities knocked so frequently at his door because his door said "SHULA" on the nameplate.

"But it's a matter of, 'What have you done with the opportunity?' he said in October 1990. "In my case, that remains to be seen. A lot of people say I haven't done shit with it."

Johnson might not have put it that harshly. But Shula was judged a failure at forwarding Aikman's development, a fact discussed in a conversation between Johnson and Aikman a week after the season was over. That six-carry game for Rookie of the Year Emmitt Smith in the loss to the 49ers kept popping up in Johnson's mind. The fact that the Dallas offense was ranked twenty-seventh in the league in 1989, then twenty-eighth in 1990, was a major consideration.

"Even though we started doing things offensively at the end of the year, when we had that streak where we beat the Rams, Redskins, Saints and Cardinals, I still felt we needed more offensive input," says Johnson, who explains "offensive input" as meaning "I wanted more ideas from my offensive coordinator."

And then there were the players who claim they approached Johnson to inform him that Shula, whose youth would figure to help him relate to athletes, was the least communicative and among the least respected of Johnson's aides. Johnson denies receiving complaints from players, but says, "That wasn't necessary, anyway. I can sense things."

Johnson's solution was announced on January 9. Two assistants, Dick Nolan and Alan Lowry, were fired. Shula was demoted to something called "wide receivers, tight ends and passing game assistant," a poorly defined, poorly disguised move designed to quicken his departure. "It's disappointing and not at all that easy to accept," Shula said. "This isn't exactly the highlight of my career. We made progress, even if some statistics don't show that. Jimmy didn't win Coach of the Year because the offense did nothing. But scapegoat is something I think I've been since I've been here."

On January 29, Shula escaped, taking a position as receivers coach with Sam Wyche's Bengals. (A year later, Wyche would be dismissed. Shula strolled into general manager Mike Brown's office to inform him of his vacation plans and of his desire to remain with the staff in some capacity. Five hours later, Shula was promoted to head coach, a turn of events that had many Cowboys players laughing wickedly. "There are some guys on that team that'll eat him up," predicted one Cowboy.) Meanwhile, Johnson was biding his time waiting for Dolphins quarterbacks coach Gary Stevens, his former University of Miami aide, to officially accept the Cowboys' offer of the offensive coordinator job. But the incestuous goings-on in the NFL stung the Cowboys.

Dolphins coach Don Shula blocked the move of Dolphins assistant Stevens to Dallas, where he would take the old job of Shula's son, Dave. The fact that Stevens backed out of what had been an all-but-done deal (Stevens had promised Johnson he'd take the post) leaves Johnson with a residue of bitterness. "Gary calls Jimmy," a friend of both said late in 1992. "Jimmy won't return the calls."

For a time, Johnson was busy making more pressing calls. Stevens was out. So Johnson called San Diego Chargers aide Ted Tollner and Kansas City Chiefs aide Joe Pendry, who both came highly recommended by Dave Wannstedt. Neither of their teams would free them. Johnson conducted a courtesy interview with Bob Schnelker, the fired Minnesota Vikings coordinator, who scored well in Johnson's X's and O's test but told Johnson, "I'm not a players' coach type." So he was out.

Then Johnson started receiving calls. From Rams passing guru Ernie Zampese. From former Chargers quarterback Dan Fouts. From Rams quarterback Jim Everett. From Wannstedt.

All mentioned the name of a thirty-eight-year old Rams receivers coach with the unlikely name of Norval Turner.

"People now say Norv must have been my fourth choice, but in reality, you might say he was tied for second behind Stevens, who was the only person I offered the job to," Johnson says. "And as it turned out, Norv was the best choice by far of anybody I could have considered. I'm glad things happened the way they did."

Turner almost didn't get the nod because his title with Los Angeles was "receivers coach." Says Johnson: "I always wanted somebody coaching Troy who played quarterback, or if he hadn't played it, at least somebody who'd worked with quarterbacks for a long period of time. I wanted a pure quarterbacks coach. That was the only thing that held me back on Norv. He'd coached receivers. Finally I found out he'd coached quarterbacks at USC (when he was on the same staff as Wannstedt) and that he'd played the position at Oregon. He hadn't played much (Fouts was the starter there for most of Turner's tenure), but he played. Finding that out, and then going out and having a couple of beers with the guy, made up the final part of my decision."

"Norv was perfect," says Aikman, who was consulted by Johnson before Turner's February 1, 1991, hiring. "He is low-key, but he has instant rapport with players. He doesn't force things. And he knows what he's talking about. We hit it off right away, and it was clear what was going to make the difference between that 1990 team that didn't make the playoffs and the team after we got Norv were three things: One, we just plain got sick of losing like we used to, and we started taking every loss personally. Two, Emmitt becoming a bigger part of our offense. And three, Norv coming."

The 1990 season was the last time the Cowboys would sit in front of their TV sets hoping someone else would win so they could make the play-offs. But on New Year's Eve 1990, members of the 7-9 club were powerless to do anything more.

Groups of Cowboys clustered at different spots watching the Rams versus the Saints. Some gathered at the Carrollton home of defensive tackle Dean Hamel. A dozen or so met at Cowboys Cafe, an Irving sports bar owned by linebacker Eugene Lockhart, former running back Tony Dorsett, and others.

The Rams forced a 17-17 tie inside the two-minute mark. But the Saints rebounded by marching into field-goal position for Morten Andersen. His first kick was blocked, and Cowboys' hopes were raised. But the Rams were flagged for being offsides on the play. Andersen's ensuing kick was good, sending the Saints to the play-offs and sending Michael Irvin to the bar.

Irvin is not much of a drinker in season. But he was into shots of tequila on this night.

"You shouldn't drink so much," cautioned a waitress. "You need to stay in shape."

"Not anymore, I don't," Irvin replied. "Bring me two tequilas. School's out."

Maybe to guys accustomed to being under the thumb of Jimmy Johnson, tying their ankles to a rubber band and then jumping 100 feet with nothing but asphalt below is a freeing activity.

But no Cowboys dared let Johnson know a bunch of them reacted to the troubling 26-23 overtime loss to the Houston Oilers on November 10, 1991, by visiting a topless bar in Arlington for some bungee-jumping.

"To this day," says one, "if Jimmy knew about us bungee-jumping, it'd be much more dangerous than bungee-jumping itself."

By 1991, the Cowboys had developed to the point where losses actually deserved to be taken seriously. Johnson wanted his team to have the mindset of a winner — which to him means somberly reflecting on every detail of every defeat. When running back Emmitt Smith, whose overtime fumble while within field-goal range cost Dallas the game, was on the verge of sobbing when he said, "There are no bright spots," his coach certainly nodded somewhere in mournful approval.

The new-regime's third season featured tears and beers. On Saturday, August 10, 1991, Irving voters approved a referendum that allowed beer and wine to be sold at Texas Stadium for the first time. On Monday, August 12, the day the Cowboys were to play host to the Los Angeles Raiders in a nationally-televised preseason game, Cowboys owner Jerry Jones balanced a phone on one shoulder waiting for Raiders boss Al Davis to respond to a trade offer for quarterback Steve Beuerlein, and balanced paper cups in the palms of his hands.

"They're both sixteen ounces," he said, eyeing the two sample cups while Davis had him on hold. "But one is squattier than the other. Does the fat one look like more beer, or does the tall one?"

Appearance may be everything in the paper cup business, and in the mourning-a-loss business. But on the field, the Cowboys entered the 1991 season believing they possessed both style and substance. "The feeling now is totally different," Aikman said on the eve of the regular-season opener in Cleveland. "I think everybody believes this is a play-off club."

"We're more confident of success than a year ago," Johnson added. "We know now that success is near. We were hoping for success last year — but we were only hoping. Now we expect to win."

Of the twenty-four starters (including kickers) from Opening Day 1990, only ten lined up in the same position in the September 1, 1991, contest against the Browns. Back at the same spots were Aikman, center Mark Stepnoski, left tackle Mark Tuinei, right tackle Nate Newton, tight end Jay Novacek, right defensive end Jim Jeffcoat, right defensive tackle Danny Noonan, left cornerback Issiac Holt, kicker Ken Willis and punter Mike Saxon. Every other position underwent either complete overhauls, or at least modifications. "We've stepped it up from last year," Aikman said. "And we're light years from where we were in 1989."

Dallas beat the Browns, 26-14, calmed by a pregame speech from Johnson in which he dismissed the intimidating woofing of 78,860 Dawg Pounders audible through the Cowboys' locker room walls. "Just dominate your man," Johnson yelled above the din. "Do that, and this'll be our house."

The Cowboys did look right at home. Smith, given six carries in that infamous 1990 loss to the 49ers, carried the ball 32 times, tying Calvin Hill's franchise record. Aikman, burdened by the team's No. 28 ranking in offense in 1990, was 24 of 37 for 274 yards and two scores. "This was as prepared and relaxed as I've ever been going into a ballgame," said Aikman, whose only flaw came in the form of the seven stitches woven into his Dudley Do-Right chin. Aikman was asked a loaded question about the difference between the Dave Shula offense of 1990 and this new, quick-read, quick-throw Norv Turner version.

"I'm smarter this year," Aikman smirked, fighting back the temptation to rip Shula.

The Cowboys might have started the season 2-0 had Emmitt Smith been smarter about how to treat his body. It wasn't the opening week's 32 carries that did him in, but something called a "carbohydrate nutritional supplement" that is designed to help the body retain fluids. The supplement is supposed to be ingested twenty-four hours prior to physical exertion in hot, humid conditions.

In the September 9 Monday night game against the Washington Redskins in Week Two, Smith totalled 104 yards on five carries, including one 75-yard touchdown run, in the first half alone. He might have doubled those numbers (instead of finishing with only 112 rushing yards on 11 carries) and prevented a 33-31 Cowboys loss had he not spent most of the second half retching on the sideline.

Emmitt, neglecting the instructions on the can, drank the junk right before pregame warm-ups. "I will never take that crap again," vowed Smith, forever losing endorsement bucks from the carbohydrate nutritional supplement industry.

The Cowboys offensive line was sickened by their Week Three performance. They allowed the Philadelphia Eagles 11 sacks in a 24-0 loss at Texas Stadium, turning Aikman into road kill, limiting the Cowboys to a franchise-low 90 offensive yards. Some players blamed a Monday Night Football hangover, saying they'd put so much energy into the the Redskins game that showing up flat for the Eagles was predictable. "People can make up all kinds of excuses," Johnson snapped. One positive came of the loss: Johnson decided to re-evaluate his starting lineup, thus triggering a flood of rookie contributions starting with the birth of the unlikely career of Texas Christian University cornerback Larry Brown.

A few months before, the five-foot-eleven, 183-pound Brown was so lightly regarded by coaches that when he asked for a few days off from training camp to visit his ill mother in Los Angeles, they didn't blink an eye. A few days off? They seemed to be suggesting to Brown that he had permission to take the rest of his life off from the Cowboys, if he wished.

"He's got no shot here," said one coach. "We don't know if he can tackle, because even after two weeks here, we still haven't seen him try."

But Brown was a Week Four starter against the Cardinals, replacing right cornerback Manny Hendrix. Brown certainly has his flaws — even as a second-year starter in 1992, his inability to hang on to potential interceptions allowed him to retain the derisive "Edward Scissorhands" nickname teammates had tagged him with — but his successful debut in the 17-9 victory opened the coaches' minds to more youthful experimentation later.

"For a twelfth-round pick to be allowed more starts over his time than all the team's first-round picks, that says something about the way the organization thinks," Brown says. "Now it also says something about that twelfth-round pick. I'm entering my third season, and I still hear people call me a long shot. I can see being a long shot that first year, and maybe that second year. But when does a long shot who has made it finally get to be called just a good player?"

Johnson is willing to give Brown his due. But his open-mindedness did not extend to a willingness to receive lineup suggestions from the media.

"Who do y'all want to start at guard? You want a new punt returner? How do you feel about kick returner? Just give me your starting lineup and we'll go with it," snarled Johnson in a September 24 press conference opened with questions about the ineffectiveness of first-team receiver Alexander Wright. "And tell me what substitution packages you want. Two tight ends? Three wide receivers? Also let me know what group you want us to name as starters. Do you want Standard package, or do you want us to introduce the Nickel package? With three wide receivers, or do you want us to introduce two tight ends, with Alfredo Roberts and Novacek? One back or two backs? Give it to me. What do you want?"

What reporters wanted was an explanation for why Wright managed just three catches in four games.

The Cowboys moved to 3-2 with a landmark, 21-16 victory over the New York Giants on September 29. Dallas had lost six straight to the defending Super Bowl champs, and hadn't even been ahead in a game against New York in four years. Safety Ray Horton ran a fumble into the end zone for one touchdown, and cornerback Issiac Holt prevented a score at game's finish with an end-zone interception. Aikman found Irvin for a 23-yard touchdown with 2:13 remaining to cap a needle-sharp 84-yard march. "A comeback touchdown drive, that means a lot to me because that's how quarterbacks seem to be evaluated," Aikman said.

In a 20-17 victory over Green Bay in Week Six, another rookie, tackle Erik Williams, joined Brown as a peach-fuzzed contributor. Williams rumbled onto the field to spell the injured Nate Newton, and though he admitted to stage fright — "I'm a rookie from a little NAIA (National Association of Intercollegiate Athletics) school (Central Ohio State) who is trying to make a very big jump, so naturally I was scared," he said — teammates said he talked more trash than any player on the field.

One of the Cowboys' most senior citizens, thirty-one-year-old Ray Horton, scored for the second week in a row, this time on a 65-yard interception return. His path was a curious one, because he had to throw Larry Brown out of his way in order to score. But, explained the aged Horton, "You get there any way you can when you have cobwebs between your legs."

Inspired by some badmouthing by a Cincinnati Bengals team that before its Week Seven match at Texas Stadium called the patchwork Cowboys' defense "The Castaways" (the Bengals were 0-5, so maybe they had some of Horton's cobwebs between their ears), Dallas won its fourth straight, 35-23. The eye-catching contribution came from many-leagued refugee Ricky Blake, a 250-pounder who spelled Emmitt Smith with a running style that reminded one of a barrel careening over Niagara Falls. "I hope my mom was watching on TV," said the guileless Blake, who scored from 30 yards out on his first NFL carry.

The Cowboys reached their bye week with a 5-2 record. Johnson refused to issue predictions of what was to come. "I did that at Miami," he said. "And I was fairly accurate. Of course, most of our games at Miami were 'W's. I don't think I ever put down an 'L'."

But he would have to put down an "L" for the Cowboys' October 27 date against the Detroit Lions in the Silverdome, a venue that would create double trouble for Dallas in the 1991 season. "We made a lot of mistakes and they did a lot of things right," said Cowboys middle linebacker Jack Del Rio after the 34-10 loss. "But any team is going to have a tough time if it gives up points just as it's expecting to score points."

Dallas was ahead 7-3 and was positioned for a 48-yard Ken Willis field-goal try just before halftime. But the Lions blocked the kick, William White scooted 55 yards for the touchdown, and the Cowboys were too stunned to recover. In retrospect, Steve Beuerlein said of his Sunday morning breakfast with two Catholic nuns: "Maybe the whole team should have joined me."

The Cowboys promoted three members of the Class of 1991 to the first team in preparation for the Week Nine game against Phoenix. Wide receiver Alvin Harper would replace Alexander Wright. Linebacker Dixon Edwards would replace Vinson Smith, who had hepatitis A. And offensive tackle Erik Williams would step ahead of Alan Veingrad, who'd been effective subbing for the injured Mark Tuinei at left tackle. "We didn't make the moves for down-the-road thinking," Johnson said. "We did it because we think it will make us a better team against Phoenix." What Johnson did not mention was that the move was also made to save the club $25,000, the bonus that Veingrad would have earned for making four starts during the season. He'd made three starts previous to the Phoenix game, and finished the year with the same number.

Dallas won, 27-7, after coordinators Turner and Wannstedt lit a fire under an uninspired Cowboys team that led the woeful Cardinals by 10-7 at halftime. "I didn't say much," Johnson said. "But boy, Norv and Dave were pretty hot."

Some of the problems were the fault of Williams, who allowed three Ken Harvey sacks of Aikman in the first half. Harvey did not spare the rod while trying to spoil the Cowboys' man-child. But Williams and most of the rest of the kids, including soon-to-be starter Russell Maryland, survived. Unfortunately, Ricky Blake fractured a hip on the game's final play, an injury that would eventually kill his football career.

Maryland was effective while working with the first team in the overtime loss to the Oilers that bumped Dallas to 6-4. Once a self-described "sloppy fat kid" who figured his future would be working at a McDonald's in his native Chicago, the six-foot-one Maryland scared off most college recruiters when he ballooned to 327 pounds as a senior at Whitney Young High School. Indiana State made him his only scholarship offer until University of Miami assistant Hubbard Alexander stumbled onto him. Alexander was in Chicago to find a defensive lineman. He wanted Mel Agee, but he opted for Illinois. He wanted Chris Zorich, who instead signed with Notre Dame. Alexander was left with the sloppy fat kid.

"Any time you see an athlete, you see if he passes the eye test — how does he look to the naked eye," says Butch Davis, then the Hurricanes defensive line coach. "The first day I saw Russell at school, he didn't pass the eye test. I was sure it was a wasted scholarship."

Maryland earned his scholarship, and later the Outland Trophy as the nation's best college lineman, through self-discipline. "Russell is a saint," says Jimmie Jones, a linemate at Miami and in Dallas. Says former teammate Mike Sullivan: "Russell invented right from wrong."

But as was the case against the Lions, even Maryland's presence wasn't enough to help the Cowboys defense invent a way to stop the Run-and-Shoot. Maryland recorded five tackles and a key sack on Houston's Warren Moon, but Dallas permitted 583 yards of offense. That Emmitt Smith fumble created concerns, as did the rushing totals that suggested he'd dropped into a slump. The second-year back had 878 rushing yards, good for second in the National Conference and third in the NFL. His 1,079 total yards were first in the NFC and second in the league. And no NFC running back could match his 40 receptions. But Smith, who'd averaged 106.5 yards in his first six games, had failed to run for more than 66 yards in averaging 59.7 yards per game in the Cowboys' last four outings.

"That ain't good," Smith said, scanning the numbers. "Wow. That stinks."

The odor wafting from Giants Stadium on November 17, however, had nothing to do with Smith's numbers. Blame the referees, said Jimmy Johnson, who absolutely came unglued after a 22-9 loss to the Giants. "In all my years in football, I have never, ever, ever seen a game officiated as poorly as that," screamed Johnson, whose head seemed about to explode. "Never. Ever. Ever. Since my daddy said, 'This is what you call a football.'"

Defensive tackle Tony Casillas suggested the Cowboys were victims of the referees' "home cookin'." Offensive lineman Kevin Gogan said, "Let's face it. You've got weekend warriors in little hats out here taking your game away."

On Monday, commissioner Paul Tagliabue decided against slapping Johnson with a $7,500 fine for ripping the officials. Why so lenient?

"Paul Tagliabue was at the game," Jerry Jones said. "He saw what went on."

The Cowboys were now 6-5. Their final five games of the season were against Washington, Pittsburgh, New Orleans, Philadelphia and Atlanta. Pittsburgh was the only club in that group not headed toward a ten-wins-or-better season. Despite the difficulty of the upcoming schedule, and despite the fact that they'd lost two straight, the Cowboys did have one major advantage they lacked down the 1990 stretch: a healthy Troy Aikman.

But not for long.

"Getting hurt in the Washington game is one of the most devastating things that's ever happened to me," Aikman says. "And I'm not talking about the pain of the knee injury. In 1990, I thought it was a wasted opportunity to see what we might be able to do in the play-offs had I been able to stay healthy and helped us get there. But in 1991, I started wondering how many times you can get away with saying, "Oh, well, we'll try again next year. I mean, you talk to some of these guys who play their whole careers without making the play-offs, and you feel for them. I was getting to thinking I might be one of those guys."

The Cowboys led the Redskins 14-7 when, on the fourth play of the third quarter, Washington defensive linemen Jumpy Geathers and Charles Mann converged on Aikman after a completion. Aikman's right leg was extended and his knee was locked. Geathers enveloped Aikman around the waist. Mann drove through his back, causing Aikman's leg to bend forward gruesomely.

"I heard him holler," Geathers said, "and I knew it was bad."

In a stupidly valiant move typical of Aikman, he ordered the shredded knee wrapped in anticipation of re-entering the game. Aikman's reluctance to rest this partial tear of the lateral collateral ligament would become an issue for the remainder of the season. He practiced his footwork in his living room at a time he should have been on crutches; he issued weekly proc-lamations of readiness to the newspaper; and, in an action his superiors must share the blame for (but still don't know about), there was the night the club instructed him to visit Baylor Medical Center, but let him go alone. Which meant Aikman used his one good leg on the drive to a hospital parking lot that was about eighty yards from the front door of the hospital lobby. Which meant this 11.037-million-dollar man dragging the two-bit leg was meandering in the dark about the Baylor grounds, searching for wherever the hell he was supposed to show up for his appointment.

In Aikman's stead, Beuerlein was reinventing himself into a folk hero. As the Cowboys' third Aikman understudy in as many years, he'd been anxious to demonstrate he had more skill than Babe Laufenberg and more savvy than Steve Walsh. Three months before, back when Jerry Jones and Jimmy Johnson were trying to coyly swing a deal with Al Davis for Beuerlein, the quarterback played it so cool that he actually exchanged sideline-to-sideline winks with Johnson during a break in that August 12 preseason game.

"I just wanted to send him a little sign to let him know we were still working on getting him," Johnson said.

It became one of Dallas's most productive swaps. Beuerlein helped beat the Redskins 24-21, a loss at RFK Stadium that ended Washington's hopes of continuing what had been a perfect 11-0 start. Aided by a spectacular juggling touchdown catch by Michael Irvin (nine catches, 130 yards while terrorizing All-Pro cornerback Darrell Green), Beuerlein completed seven of 12 passes for 109 yards. And he attempted to halt any Beuerlein bandwagoneers with a statement of political correctness befitting the site of his triumph.

"Anybody who talks about a 'quarterback controversy' needs to have some sense slapped into them," Beuerlein said.

As is often the case when dealing with their constituency, the pols didn't listen. The United States House of Representatives, full of Redskins fans, formed a captive audience for Representative Dick Armey of Lewisville, Texas, who took the floor to read a poem:

The loss took place at RFK
But evokes the words of JFK
Cowboy fans can chant this one-liner
Say it loud: "Ich Bin Ein Beuerleiner"

Al Davis, who speaks fluent Brooklynese, once said of Beuerlein, "He can't drive the cahr." The dig meant he's a quarterback who can't run the show. But Davis was wrong about Beuerlein, who was 14 of 25 for 217 yards in his first Cowboys start, a Thanksgiving Day win over the Steelers on November 28.

Davis is still trying to find a quarterback as good as the one he gave up on August 25, 1991, when the Cowboys shipped to L.A. a fourth-round pick for the guy who would steer Dallas to the 1991 play-offs. In 1992, it would be the way Beuerlein corralled his desire to play — never issuing demands or challenges that would threaten Aikman's position — that made Davis' accusations of selfishness seem ridiculous.

"Of course I'd like to be the No. 1 guy somewhere," says Beuerlein, kept from playing in 1990 by a vindictive Davis, but after 1992 a free-agent plum. "Hell, I'd like to be the No. 1 guy in Dallas. But I don't look at my time in Dallas as being wasted. Staying in Al Davis' doghouse, now that would've been a waste."

Beuerlein enjoyed the fact that his success was driving Davis up the wall. A day after the Redskins game, Beuerlein got a phone call from some of his Raiders buddies who said they sat in a Cincinnati airport bar watching tape of Beuerlein's winning performance on ESPN. They raised a toast to their old mate. Meanwhile, sitting alone in a corner of the establishment lit only by the flicker of Beuerlein's performance was Davis, disgustedly wadding up a paper cup and slamming it into a garbage can.

Beuerlein could drive the cahr. And the Cowboys were proving to be a cahr that handled well.

Throughout Jimmy Johnson's time in Dallas, players griped about being overworked. Of course, griping about being overworked is the football player's perpetual state. They are required to gripe, it is believed, by a clause in the new collective bargaining agreement. But in the case of the Cowboys, the moaners might have had a case. By the time they'd beaten Pittsburgh 20-10 and achieved an 8-5 record, Cowboys players had endured the NFL's most demanding "voluntary" off-season program, its most grueling training camp, its most physical daily in-season practice regimen and now, two games in five days thanks to the Turkey Day sandwich.

The eleven months of pounding their heads against a wall made the two games within 120 hours seem like pecks on the cheek. "We may be hurting," safety James Washington said. "But we're too numb to know it."

Said assistant coach Butch Davis: "Maybe it's easier to ask these players to make sacrifices like this because we ask so much of them every day. What they've done, in effort and preparation, is amazing. Play away from home all month, then play on a Thursday. Travel, pack, unpack, bus rides, plane rides. Show up for three road games and play your heads off. And then, against Pittsburgh, we ask them to play their heads off even more."

But, Davis added, "We're at a stage in our development where we can't afford to do it any other way."

When the Cowboys' record jumped to 9-5 with a 23-14 win over New Orleans in Week Fourteen, players and coaches seemed to sense they'd elevated themselves to a more developed stage. "I throw out enough 'I told you so's' during the week," said a beaming Jimmy Johnson, who knew that his team had inched very close to clinching a play-off berth. "But I'm sure you'll hear a few more as the week goes on."

But offensive lineman Nate Newton added one somber note. In Week Fifteen, Dallas had to travel to Philadelphia, where it had lost four straight, to oppose the Eagles, whom they hadn't beaten in a non-strike meeting since 1986. "You know why we can't be sure how great we are yet? Because we haven't beaten Philly," Newton said. "If we go in there and win that game, then maybe the party can start."

Actually, many Cowboys did not know that their play-off-clinching 25-13 victory over the Eagles on December 15 was permission to party. Many Cowboys, unfamiliar with the whole business of magic numbers and such, didn't know the victory was play-off-clinching.

"We're in? No, I'm not believing it yet," linebacker Ken Norton said. "I'll believe it when I hear it from the big guy."

"The big guy" — Jimmy Johnson — had purposely failed to inform his team of the exact implications of a win at Philadelphia. He knew a 10-5 record would propel his Cowboys into the postseason. But he wanted his club peaking, not peeking.

Dallas's game plan was to play not to lose. Johnson wanted to avoid permitting the omnivorous Eagles defense from gaining momentum with turning-point plays — sacks, fumbles and interceptions — so he attempted to completely erase those as possibilities. Beuerlein responded by making almost no plays at all. "The whole idea was to not make any mistakes," he said. Still, no team intends on its quarterback starting the game zero-of-11 passing and finishing the first half two-of-17, as Beuerlein did. No team can plan on earning seven sacks, as the Dallas defense did. No team can count on a safety from its kickoff coverage team, or on an 85-yard Kelvin Martin punt return that to this day causes sleepless nights for Eagles coach Rich Kotite.

For starters, Martin is intelligent enough to know that five-foot-nine, 160-pound men who want to play football are supposed to be on the initiating end of kicks, not on the receiving end. "It's suicide," says Martin, who was the club's leading receiver in 1990 with 64 catches but caught just 16 in 1991. "But you do what you're told to do."

What special-teams coach Joe Avezzano told his punt-block unit to do was "Buzz," that is, shift into an alignment that dumps his standard block-that-kick mentality and instead double-team the Eagles' outside coverage men. Philly punter Jeff Feagles drilled the kick 62 yards. Martin trotted back and fielded it at his 15-yard line. "As high as it was, I still decided not to fair-catch it because I didn't see any green (jerseys)," said Martin, who would turn upfield to see nothing but green (turf). Martin slid through the first wave of pursuers, then skipped away from Feagles's tackle attempt. Finally, he cut behind

Issiac Holt's pancake-like flip of Robert Drummond and sailed into the end zone for a 15-10 Dallas advantage.

The Cowboys would add Ken Willis'sz third field goal and a short Beuerlein-to-Irvin touchdown pass as part of a 17-point final quarter that should have triggered a Cowboys' Mardi Gras. For the first time since 1985, the Dallas Cowboys were in the play-offs! The fools were foolproof! Jerry Jones and Co. had gone from Jethroes to Geniuses in three short seasons!

Except these geniuses still weren't sure they'd qualified for the postseason. Troy Aikman and Ray Horton walked off the Veterans Stadium field calmly debating the issue. Jerry Jones himself pleaded ignorance.

"We're in?" the owner asked. "Are you sure? Are you absolutely sure?"

Four of the Cowboys bound for the play-offs were also Pro Bowl-bound. Emmitt Smith, who earned enough votes from his peers in 1990 to be the lone Cowboy to make it to the postseason all-star game in Honolulu, was joined this time by Aikman, Irvin and Novacek. "The greatest thing," Smith said, "is that this time I'll have somebody to socialize with."

In the regular-season finale, Dallas finished with the Falcons, as they did in 1990. This game, a 31-27 Cowboys win, was more entertaining but completely meaningless to Dallas. It did, however, prevent coach Jerry Glanville's Falcons from winning the NFC West, and memories of how Glanville rubbed it in a year ago made the victory a bit sweeter. CBS-TV reporter Leslie Visser, who gets along famously with Johnson, informed him before the game that while the Cowboys spent Saturday night studying, Glanville's Falcons boot-scooted around their Irving hotel at a private concert conducted by Jerry Jeff Walker.

"We were in meetings, they were listening to country-and-western music," Johnson remarked. "I guess some teams prepare differently than others."

The Cowboys had prepared so thoroughly for this one that they found a way to save themselves a sixth-round draft pick. Casillas, acquired from Atlanta at the start of the year, cost Dallas a No. 2 and a conditional pick based on playing time. Had he been in on 75 percent of the Cowboys' snaps, Dallas would've given up a No. 6. By monitoring his participation in the final game, the Cowboys kept Casillas below 75 percent and forfeited only a No. 8 pick.

"It's just keeping inventory," Jerry Jones said.

During the Cowboys' season-ending, five-game winning streak — a period when someone had to step up in Aikman's absence — Michael Irvin caught 37 passes for 649 yards and four touchdowns. In Dallas's final eight games, he lined up opposite five of the league's six Pro Bowlers. Against Houston's Cris Dishman (seven catches, 84 yards, one touchdown), Washington's Darrell Green (nine catches, 130 yards, one touchdown), Pittsburgh's Rod Woodson (eight catches, 157 yards, one touchdown), Philadelphia's Eric Allen (five catches, 92 yards, one touchdown) and Atlanta's Deion Sanders (10 catches, 169 yards, one touchdown), he fared phenomenally well. Later, he'd get the league's sixth Pro Bowl corner, San Diego's Gill Byrd, in Hawaii. Byrd was covering Irvin when he caught a 13-yard touchdown pass, one of the eight receptions for 125 yards that gave Irvin the Pro Bowl MVP award.

Smith totaled 160 yards against the Falcons while being kept updated by Texas Stadium public-address announcer Murphy Martin on the ground-gaining progress of closest rival Barry Sanders of Detroit. Irvin (1,523 yards) and Smith (1,563) became the first same-team duo to lead the NFL in receiving yards and rushing yards. "Our offensive line might not have any Pro Bowlers," Nate Newton said. "But at least we block for two kings."

The Cowboys had royalty at quarterback, too. But King Aikman was left scratching his crown after not getting on the field in preparation for the next week's play-off opener in Chicago. Jimmy Johnson said the decision to keep Aikman under wraps had something to do with not wanting him to hydroplane himself into another injury on the wet turf, and something to do with not wanting Cowboys players to think Johnson "is not taking this game seriously." Aikman did take the field once; oddly, when first-teamers were introduced in the pregame, he and Beuerlein were trotted out.

Who would start at quarterback in Chicago? "I've kind of been left in the dark," Aikman said.

Johnson decided to open with Beuerlein. The Bears, like Dallas a wild-card after an 11-5 regular season, countered with those three fat guys from that "Da Bears" skit on "Saturday Night Live." Cowboys players who caught their Dallas-bashing act at midfield before the game at Soldier Field were not amused. So even after the three fat guys retired somewhere in the stands to their six seats, Dallas let off some America's Steam. In winning their sixth straight game, the Cowboys forced a first-drive fumble that led to a field goal, blocked a punt that led to a 10-0 lead, cemented together three goal-line stands, swiped two interceptions, blitzed like escaping convicts, committed no turnovers and permitted no sacks.

"Hey, those 'Da Bears' routines are cute," said guard John Gesek. "But go tell those fat bastards to get with the program."

The Cowboys advanced to the divisional round of the NFC play-offs, and a chance to gain revenge against Detroit. Dallas had avenged its first embarrassing loss of the year, that 24-0 nightmare against Philadelphia on September 15, by rebounding with the play-off-clincher three months later. Now was a chance to erase memories of the 34-10 loss in Detroit back on October 27.

119

"We didn't think the best team won that day, and I'm still not sure they're the best team," said center Mark Stepnoski before the January 5 play-off at the Silverdome.

The Cowboys made fun of Lions quarterback Erik Kramer, calling him a "scab" for crossing Players Association picket lines in 1987. They burned at the thought of Lions cornerback Ray Crockett's 96-yard interception return for a touchdown, how he strutted and posed his way down the sideline. "That makes me sick every time I watch it," guard John Gesek said.

The teams seemed remarkably well-matched. Dallas had Emmitt Smith and his 1,563 yards and his 12 touchdowns. Detroit had Barry Sanders and his 1,548 yards and 16 touchdowns. Dallas's Beuerlein was a backup-makes-good story, having completed 49 percent of his passes and throwing a touchdown in each of his six games. Kramer was completing 51 percent, with 11 touchdowns in his eight starts. Both clubs were riding six-game win streaks. Neither had extensive postseason experience (Dallas had ten players who'd been in the postseason; Detroit hadn't hosted a play-off game since 1957).

"It's like we're looking in a mirror," said Cowboys linebacker Jack Del Rio.

Then the mirror cracked.

The Cowboys' "family" turned dysfunctional in a 38-6 loss in which the Lions pointed only at the goal line while the Cowboys pointed fingers at each other. Cornerback Issiac Holt refused to follow the direction of coaches and was tugged to the bench, where he was belittled by Jimmy Johnson. "I only got beat on three plays," Holt said, deflecting blame toward the other corner, Larry Brown. Said Brown: "I D'ed up. I don't think (Willie Green) was a factor. I took him out of the game." All Green did was catch eight passes for 115 yards and two scores. All Kramer did was throw for 341 yards. The game

seemed over in the first quarter, when Melvin Jenkins intercepted Beuerlein and returned the pick 41 yards for a touchdown and a 14-3 lead.

"He guessed right," Beuerlein said. "He wasn't supposed
to be there."

It wasn't any consolation for the Cowboys at the time, but
their failure to advance to that NFC Championship Game was
excusable. Because, to paraphrase Beuerlein, they weren't supposed to be there, either. Not yet.

6 THE PUPPETEER ★

Chuck Fairbanks once revealed to Jimmy Johnson a secret of football success.

"Every now and then, you need a crisis," said Fairbanks, the head coach at Oklahoma when Johnson was his defensive line coach at the start of the 1970s. "And if you don't have a crisis, sometimes you need to create one."

The way Johnson sees it, he is the Puppeteer of Valley Ranch. Anyone who comes in contact with him — players, staff members, media people and ideally, opponents — are the marionettes. If Johnson believes a certain atmosphere is necessary to make his wishes come true, that certain atmosphere is achieved.

It is manipulative, Johnson admits. "But I know best how things need to be," he says. "Doing it my way, that's what makes me happy. I feel like things stay in order that way. If I'm not doing that, there's not the sense of order that I need."

Says Michael Irvin: "Jimmy persuades people to do what he wants done. But who doesn't try to do it? He does it with players like I used to do it with women. Maybe he's a user. But the only difference between him and everyone else is that he's more persuasive."

Says Troy Aikman: "By now, I suppose we're all believers. All we have to go off of is the results. So obviously what he does works."

Cowboys players were devastated by Johnson's reaction after the December 28, 1992, victory that ended Dallas's NFC East-winning regular season with a club-record thirteenth win. The Cowboys had finished 13-3 with an imperfect 27-14 win over the Chicago Bears. As is customary, Cowboys players and coaches gathered around Johnson in the postgame Texas Stadium locker room to kneel in prayer before hearing some words of wisdom from the coach.

"Sick call is at 10:00 a.m. Make sure you get your two weightlifting sessions in this week. See you tomorrow," Johnson muttered.

There were no congratulations, no atta-boys, no back pats. Johnson's purpose was obvious; he wanted the players to forget about their past accomplishments and focus on the upcoming postseason. And he wanted them to know of his dissatisfaction with their sloppy performance, in which three fumbles allowed the Bears to storm back into the game with 14 fourth-quarter points. But Johnson's words eclipsed what players believed was their brightest hour, and caused the men who'd just finished their prayer — men who obviously were on the edge of their seats in anticipation of praise from the Puppeteer — to use the coach's name in vain.

"Why not take five seconds to say, 'Congratulations'?" center Mark Stepnoski wonders.

"That," says linebacker Ken Norton, "was a matter of us knowing our coach. We should have known not to expect a bunch of pats on the back from him. Whether we like it or not, he's the way he is. And whether we like it or not, and no matter how much we fight him or disagree with his methods, he was succeeding in turning us into being like him. We were almost turning into having his personality."

That was the permanent result of Johnson's snub. The temporary result was a mini-crisis that magnetized players into bonding with each other against the "enemy." The NFC East-champion Cowboys didn't have a game for two weeks. For fourteen days, who would the Cowboys players rip and snort at? Who would be "the enemy?" For the moment, the coach would volunteer.

"It's brainwashing, and he's good at it," tight end Alfredo Roberts says.

Johnson prefaces an observation by saying he's not a base-ball fan. But he correctly recalls the aura of the Oakland A's in their championship years of the early 1970s. He notes that their volatile clubhouse seemed to "help them win championships because it keeps them alive and on their toes. You never knew what to expect around that place. I like that."

Johnson says he intentionally strives to be unpredictable as a way of keeping his Cowboys off their heels: "I'm more effective as a bad guy because I'm not always the bad guy. I'm the bad guy rarely. If you're the bad guy day-in and day-out, you're truly not the bad guy. You become the same voice every day, predictable. So it doesn't have the effect.

"Reward and punishment. You've got to combine them. That's the best way to teach. Studies have shown the most effective way to achieve long-term retention of knowledge is a combination of reward and punishment. If you only use re-ward, studies show the individual will retain what you're trying to teach him for a shorter period of time.

"So I use both. Reward and punishment."

This man handles everyone in a similarly calculating man-ner. He is careful to make himself familiar on a personal level with every player, every coach, every trainer, every equipment man, every scout. He gives them the time of day, they give him loyalty.

"I surround myself with people who are quality, intelligent, loyal people," he says. "I create an environment where someone who wants to get ahead can get ahead. I give them freedom to be as outstanding as they want to be."

Johnson revels being in position to "give the freedom." In January of 1993, the New York Giants and Chicago Bears were seeking a head coach and were elbowing their ways toward interviews with Dallas defensive coordinator Dave Wannstedt. As far as Wannstedt knew, their interest was not yet public knowledge when, one afternoon, the phone in Wannstedt's Valley Ranch office starting sounding off.

"I was in there watching Eagles film (in preparation for the Cowboys' play-off opener against Philadelphia)," Wannstedt said. "The phone was ringing off the hook. What had happened was, Jimmy had just stood up in a press conference and announced that teams would have permission to interview me immediately. Only he forgot to tell me about it."

Johnson labors furiously to achieve such shot-calling positions, just as he once labored to be hired for any coaching job, then to be labeled a coaching "prospect," then to be identified as a coaching "phenom," then finally, at both the University of Miami and in Dallas, to be a muscle-flexing mentor, boss and puppeteer. Johnson spent years climbing the ladder, doing what he calls "grinding" for years in the shadows of others. ("Grinding," chuckles Dallas assistant Joe Avezzano, "is the catch-phrase around here for what I used to just think was called 'working hard.'")

Johnson was, and is, bothered by being passed over at his alma mater in 1976. He was the Arkansas defensive coordinator when athletic director Frank Broyles, Johnson's old coach, opted instead to hire Lou Holtz. When Johnson did finally get his big head coaching break, in 1979 at Oklahoma State, he had spent fourteen seasons bouncing around as an assistant, from Louisiana Tech to Wichita State to Iowa State to Oklahoma to Arkansas to Pitt, to OSU, then Miami and then Dallas.

Always there was Johnson fighting for the control that would allow him to avoid the problems created by those he considered less competent. Or to personally and purposely orchestrate the problems, the crises, when the need arose.

"I've taken some heat wherever I've gone," Johnson says. "At Oklahoma State, they were on probation, so it was guilt by association there. That definitely set up a situation where the people in the program, the people who supported the program, had to circle the wagons. At Miami, there was this idea that I was some hick from Oklahoma, and when I left there was this renegade thing. There were dozens of times when our image was manufactured by outsiders, but was used by us as an advantage. Those teams definitely bonded together because of what they had to deal with. And when I came to the Cowboys, it was, 'Aw, he's just a college coach.' And as far as a crisis or two, we had plenty. Of course, early on not all of them were created on purpose."

In February 1992, when the complicated rules of NFL free agency were finalized, Johnson educated himself into being an expert on the subject. After study sessions with Jerry Jones and team vice-president Stephen Jones, no one in the league knew more than Johnson did. The Puppeteer should not have been surprised when other head coaches in the league contacted him seeking rule clarifications. Says Johnson: "I am completely loyal and as cooperative as possible with people who work for me, and with me, on one condition: that they be completely loyal to me back."

Johnson's dealings with the media — an area where allegiance to a coach is ethically forbidden — are especially instructive. It was Chicago Mayor Richard J. Daley who said, "A newspaper is the lowest thing there is." Johnson surely wishes he would have thought of that line first. Says broadcaster Dale Hansen: "Jimmy tolerates the media. If he could eliminate us, he'd do it in a heartbeat. Tom Landry treated us all equally like crap. At least Jimmy treats us selectively like crap."

A number of reporters think Johnson's selectivity is based on his personal feelings for them. They are foolishly mistaken. The Cowboys coach views the media as another executing arm of his "reward-and-punishment" system. When he thinks it's time to feed his Cowboys, Johnson uses the media like so much Puppy Chow. When he deems a slap on the nose necessary, he uses the media like (fittingly) a rolled-up newspaper.

"The media's job is to give out information and I just try to help out any way I can," Johnson says, smiling.

Johnson's strongest media relationships, for the most part, are with the media members who are strongest; that is, the reporters who reach the largest audience. Among the top sports media personalities in Dallas/Fort Worth are Randy Galloway (the *Dallas Morning News* columnist and WBAP-AM Radio talk-show host), Brad Sham (the KVIL-FM Radio play-by-play announcer) and Hansen (the Channel 8 sports anchor and game analyst on KVIL). Not coincidentally, Johnson says Galloway, Hansen and Sham top his must-talk-to list.

"Whatever access I have to Jimmy has absolutely everything to do with the circulation of my newspaper and the size of listenership to the talk show," Galloway says. "Jimmy can give you newspaper circulation figures and talk-show ratings a heck of a lot quicker than I can. I know he doesn't talk to me because he considers me a true friend. I've seen his list of top five friends, and I'm not on it."

Hansen says Johnson sometimes "colors his view of somebody by what he thinks of their lifestyle. If you don't like some of the things he likes, you might not be allowed to get too comfortable with him. I believe I get better stuff from Jimmy because I go to (the training-camp media parties at) Hooters and drink Heinekens with him back in the corner and laugh and joke. Jimmy is the kind of guy who if you don't have a beer once in a while he has a question about you. So a guy like myself, or Galloway, talks his language and drinks beer with him. We tend to find Jimmy talking to us about some very useful information. But I don't think it has as much to do with who he likes as it does who he needs."

The first time Hansen had an in-depth conversation with Johnson was at the 1989 Cowboys training camp in Thousand Oaks, California. Hansen was intent on finding out Johnson's plans for the quarterback position. Many people in the media assumed the Cowboys had to sign veteran Steve Pelluer rather than start rookie Troy Aikman. Hansen sought out Johnson one night and they found themselves together at a Mexican restaurant sipping margaritas and dipping chips. Then Johnson starting spilling the beans. Not the pinto kind, either.

"You can't possibly start Aikman," Hansen said.

"The hell I can't," Johnson said.

"But what about all the media reports about you guys wanting to sign Pelluer?" Hansen asked.

"Pelluer," answered Johnson, "has balls the size of raisins."

Recalls Hansen: "Johnson was saying all these sort of inside-info things that I couldn't believe he was saying to me. I finally had to stop him and ask him if he realized I was in the media. That talk allowed me to go on the air and be right about their disinterest in Pelluer. But for a while, it had me thinking,

'Hey, aren't I something? Look at me, I'm tight with Jimmy Johnson.' The truth is, for a while I got sucked in."

Much to the consternation of some local media higher-ups blinded by their own self-importance and unwilling to comprehend Johnson's motives, the bigger you are the harder Jimmy sucks. *Sports Illustrated* is granted far greater access into Johnson's supposed "inner sanctum" than are the two major Metroplex newspapers. A CBS-TV broadcaster will more readily get an audience with him, will get more time from him and will get better answers to questions from him, than, as Johnson frankly puts it, "someone from a radio station in Tyler or Waco. Now, I might personally like that guy or woman from Tyler. I might not be able to stand the CBS guy. But dealing with the CBS guy is a more effective way of getting my message out there, and of accomplishing what I have to get accomplished."

Galloway knows that if he lost his position, he'd lose his place in line. "If I moved to a job in West Texas, Jimmy would probably talk to me about as often as he talks to Don Shula," he says.

As was the case with the Cowboys under old-regime president Tex Schramm, the Johnson Administration is acutely aware of what is written and said about it. Johnson monitors the TV and radio shows, or enlists help in doing so.

"It was evident early in the game that Jimmy would be different than Landry in the sense that not only would he listen to every word, but that he would readily acknowledge doing so," Sham says. "Tom would very rarely acknowledge that he'd heard something by issuing some sly remark the next day. But Jimmy doesn't have to rely on a sly remark the next day. He calls the radio shows. He'll just flat pick up the phone and call you. Randy is so aware of this that he makes sure Jimmy has the radio station's private number so he can get in when he wants to."

The public relations staff clips out every single Cowboys-related newspaper and magazine article on the club it can get its scissors on, Xeroxes off a few dozen copies and puts a packet of clippings on the desk of every Valley Ranch employee. One of the first things Johnson does every morning is devour his clippings.

"He is so intelligent that I would hate to insult him by claiming he didn't know what Bosnia is," says Sham, when asked how far beyond the sports section Johnson reads. "But I'm not so sure about Herzegovina."

Johnson scans and commits to what friends say might be a photographic memory every single inch of what most readers know is one step from being bird-cage liner. "I read your notes today, and not that it matters," he'll tell a writer, "but there was a factual error in there." Imagine: arguably the hardest-working head coach in the National Football League finds time to copy-edit newspaper stories!

"Not that it matters"? Johnson can be unforgiving, not as much when his sensibilities are offended as when he views a story as an unnecessary obstacle to his football team's success. In 1990, after WFAA-TV reporter Gerry Oher broadcast a "negative" story, Johnson made a conscious decision to overtly blackball him. Oher's presence at press conferences was ignored. Oher would ask a question. Johnson would pretend not to hear. "Are there any questions? Any questions at all?" Johnson would respond.

After a 1992 newspaper story revealed how one of the Cowboys' draft-day plans had gone awry, Johnson met with the responsible reporter to vent his anger. "I don't expect you to help me row the boat," he said. "But I don't need you punching holes in the bottom of the boat, either."

Metroplex reporters should have learned their lesson about Johnson in 1989, when he and Jones puffed smoke screens all around the Herschel Walker-to-Minnesota trade. Rumors of the blockbuster deal began to ooze out seven days before the October 12 swap. The first report came out of Miami, of all places, and suggested the deal was done. After Johnson issued a denial, he asked a group of reporters to confidentially let him in on the source of the report. They told him the source was reputed to be none other that Linda Kay Johnson, his soon-to-be estranged ex-wife.

"Well," Jimmy cleverly bluffed, "you'll have to come up with a more reliable source than that. I haven't talked to Linda Kay in six months."

The media nevertheless went with the story. By the weekend, when the Cowboys were in Green Bay to play the Packers, Walker had even joined in the deception. Ed Werder, then of the *Fort Worth Star-Telegram* (now with the *Dallas Morning News*), approached Walker in the lobby of the Paper Valley Inn in Appleton, Wisconsin, on the eve of the game. Werder, fighting his way through prepubescent autograph-seekers a foot shorter than him, asked a question. Walker started to answer, then paused to accuse the six-foot Werder of trying to pry information from him while disguising himself as an elementary schooler.

In the locker room after Dallas's 31-13 loss, Walker was engulfed by more reporters. Again following the lead of his Cowboys superiors, he took the offensive and questioned the reporters' motives and integrity.

"What school did you graduate from?" assailed Walker, who had quit the University of Georgia early to turn pro.

"At least," counter-punched writer Mickey Spagnola, "we graduated from somewhere."

Walker decided to challenge the reporters to a duel of sorts. That week, he was to fire questions at them for a change.

Werder, Spagnola of the *Dallas Times-Herald* and Tim Cowlishaw of the *Morning News* were invited to a downtown Dallas TV studio to be grilled on "The Herschel Walker Show." They made it. Herschel didn't. By the time the director yelled "Lights, camera, action!" Walker was a Viking, sitting in a Minneapolis TV studio. The round-table discussion was conducted via satellite.

Until the end, Johnson and all involved did their best to camouflage their intentions with Walker. Jerry Jones was not wildly successful at this. Guidance from Cowboys public-relations director Greg Aiello had convinced Jones that out-right lying was not advisable. He urged Jones to issue "no comments." Thus came Jones'sss line to Werder on the Sunday morning of the Green Bay game. Upon exiting a coffee shop, Jones prefaced Werder's questioning by saying, "I'll talk to you about anything except the Herschel thing."

"But the Herschel thing is all I want to talk about," Werder said.

Feeling cornered, Jones said, "I don't want to lie to you. But I can't tell you the truth."

Vikings general manager Mike Lynn found himself in the same dilemma by Tuesday, when the NFL owners meeting was held at D/FW Airport. Lynn was hemmed in by reporters in a stairwell and talked to them for a time before making his escape through the hotel kitchen, with newshounds in hot pursuit. Johnson, displaying the same shrewdness that helped Dallas swing the deal, waited out the mob before tiptoeing undetected down an alternate stairwell.

Hansen, recalling Johnson's earlier denials, says he "told Jimmy point-blank that he lied to me. I used that term. He always felt that term was too strong. I just said telling me that there is no truth to a story I ask him about, and then turning around and doing it forty-eight hours later, hangs me out there. Just say, 'no comment.' Otherwise you make me look stupid. You hang my ass out to dry."

Better yours than his, Dale. Johnson knows the ins and outs of journalism better than many of its practitioners — and not because of that hokey weekly newspaper column that is ghost-written for him by his public relations staff. Simply, Johnson believes his job as coach supersedes his responsibility to play by any reporters' rules. For instance, he understands the boundaries that must separate reporters from the subjects they cover. But he believes those are the ethics of someone else's profession, not his.

"What happens," Johnson says, "is that a reporter writes something negative, and that may become something that negatively affects my operation. Because a player might pick up that newspaper and read this negative story about himself, and maybe he thinks the information came from me. Now I've got a little brush fire I've got to go put out.

"So my dealings with members of the media are a lot like my dealings with the players. It's important that if I send a message to someone, that they pass that message on in the way I want it conveyed."

And Johnson beats the hell out of Western Union when it comes to sending messages. Does Johnson publicly "lose his temper"? Very rarely. He displays it, but he rarely loses it.

In a Monday press conference after the Cowboys' 20-17 loss in Washington on December 13, 1992, Johnson reluctantly plodded through the rudimentary questions and answers about the defeat. As he was wrapping up a session he purposely had conducted with a funereal gravity, Johnson spotted one beat writer whose crime was that his face wasn't mirroring the coach's grimace.

"Somethin' funny?" he snapped, all but commanding the army of TV cameras to pan from his face in the direction of the smiling offender. "Somethin' humorous?"

Had Johnson gone out of control? Of course not. His reaction — as with his snubbing of Oher, as with that 1991 blasting of the officials after a loss to the Giants, as with any number of explosions acted out in front of an edge-of-its-seat audience — was a scene inspired by anger but performed almost by calculated rote.

"I show that I'm upset. I show that I'm irritated. It might look like I'm out of control, but in that case and in every case, I knew what I was doing," he says. "Are media people offended by that? They need to understand that sometimes it gets my point across for me to react in specific ways."

Johnson admits to possessing a "file folder" crammed with appropriate responses for when he senses his team is in need of a "crisis" or his players in need of "getting his point." The folder is not in the little white safe located beneath his Valley Ranch desk; it's in some oft-visited sector of his brain. He agrees that the "Somethin' funny?" performance might be a repeat of a "Somethin' funny?" performance he gave, say, back when an Oklahoma State beat writer smiled in a postloss press conference. He agrees that calling the work of the New York refs the worst he's seen "Ever. Ever. Since my daddy said, "This is what you call a football" might have come out of his mouth because he'd stored it in the mental file after using it back when he felt his University of Miami team had been screwed by the stripes.

"I've heard every one of Jimmy's speeches before," says receiver Michael Irvin, who played for Johnson both in Miami and now in Dallas. "He practices them on the banquet circuit, then gives them to us when we need them."

Players might see through Johnson's act. But like a kennel full of Pavlov's dogs, they are still moved by it. "If we practice hard, he might let us have a half-day off sometime," guard Nate Newton says. "He'll throw us a bone here and there. But I tell the guys, 'Don't get it confused. All he's telling you is that if we do what we're told, he can be a nice person. And if you don't, you'll see the dark side.'"

Once, Johnson's motivational techniques included fathering. Now, that tool has been replaced by instilling fear. Johnson, chameleon-like, had to rebuild himself from players' coach into taskmaster.

"My reputation in college was always as a players' coach," Johnson says. "But I don't know if in pro football you truly have any players' coaches. In the pros, it's made even more difficult because of the financial situation. I really tried to fight for what is right for both sides when a player is up for a contract. That is a difficult gap to bridge."

The professional athletes who in 1989 counted on Johnson to operate using a "permissive parenting" style found out quickly how Johnson had necessarily altered his demeanor from college coach to pro coach. In his first Cowboys' team meeting, Johnson ordered players to introduce themselves. Name, rank and serial number, that sort of thing. Players thought it sophomoric and demonstrated that in their orations. Johnson was not amused. His players, who'd grown accustomed to the stoic Tom Landry standing at the head of the class, seemed to be under the impression that Johnson was like a substitute teacher, that they'd spend the season throwing spit wads and drawing cartoons on the blackboard.

After the final player had completed his stand-up routine, some joker actually called out to Johnson, "Hey coach, who are you?"

"I'm the guy who decides whether or not you get a paycheck every week, and whether or not you have a career in this league," Johnson answered sharply.

Says Newton: "Coach Johnson isn't a con man. He's more like a hit man."

Another reason Johnson tempered his players' coach side is the quality of opponents at his new level.

"It is very easy to be a players' coach when you're winning every week as we did at Miami," he says. "Show me any place in the world where there's a players' coach whose team is losing every week. That doesn't exist. At Miami, we lost four games in four years. So all the players loved me. And the ones who didn't love me wouldn't say so in public."

Beyond his passion for blackjack, Johnson is not interested in leaving anything to chance. "I don't think I've ever put down even a five-dollar chip on roulette, or any other game," he says. So it is understandable that his announcements, pep talks and tongue-lashings in team meetings follow a precise and thought-out pattern. "I call it planting seeds," he says.

Here's a typical in-season week's oratory itinerary for Jimmy Appleseed:

Monday — The Cowboys won on Sunday. Johnson addresses players in the big meeting room for a team get-together at 1:00 p.m. First, special-teams coach Joe Avezzano speaks. Then Johnson takes center stage to award game balls (he doesn't give them out after losses). It is here when he introduces his unofficial "theme of the week."

"Don't spend too long thinking about that victory," he'll say. "This week's game is the one we've known all along would be the tough one. Isn't that right, Norv (Turner) and Dave (Wannstedt)? Isn't that what I've been saying all along?"

Says Irvin: "It's scripted, sure. But it's not a head game. To Jimmy, it's communication."

Then comes a 2:00 p.m. session with the media. It is conducted in the cozy press library and generally has an informal flavor, right down to Johnson's outfit, either a nylon jogging suit or slacks and a sweater. Johnson gives an injury update, answers specific questions about the previous day's game, and the game ball announcement is made again. Then the "theme" is repeated for the benefit of the cameras, which means his players will have heard it at least twice by 10:35 that night, when the local sports broadcasts all dutifully replay it.

"A lot of guys say they don't watch TV or read the papers, but most of us are pulling your leg when we say that," says defensive back Robert Williams. "We want to know what's being talked about, too."

Tuesday — Players are off. But they will still hear Johnson's echo eventually, because he's available at the Tuesday press luncheon, pushing headlines and story ideas onto the Fourth Estate. Johnson takes the podium in the big meeting room and faces approximately sixty reporters interested in both scribbling down everything he has to say ("As I told the team, this is the game we've been concerned about all year") and what Jerry Jones'sss caterers will be serving as soon as Johnson's session is over.

Johnson has traded in the jogging suit for a tailored navy-blue suit, pairing it with a sharp white shirt with blue pinstripes and a red silk tie. Again, through sheer will he controls the mood of the room. His eyebrow-furrowing is an especially intimidating sight. Equally daunting is his lip-pursing. "If I'm in a serious discussion and I don't expect laughter," he says. "In a serious discussion, I want it to be taken seriously."

Usually after a win, Johnson expects laughter because he can successfully court it. Four decades on the recruiting circuit, the banquet circuit and the late-night-crawl circuit have honed his public-speaking skills.

In 1991, Jones was lampooned in a ceremony that featured almost a dozen celebrity roasters. Johnson was among them. But unlike the men and women who joined him onstage at the

Meyerson Center in Dallas, Johnson hadn't been given weeks to prepare. He went to the microphone cold, without notes. He knocked 'em dead. Same thing happens most Tuesdays — especially if he spots an influential out-of-town journalist in the audience. "Jimmy perks up a little bit if a national guy rolls into town," Galloway says.

Wednesday — Johnson meets with the players at 1:00 p.m., right after many of them have popped in and out of the locker room in attempts to elude reporters, who are allowed to roam about from noon to 1 o'clock. The team is given the game plan, and spends the afternoon implementing it on the practice field. Then Johnson calls them together.

Roberts started his college career under Johnson in 1984, as a freshman at Miami. "It's always been like this," Roberts says. "Invariably, on the Wednesdays I thought we had a good practice, he'll call us up and say, 'Y'all didn't practice worth a damn.' And the times we practiced like shit, he'll say, 'It was a great day of work.' It's all designed to set whatever tone."

After practice, reporters are summoned to the edge of the practice field, where they can observe a few actual plays. Practice-squad quarterback Jason Garrett throws a pass to practice-squad receiver Tyrone Williams. Incomplete. Both practice-squadders need more practice. But not today. The session is over, and Johnson doesn't have to say anything to communicate to the media his mood. You can see it in that funny way he swings his arms when he walks. If his arms chop up and down purposefully, it means he'll say, "We were sloppy today, but we'll get better." If he skips over, then leaps up atop a two-foot-high ledge rather than trudging up a slight incline, it means he'll say, "Good practice, good practice. We were very sharp. ... Let's see. What else y'all got for me?" Then he'll entertain questions almost endlessly.

Another telltale sign comes after his mini-conference, when Johnson walks up the track toward the locker room. Are reporters allowed to walk up the track with him, possibly to speak briefly with a player or coach? It depends. If it's "Eagles Week," they needn't bother. Track-passers will be shot. However, if the upcoming opponent is, say, the Seattle Seahawks, the coach won't bat an eye if the media boys want to drop their tape recorders, ask equipment man Buck Buchanan for a football, and play a little catch.

Thursday — The ritual is virtually unchanged from Wednesday except that Johnson picks his game captains and adds two-minute-drill work to the practice. If the normally physical workout is an especially good one (or as Roberts says, if it's a crummy one but Johnson wants his Cowboys to think it's a good one), he'll call the fellas up and then holler, "Take it to the house." This is Johnsonese for "You have permission to end practice and go into the main building." But to the Cowboys, it seems to mean "Act like this is the day of your high-school graduation, the day of your escape from prison and the day your agent got you a guaranteed contract, all rolled into one."

"You whoop it up on Thursdays because you know Friday and Saturday aren't going to be physically demanding," says guard John Gesek. "You get to have two days where your body doesn't feel beat to death."

Johnson hasn't said whether it is part of his script or not, but another trend that oddsmakers might want to follow in the future developed in 1992. Johnson's tension level right around Thursday seemed to reveal his confidence in the Cowboys' ability to win on Sunday. The Jimmy-O-Meter served as an inaccurate gauge only three times: before the season-opening 23-10 win over Washington on September 7, the 20-10 win over the Eagles on November 1 (Johnson was proven to have been unnecessarily tense) and the 27-23 loss to the Rams on November 15 (when he was proven to have been mistakenly loose).

"The only reason I can't buy your Jimmy-O-Meter thing," Aikman says, "is that while I've seen him uptight, I've never seen Jimmy where he didn't think we were going to win that week's game."

Friday — The Cowboys go through a light morning workout. Johnson repeats the "theme of the week," reflects on the recent days of work and dismisses the players. He wants to keep it short with the media, too, and does so.

A hint. If you ask him a question and he answers with a befuddled-sounding, "Do, do what now?" it means he's blowing you off.

It is Johnson's contention that "the game is won on Wednesday, Thursday and Friday. By Friday, the deal is done." Nevertheless, he shows up on Saturday.

Saturday — The team meets for a walk-through. Ideally, this happens in the morning so Johnson is free to watch college football on TV in the afternoon. At 7:00 p.m. the Cowboys comes together for dinner at the team hotel. At eight o'clock, they study in meetings for about ninety minutes. Johnson keeps a low profile throughout. This is the only day of the week Johnson, probably the most media-accessible coach in football, is generally off-limits to reporters (except for the networks, whose broadcasters receive a pregame briefing from the coach and key players). A scribe may bump into Johnson in the hotel lobby or hospitality room, but Saturday is when he rests his voice from the public at large.

"Not even the players hear much from him on Saturdays," Aikman says.

Sunday pregame — With about two minutes to go before the team takes the field, Johnson calls everyone up in the locker room. His most memorable postgame speeches are set up here.

That "When you go up against a big gorilla, you hit him with everything you got" postgame spine tingler after the 1991 play-off clincher in Philadelphia was set up by similar pregame remarks. "He's always got one zinger to hit you with," Roberts says. "When we play a team like Philly, a team that tries to be intimidating, he says, 'First play, you hit Philly right in the damn mouth.'"

Sunday postgame (win) — Johnson is at his most predictable here. A prayer with his team behind closed doors is followed by a few encouraging words and another of his endless reminders to "enjoy this one, but remember, we've got more work ahead of us." Then he crosses the hall to an interview room to meet the press. He'll joke about the microphones being positioned too high on the podium. Then he'll credit the losers, refuse to single out individuals, instruct the reporters as to what the key point in the game was, kid a media member who picked against his Cowboys, and, when he's had enough, say, "Okay?" That means he wishes the interview to be over.

But first, a member of the electronic media who wants to record himself asking a question says, "Coach, how big a win was this?"

"It's big," Johnson will say. "But not as big as next week's."

Says Cowboys staffer Bruce Mays, who has worked for Johnson for fourteen years: "Jimmy says that just like Raphael, the great painter said it. When they asked Raphael which of his works was his favorite, he always said, 'The next one.'"

Sunday postgame (loss) — The prayer is followed by that frightening furrowed brow and those scary pursed lips. The press conference leads the league in brevity. "Can you talk about what you're upset about?" the reporters ask. "I'm upset about a lot of things," Johnson says as he backs away from the microphones and toward the dressing room.

"Every time we lose, the guys expect him to go off," Roberts says. "He usually doesn't. He'll just say (after road games), 'Let's shower and get back to Dallas.'" Then Johnson will hurry to his customary front seat on the bus. And he'll mope.

"He's thinking of how he'll handle the week," Roberts says. "He didn't go off on us in the locker room. But he'll go off on us Monday or Wednesday."

Says Aikman: "We're not blind to what needs to be done and what needs to be corrected when things go wrong. I mean, we get ourselves prepared, too. But you've got to admire the fact that Jimmy has the courage of his convictions. It's easy to say things are being done the right way when you're winning, but he acted like he knew they were right even when we were losing. He follows his plan every single day."

As an offshoot of his plan, Johnson seems to have nurtured an infallible knack for seeming to lie while telling the truth and for seeming to be truthful while fibbing around the edges. Ask Johnson how a player is doing in training camp. If all he says is, "Murphy's doing some good things," Murphy might as well consider himself cut right there. Suggest to Johnson that his divorce after twenty-six years of marriage, the parade of different sports cars he eases into his personalized parking space at Valley Ranch and his addiction to dominating those around him seem like symptoms of what psychologists call a "midlife crisis," and Johnson feigns ignorance. "A midlife crisis? What's that?" asks a man who has spent thirty years studying the human condition.

On January 26, 1993, a few days before the Super Bowl, Johnson announced to the national media that he was presently poring over a book about positive thinking, "something about positive experience." And then he smoothly used the theme of the book to glide into relating a funny or ironic anecdote. Veteran Johnson-watchers were sure the coach had invented this book to set off his message-sending food chain: feed theme to reporters. Reporters write of theme. Players read of theme. Players obey theme.

This whole "positive experience book" thing smelled especially fishy when someone pressed Johnson on more literary details. "I can't pronounce the author's name," Johnson said in what seemed like a weak alibi.

The book actually exists. It is *Flow: The Psychology of Optimal Experience*. The author is University of Chicago psychologist Mihaly Csikszentmihalyi. Mihaly Csikszentmihalyi? Johnson's truth really is stranger than fiction.

Johnson achieves flow the way a river does. He's a force of nature.

There is his "I don't believe in luck" address of December 1, 1992. Someone mentioned to Johnson how "lucky" any team needs to be in order to rocket to a 10-2 start, as the Cowboys had. Lucky? Johnson roared head-first into a stirring speech.

"I don't think there is any such thing as luck," Johnson said. "Injuries, who you face when, all those things, that's part of football. ... Our players work hard in the off-season on conditioning and strength. Our practices follow a routine that used to be questioned. But we work hard during the week so we're not soft during games. That was, maybe it's the other team that has the injuries. ... You can't sit around thinking you're going to get lucky, 'cause you do that and you'll get your rear end beat. Think that way, you're not going to win a damn thing. ... I don't believe in luck."

This was another bit of Morse code for the benefit of Cowboys players. Read Johnson's dots and dashes, and you understand that he wasn't railing against luck, but against reliance on luck. (It might be only coincidence that on the morning of Johnson's speech, the front pages of the newspapers featured a story on a retired nurse who'd just won

$21.7 million in the Texas Lottery. She presumably accomplished this without the benefit of off-season instruction from Dallas strength-and-conditioning coach Mike Woicik.)

The message was received — by everyone.

Shortly after Johnson's "no luck" speech, Jerry Jones was asked to detail the key points in the Cowboys' drive to the top. Jones spoke at length about Dallas's installation of a quality coach, the acquisition of a stand-out quarterback, the building of a capable defense, ad infinitum. And then he cited something called "serendipity." In fact, three times in answers to three different questions, Jones — not usually given to two-dollar words — mentioned this business of "serendipity."

"Serendipity" is a word derived from the 1964 Persian fable "The Three Princes of Serendip." It means having the ability to find valuable or agreeable things not sought for. In short, it means "fortunate." "Blessed."

You know, Jimmy. Lucky.

Johnson the Puppeteer has had things he couldn't possibly have planned on, things no human can control, fall his way. But more often, he's tugged on them until they've toppled his way. After the Cowboys' 52-17 Super Bowl XXVII win over Buffalo, assistant coach Joe Avezzano read a 1989 newspaper column that predicted Johnson wouldn't rack up wins by scores like 50-7 in the NFL as he had in college. "No, not 50-7," Avezzano says. "More like 52-17."

This is Johnson's ship. You are either a passenger or a crew member, which means you're one of the guys "rowing his boat," as he says, or else you're a stowaway. You want to kiss Jimmy Johnson's ring? You may — as long as you're willing to set up shop under his thumb.

At training camp one year, Johnson strolled across the campus at St. Edward's University with his strings attached to most of his favorite things in life. He was balancing a stack of

Styrofoam boxes loaded with Mexican food. He was joined by his girlfriend, Rhonda Rookmaaker, who was toting a plate of barbecued ribs. And he was headed toward his room, where the Heineken was on ice and a Monday Night Football game was on TV.

A passerby commented that it appeared Johnson, whose Cowboys had won a preseason game the night before, had armed himself with all the essentials of a perfect evening.

"Yep," Jimmy said. "What a great day it is! We got a win. I got my Mexican food, I got my ribs, I got my football game on."

"And you've got me!" reminded Rhonda.

Johnson couldn't let slide the opportunity to chillingly master the situation.

"Oh. ..., uh, yeah," deadpanned the Puppeteer.

7   CAMP COWBOY   ★

Under the flamethrowing daytime heat in Austin, Texas, Cowboys training camp is like the Bill Murray movie "Groundhog Day." In the movie, Murray wakes up every morning to the exact same day he woke up to yesterday. The same occurrences, the same conversations, the same everything. Nothing changes, no matter what.

But by night, Cowboys training camp is better described by the bartender to Henry Fonda in the old movie "The Ox-Bow Incident." Fonda wants to know what there is to do in this small town. The bartender replies, "Eat. Sleep. Drink. Play poker. And fight."

Welcome to Camp Cowboy, where the days are long but the nights are longer if a player can avoid being caught out after curfew. Where men are men and their wives are 200 miles north in Dallas.

This is where receiver Kelvin Martin and offensive lineman Freddie Childress are packing heat, and quarterback Babe Laufenberg is packing forty-seven pairs of underwear.

This is where defensive tackle Dean Hamel tells Jimmy Johnson "I feel like tearing your head off" because of his contract dispute with management, but because he's hungry decides to think about it over the free lunch provided, of course, by management.

This is where running back Tony Boles decides to, um, "borrow" teammate Emmitt Smith's Nissan Pathfinder. And Smith's credit card. And fails to come back with it. For two days.

This is where frustration caused when 300-pound men failing to hit a tiny white ball more than thirty feet off the tee transforms day-off golf outings into club-tossing contests. This is where the pace of the Cowboys coaching staff's jog is quickened by an angry stray goat that patrols the St. Edward's University campus.

This is where cafeteria food eventually seems bland enough to prompt Michael Irvin to climb atop a lunchroom table and announce, "How can you expect a Ferrari to run right if you feed it regular gas?" This is where Troy Aikman can sense camp is nearing an end "because the cooks start clearing out the cabinets, making us use chocolate milk on our cereal." This is where receiver Jimmy Smith misunderstands a thick-accented cafeteria worker and passes on some mystery grub she calls "turkey roll" because he thought she said "donkey meat."

This is where "Autograph Alley" fans not yet familiar with their heroes show their appreciation for the signature of punter Mike Saxon by saying, "Thanks, Mr. Aikman." This is where Saxon can finally be identified by the almost traditional black eye given him each and every summer as punishment for too much dorm-room revelry.

This is the home of the state capitol, the home of the University of Texas, the home of Bubbas. This is where 750,000 bats reside (they stay near Hidden Hills). This is where nude sunbathers hang out (they stay by Lake Travis' Hippie Hollow). This is where every July and August for five weeks, 100,000 Cowboys fans and 100 million dragonflies converge (both types of God's creatures fight for room near the St. Edward's University practice fields).

This is where the threat of roster moves means no job is safe, and the threat of golf carts careening wildly around the campus of St. Ed's means no life is safe. This is where jazzy, funky Sixth Street and the other aspects of nightlife in Austin (proud of the fact that it has more bars per capita than any city in the United States) change the daytime's monotonously hellish inferno into a tempting Garden of Eden.

"Austin gives players one more reason to 'go over the wall,'" says ex-Cowboys quarterback Babe Laufenberg.

Most NFL training camps are staged as far away from civilization as possible. Platteville, Wisconsin; Greeley, Colorado; Rocklin, California. Conventional wisdom drives teams to find trouble-free, well-scrubbed, God-fearing towns where the idea of a social event is visiting the twenty-four-hour bakery at the Tom Thumb; where church steeples provide the only shade; where the water needed to replenish the body after a draining workout isn't customarily supplemented by hops and barley.

Instead, Cowboys owner Jerry Jones uprooted another tradition in 1990 by shifting his team's training camp headquarters from Thousand Oaks, California, where it had been for twenty-seven seasons, to Austin, where he found the antithesis of the standard training-camp site.

"Austin is a great place for training camp, almost too great," says former Cowboys defensive tackle Danny Noonan. "It's a young town, a party town. When the Cowboys were in Thousand Oaks, you had to drive clear to L.A. to get in the same kind of trouble."

Austin is a mishmash of hedonism, alcoholism and intellectualism. And in terms of finance and promotion — two categories dear to Jones's heart — locating a football team there for five weeks every summer was a genius stroke. You want money-making schemes? Remember, this is the man who tried to organize a "Superstars" competition at the 1991 camp between members of the Cowboys and visiting Raiders. Troy Aikman, Emmitt Smith, Marcus Allen and Howie Long racing one another on an obstacle course, muscling up in a tug-of-war, long-distance-throwing a softball! It took considerable horsepower to pull Jones off the idea, the overriding logic being that the football team's fortunes might be marred slightly should Aikman pull a hamstring while doing competitive somersaults. This is the man who before the 1990 game against the 49ers considered allowing bungee-jumpers to perform at halftime by dangling themselves from the rafters at Texas Stadium.

"Problem was, we didn't know if insurance would cover us if something went wrong," vice-president Mike McCoy says.

There were surveyors of the move to Austin that promised it would cause Jones's Cowboys to go "splat!" Tom Landry and Tex Schramm were first in line to naysay.

Said Landry: "You could look the world over and not find a more perfect place to train than Thousand Oaks. July in Texas wears your players down. You're not only contending with 100-degree heat, but you have to deal with the humidity."

Thousand Oaks, said Schramm, "was the perfect place to train. The weather was cool enough where you could go all out in the workouts. Also, it never rained in Thousand Oaks. We never missed a workout. The Texas heat is too debilitating. They're going to find out they made a big mistake."

But the decision to summer in Austin was a brilliant one. The Cowboys save themselves almost $400,000 a year by dumping on California Lutheran College. They pocket a similar amount annually by drawing followers of one of Texas' most recognizable symbols to a city in Texas. The Cowboys wrap practices around benefits and parties and golf tournaments. They cover the fences surrounding the two practice fields with commercial billboards, like in a minor-league baseball park. Lining the field are enough full bleachers and busy vendors to inject into this most mundane nonevent a festive aura. "As soon as I saw beer was sold on the sidelines, I was sold on the place," offensive lineman Kevin Gogan says.

It is a chili cookoff, a bearded woman and a Ferris wheel away from being a county fair. Practices are free to the public, but equally boring scrimmages are viewed at a price. A crowd forms every year on the day before camp opens to watch workers paint stripes on the field. Johnson once surveyed a mob of five thousand watching his team stand around during stretching exercises and pondered Austin's unemployment rate.

The team's presence in Austin also works to the benefit of the football program, which Johnson desired to craft into a more metallic-blue-collar one. Johnson is convinced that conditioning is aided by the sort of brutal weather that can draw sweat beads from a cactus. "Most of the players are for it," Johnson said in December of 1990, when the move was announced. "Except the fat guys." Travel by staffers and players and their families is aided by the fact that camp is a three-hour car ride from Dallas rather than a three-hour plane ride, as Thousand Oaks is. "The only advantage to Thousand Oaks is that my mom lives thirty minutes away from there, so she did my laundry," Laufenberg said after the change in location. "Now, I have to bring forty-seven pairs of underwear to camp."

Training camp is more than just three-point stances and square-outs. It is as critical to the bonding of a team as it is to the choosing of the team. It is the peace-time equivalent of a foxhole.

"Training camp is the time for the players as well as the coaches to learn about each other," Johnson says. "When we have our daily staff meeting, we'll sit around and talk personnel, because that's what the meeting is officially designed for. But eventually, we'll get to drinking a couple of beers, and we'll get to talking three or four hours into the night. And that ends up determining how we're going to deal with one another for the rest of the year. If it's four hours of serious talk, that's important to the football team. But if it ends up being a talk about something that happened on the field with a player, or a funny story, that's important, too.

"It's a time to build relationships. Training camp doesn't have to be a concentration camp."

In preparation for Austin, Cowboys management does not erect barbed wire or unleash German shepherds. They simply stock up, as all NFL teams do, with 50,000 pounds of ice, 300,000 feet of athletic tape, 100,000 pounds of breakfasts, lunches and dinners and eighty thickly muscled job applicants. They load the lunchroom VCR every day with that same 1991 highlight reel, the one that opens with Johnson pouring some extra syrup on that "Poht Ahthuh" drawl and telling campers day after day after day, "The mind controllin' the body, not the body controllin' the mind." (Nobody informs the new campers that this will eventually mean Jimmy's mind is controllin' their bodies).

And then they allow the human drama — not to mention the human comedy — to play itself out.

A quaint Cowboys training camp tradition is the Bloodletting of the Punter. This involves six-foot-three, 200-pound Mike Saxon as the victim, and a series of beefier Cowboys as the executioners.

"This thing with Sax became a ritual," Noonan says. "Sax gets beat up every year. Let's see. ... Todd Fowler beat him up one year. Crawford Ker did it. Mark Walen did it. And then in '91, Jack Del Rio really did it. He screwed Saxon up bad. Part of it comes because Sax turns into a different man when he gets a little firewater in him. And part of it comes because Saxon, who is a hell of a great punter, knows he's not going to hit or get hit all year, so this is his one chance to do it with his friends."

Noonan was riding back to Dallas with Saxon after the 1991 conflict with Del Rio in which Saxon stayed on his feet long enough to sustain a list of injuries that would have sent trainer Kevin O'Neill into fits. Saxon did his best to hide his two black eyes behind sunglasses.

"He had the black eyes, his knuckles were all messed up, even his punting foot was all cut up," Noonan says. "And he was as happy as can be. To him, it was like he hadn't gone through training camp unless he got beat up."

"I'm quitting it this year," Saxon says. "Not that I didn't get a few shots in on those meatheads. But things are different now that I've turned thirty."

The marriage of guns and cars seems to be one in need of a divorce every summer. Kelvin Martin's problem in 1990 began when he realized it was 10:59 p.m. and he was supposed to be tucked in by eleven o'clock. When he stepped on the accelerator and wheeled south toward St. Ed's, a police car gave chase. Martin might have pulled over voluntarily had his only problem been that he had a 9mm pistol under the front seat. But his dilemma was compounded by that curfew problem.

With which authorities would Martin rather talk his way out of trouble? Jimmy Johnson? Or Austin's finest? Martin chose the cops, but only after his attempts to elude them found him trying to hide out in a parking garage — that happened to be located across the street from police headquarters. Martin was allowed one phone call. Receivers coach Hubbard Alexander answered, and arrived to bail Martin out of trouble.

Oddly, it was just the day before that the team invited in a team of FBI agents to explain to players the dangers of carrying weapons while at camp.

In 1991, offensive lineman Freddie Childress faced a rock-and-a-hard-place choice similar to Martin's. Did Childress want to be choked to death by angry tackle Mark Tuinei, or risk being charged with reckless gunplay? "The Big Chill" decided on the gun.

A disagreement between Childress and some teammates drew Tuinei from a dead sleep in an adjoining room. Tuinei believed he'd settled the brawl when he wrapped his hands around Childress' ample neck and hoisted the 350-pound man off the ground. But once released, the furious Childress ran from the Premont Hall dorm, yelling, "I'm going to my truck and I'm getting my gun!"

The rest of the Cowboys immediately evacuated Premont Hall. Tuinei returned to his room and fell back asleep.

Cars can be problematic by themselves, too. Ask running back Tony Boles, who as an eleventh-round rookie in 1991 needed to fly straight to have any shot at making the club. He flew straight, allright: straight out of town with Emmitt Smith's Nissan Pathfinder. Boles was a young man with some problems, but now he had a shiny new car and a millionaire's credit card, too. Smith had handed Boles the card thinking he'd use it to gas up the Pathfinder. But after almost twenty-four hours had passed, Smith contacted the Austin police and reported the automobile and the credit card stolen. The police were already investigating an incident that day when gasoline was stolen from an Austin Texaco by a man driving a vehicle that fit the description of Smith's.

Two days later, Boles rolled the Pathfinder back into camp. The gas tank was empty. Boles' career was ruined, and so was his savings account. His $450-a-day salary was eaten up by his $5,000 fine.

Coming in after curfew usually draws a $500 penalty. Boles established that coming in two days late means $5,000. There is no established fine for not coming in at all, which might be why 1992 rookie defensive backs Kevin Smith, Donald Harris and Michael James once attempted to wait until dawn then stroll onto campus as if they'd been there all the time.

It so happened that around midnight, Cowboys administrative assistant Bruce Mays couldn't sleep. So he left his dorm room and went outside for some fresh air. Curfew-breakers Smith, Harris and James spotted Mays pacing back and forth outside the St. Ed's dorms. Mays is Dallas'ss "Turk," the guy who breaks the bad news to waived players. He is doubly imposing to young players because he's also considered Jimmy Johnson's henchman. "They thought I was laying out for them, but it was just a coincidence," Mays says.

Countered one skeptical veteran: "The Cowboys set up a sting operation. The rookies who went over the wall got stung."

Our young protagonists decided to park their car at the bottom of the hill and outwait Mays. But his insomnia had no bounds. It was 6:00 a.m. before their car finally lurched from its hiding place and into the players' parking lot, its inhabitants confident that any witnesses would assume they'd been early risers back from a trip to Dunkin' Donuts. Surely they felt secure by the time they reached their rooms. But it was there they saw little Post-It notes stuck on their doors. "Welcome back," Mays had written. "I've been looking forward to seeing you."

Veteran defensive back Robert Williams usually spends his free time at camp joining safety Ray Horton in the cool darkness of a movie theater. "You can't get into any trouble there," Williams says. "A lot of the younger guys end up missing curfew because they're out touring the titty bars."

A strip joint on the north side of town called Sugar's became the hottest spot in 1992, beating out Expose, a place one block away from campus that was hurriedly refurbished for the team's arrival. But, argues Mays, "Hunger makes players break curfew more than women. It's definitely food over women, every time."

The Cowboys' dizzying summer travel schedule can also create tardiness. In 1990, Troy Aikman, Daryl Johnston, Mark Stepnoski and Jeff Zimmerman left the team's temporary training camp headquarters at the University of California at San Diego in search of a nightclub.

"We got there at eleven, and curfew that night was at twelve," Aikman says. "All of us were pretty lost. But Zimmerman said he was real sure we were only fifteen minutes from the campus. Just to be safe, we left the club twenty minutes before midnight."

But Zimmerman had no clue where UCSD was. The foursome drove in circles for forty minutes, finally spotting a campus security guard, who told them to follow his car and he'd lead them to the dorm.

"We were twenty minutes after curfew, but it was so quiet, it looked like we might be able to sneak in," Aikman says. "I was so glad that security guard had helped us that I started wailing on my horn to tell him thanks."

The security guard, however, had directed the players to the wrong dorm. Aikman was honking his car horn outside the dorm where the coaches sleep. "The coaches stormed out the door," Aikman says. "Needless to say, we got caught."

Offensive coordinator David Shula followed the players into a room.

"You know you're going to be fined for this!" he said.

"Fined?" said an incredulous and intoxicated Johnston. "Listen here, I've done everything by the book ever since I came to the Cowboys. I've done everything you've said to do."

Johnston rambled on and on, finally talking himself into a rage that reached a peak when he jammed his fist through a wall that was in the vicinity of Shula's head. The punch had a sobering effect on both men.

"Sorry," Johnston said. "Ever since I've been a little kid, I've have this bad habit of punching holes in walls."

On the St. Ed's campus, Cowboys employees don't need to be at least sixteen years old to hit the streets. The team contracts with a company to supply a dozen golf carts, originally intended to be used to transport injured players and supplies. In their evolution, the carts have become wheeled weapons of destruction. The fourteen-year-old ball boys drive them. The players steal them. Those involved are injured by them. Offensive line coach Tony Wise almost lost a leg while trying to dismount a moving cart.

"There ought to be a law," said Wise, who probably realized later that there is — but that in Austin, the Cowboys are often above it.

Running back Curvin Richards violated the senses as a rookie in the 1991 camp. Richards, a native of Trinidad, was distinguished by a heavy accent, an almost cartoonish friendliness and an assortment of superstitious habits his teammates thought odd. Richards came to Dallas as a fourth-round pick from the University of Pittsburgh, where he'd left after his junior year in part because of a conflict with Panthers coach Paul Hackett.

Maybe Hackett objected to Richards' refusal to remove a string of beads from around his neck. "They give me strength," Curvin said. Or maybe the coach was offended, as Richards's

Cowboys teammates were, at his refusal to bathe regularly. "That would wash away my strength," said Richards, who did concede to a soap-down every three days. That meant six practice sessions in the sweltering Austin heat and humidity without the benefit of a cleaning. No wonder the Cowboys nicknamed Curvin "Shower Time."

The problem with the zoo-like atmosphere at Camp Cowboy is there is no escape. There is virtually nowhere in Austin to turn where the customers don't want to prod and poke at these oversized creatures. In 1992, the organization planned a party for sponsors so massive is was to be staged outside, spread over the two St. Ed's practice fields. Players were urged to attend, with a promise that the available acreage would allow them to actually enjoy themselves as guests.

But it rained. Organizers scrambled to shoehorn hundreds of people into the cafeteria. The bash was a bust, especially for the players who were now wedged tightly into a space where they couldn't circulate. The only freedom of movement they had was at their hands, which were kept busy signing the autographs they'd been assured wouldn't be part of the evening.

Finally, Aikman and Gogan decided they needed out. "You are under a microscope," Aikman says. "There are only so many times when you get asked, 'How do you feel about the season?' before it finally makes you want to throw up."

Gogan, being an offensive lineman, used his six-foot-six, 320-pound frame to shove his way through the mob, creating a path followed by Aikman. As they hopped into a car, they decided against the popular Austin hangouts, like loud-rockin' Maggie Mae's on Sixth Street and Sholtz Garten, the 130-year-old landmark, for fear that more prodders and pokers would find them there. They pulled a U-turn away from downtown and decided on grabbing a beer at the most remote, run-down hole they could find. They stumbled upon a basement in what had once been a Ramada Inn that would serve them.

"Perfect," said Gogan, as he cased the joint and spotted just one customer, a grizzled drunk who'd passed out atop a bar stool.

Aikman and Gogan were debating the merits of IQ tests, comparing truck models and celebrating their good fortune at being able to temporarily sneak away from the subject of football when they were joined at their corner booth by an uninvited guest: the grizzled drunk had regained consciousness.

"You're my favorite quarterback, and you're my favorite lineman," the unfortunate man told the two players.

"And you're my favorite barfly," Gogan replied.

The man slobbered on about Michael Irvin, the Cowboys receiver not in Austin because of a contract dispute, being his "all-time favorite player of all-time." Finally, he tugged a quarter out of his pocket and reached it toward Aikman.

"Troy, I want you to go use the pay phone," the drunk commanded, "and call Michael right here and now. And I want you to tell him to get his skinny black ass into camp on the double."

Jerry Jones and Jimmy Johnson wish it would've been that easy. Just before the start of 1992 camp, safeties Bill Bates and Ray Horton signed on. By August 12, linebackers Vinson Smith and Ken Norton, defensive end Jim Jeffcoat and safety James Washington were also under contract. But by the middle of the month, it was becoming clear that defensive end Tony Tolbert and a trio of pivotal offensive players, Irvin, tight end Jay Novacek and center Mark Stepnoski, weren't coming to Austin. And their absence become a topic as hot as Austin.

Jones postured by repeatedly noting how well backups were performing in replacement of the missing. "It takes forty-seven men to beat the Washington Redskins," Jones said, referring to Dallas's foe in the regular-season opener. "For us to think that any one or two people can make that great a difference would be like saying the Cowboys are built like a house of cards."

Jones detailed his club's plans in the event Irvin, Novacek and Stepnoski never signed. He promised success for the Cowboys even without them. "I didn't notice any drop-off," Jones said after the preseason opener in Tokyo, a 34-23 loss to the Houston Oilers. "I did notice the play of the people who were in there. Our top offense moved the ball well, And they did it against an excellent team. Who could ask for anything more?"

Well, Irvin, Novacek, Stepnoski and Tolbert could ask for more, to name four. When KDFW-TV announced that sports anchor Ted Dawson's departure was imminent, Irvin — who had started taping his weekly TV show at the KDFW studios — announced that his negotiations were progressing so poorly that he might need to change careers. "I'm going to fill out an application at Channel 4," Irvin said. "I want to start working again. I need a job. I could do the sports over there, couldn't I?"

Johnson saw the humor in none of this. He and members of his staff left the distinct impression that the people on both sides of the bargaining table were forgetting that football was the point. He saw the wordplay as another example of posturing affecting his team. He yelped at Jones, who reacted by imposing a gag order — on himself. In mid-August, Jones decreed that no one in the organization was to comment on any of the organization's contractual dealings. Of course, he'd been the one doing most of the commenting. "The purpose," Jones says, "was to control what was being said by everyone and instead concentrate on actual negotiations. But I'll admit, as much as anything else it was a reminder to myself to watch myself."

Cowboys training camp is now a time when reputations are built and a time when spirits are broken. But players say they never had it as easy as they did under Johnson in Thousand Oaks in 1989, when he was still feeling his way around pro football.

"Jimmy's first year, we called it 'Club Med,'" Noonan says. "Jimmy didn't know what was going on. We hardly had any meetings, our practices were really easy, and he had Everson Walls going to him and saying things should be set up this way and moved that way. But Jimmy sure learned, didn't he?"

"Now, you don't dare rest on your laurels," safety Bill Bates says. "I don't. No one can afford to. Not Michael Irvin, not Troy Aikman. Troy slips, there's a Steve Beuerlein sitting there waiting to move right in. The pressure I feel is the same pressure I feel every year. And it's the same everyone on the Cowboys should feel."

Says Irvin: "It's completely different than all the little mini-camps we do around here. I call Jimmy's mini-camps 'The Little Olympics.' We all run around in our underwear and show how we can run and jump. It has nothing to do with football. All the guys who really can't play football look great during the Little Olympics. Games are a different level, but all the demands of training camp make it real close to the real thing."

Ask Emmanuel McNeil, the free-agent defensive lineman who in 1991 went to Johnson and quit after the morning practice, was asked to stick it out and returned for the afternoon session, then was cut four days later. Ask another defensive lineman, Chad Hennings, the Air Force flyboy who had Cowboys executives engaging in what seemed like a competition to see which of them could produce the most colorful and outlandish analysis of his gifts. Jimmy Johnson said Hennings, an eleventh-round pick in 1988 who'd been released from his military commitment in the spring, would have been a first-round pick had he been eligible for the 1992 draft. Jerry Jones said Hennings would have been a top-five pick in the first round. Vice-president Stephen Jones said Hennings would have been a top-three pick.

Then Hennings himself, perhaps swept away by a force almost as powerful as that A-10 fighter jet he'd been steering through forty-five missions in Operation Desert Storm, chimed in. "First I want to make the team, then I want to be a starter, then I want to play in the Pro Bowl," said the still-promising Hennings, who barely achieved the first goal and fell well short of goals two and three.

"I've always had high expectations for myself," says Hennings, who was a fixture on Dallas'ss game-day inactive list. "You get told you're inactive every week, you're like a deflated balloon. No, because it's a sudden explosion, you're like a popped balloon."

Noonan's been there, too.

"Coaches bullshitting about how good their players are is part of the setup," he says. "All summer (in 1992), I knew I was going to eventually be cut. But Jimmy kept telling me I might be staying around. I knew he was bullshitting me. He knew he was b.s.'ing me. And he knew I knew it. But it's part of the game they play every summer to keep players motivated."

Another Cowboys training camp ritual is the annual burn, burn, burn over the Ring of Fire. That is, the Ring of Honor, which became a political football of sorts in August of 1990 when Jerry Jones informally invited ousted coach Tom Landry to be inducted. Landry didn't say no; as would be the case for the ensuing two summers, the Hall-of-Famer didn't say much of anything intelligible on the subject. Landry talked of having "other appointments" (he was publicizing his autobiography that fall) but it was clear what he actually had was other agendas.

"We haven't received any response at all," said team representative Charlotte Anderson, Jones's daughter, after an official invite was mailed in October. "We're almost wondering if we should make sure he even got the letter."

By July 18, 1991, Landry still hadn't turned the other cheek. But a new summer brought a new tact from Jones. Maybe, he thought, Landry had not accepted the Ring of Honor invite because he was uncomfortable with the idea of going to midfield at Texas Stadium and swallowing his pride in a ceremony in which he'd have to stand alone next to the new owner, the man who'd fired him. Jones decided that Landry might be more willing to do the right thing — that being agree to have his name where it belongs, on the facade on the second deck at Texas Stadium — if he could be joined by some of his contemporaries.

Jones let it be known through his cooperation with a newspaper that he was receptive to former president Tex Schramm and founding owner Clint Murchison being honored in a "three-Ring" ceremony with Landry. "Coach Landry is in the Hall of Fame, Tex is going, and without Mr. Murchison, there wouldn't be a Dallas Cowboys," Jones said. "All three are greats of the National Football League, and all three would be wonderful additions."

Schramm seemed to buy it. "I'd certainly appreciate the gesture," he said. "I can't give a resounding answer either way. ... I'm not anxious to carry on any vendetta at this stage in my life. ... Roger (Staubach), my great friend, feels strongly that the Cowboys are the Cowboys and that cooperation between past and present would add luster for everyone."

Landry wasn't as forgiving. "I surely don't have any hard feelings," he fibbed of his February 25, 1989, dumping. "That's something I've said even going back to the time when I was unceremoniously removed."

Least cooperative of all was the family of the late Murchison, who in 1984 sold the club to Bum Bright. Said son Burk Murchison: "My dad was careful to find the right person when he sold the team. He liked Bum Bright because he believed the style, the approach of the Cowboys, wouldn't be changed. When Mr. Bright sold (to Jones), he obviously wasn't as careful.

"There's a reason Jerry Jones wants to get old-regime people in there. There's a pragmatic reason for him wanting to attract a Landry and a Schramm. It's good business."

Finally, on July 16, 1992, Jerry Jones decided his Ring of Honor could survive without old-regime members who didn't want in. "We've got enough on our plate as it is," said Jones, shutting down the debate. At least until the summer of 1993.

Jones says, "Early on, we couldn't make a move without being scrutinized. I wanted coach Landry in the Ring of Honor in 1990. I still do. He belongs there. But at first there was the concern that there would be a perception that I was trying to ride the coattails of the past by putting him in there. That's why we didn't push too hard to do it when our team was losing. We didn't want a halftime ceremony involving coach Landry to happen at a game where we were getting blown out, or even at a time when maybe we didn't have a winning record.

"I think his reluctance to do it is based on his feeling that it would look like an endorsement, like he was giving in. I regret that. But as we really worked to get our football team where we want it, after a while, it became almost a nonissue. It became, 'Well, if he doesn't want to be in, why are we pushing it?'"

Besides, by 1992, the plate was full. A day before the Cowboys opened their 1992 camp on July 16 (Johnson's forty-ninth birthday), they had ten unsigned veterans. Many of them didn't want to be under contract yet because they had no interest in traveling to Tokyo for the August 1 preseason game against the Oilers. Irvin, Ken Norton, Vinson Smith and Tony Tolbert were among the unsigned veterans who never bothered to complete their travel paperwork (passport, visa, etc.) because they never intended to sign in time.

The hectic itinerary included a trip to San Antonio for a scrimmage against the Oilers and a visit to Austin by the Los Angeles Raiders, who would work against the Cowboys for three days.

"Al Davis better wear a helmet on the sideline," said Beuerlein, the ex-Raider who feuded with Davis in a 1990 contract dispute. "I may put one in his ear hole on a 15-yard out pattern."

Dallas also needed to adjust to a rookie starting at middle linebacker. Robert Jones, an East Carolina product taken with the twenty-fourth pick in the draft, was handed the job after veteran Jack Del Rio was allowed to leave via Plan B to Minnesota. "Around there," Del Rio said, "they seem to feel they can replace any one or two players with very little problem." And indeed, the Cowboys did seem more sure of themselves than ever. A month before training camp opened, the Cowboys hosted a Pick-a-Ticket night on July 14. The timing did not seem astute. That was the same night as the baseball All-Star Game. But late that night, Jones, Johnson and others retired to Jones's 50-yard-line luxury box and put their heads on a swivel, watching the three TV stations' live shots from Texas Stadium. There were high-fives all around, because 8,000 people had passed on the baseball game to visit Texas Stadium to watch a meaningless practice.

What makes the Cowboys such a draw? They do have their sideshows. Take Nate Newton. Or at least take 100 pounds of him, as an off-season crash diet did. Newton exited Dallas before a spring mini-camp by scribbling out notes to Johnson and Wise that vaguely explained his plans to get in shape. Newton instructed defensive end Tony Tolbert to deliver the notes as he snuck out of town. "I knew if I asked coach Johnson first, he wouldn't go for it," Newton says. "But I just remember getting on the scale and seeing a four and two 'O's.' And I said, 'Oh, oh.' I had to do something."

Newton hauled his 400-pound butt to Florida and sought counseling on proper eating and exercise habits.

"I was one of those guys who watched a pizza commercial on TV, and went and got in the car and bought me a pizza," says Newton, who once went AWOL on Jenny Craig, who once laughed off $80,000 in weight-clause incentive money, who thought his niche in pro football was as "The Kitchen," a jolly fat man enormously popular with fans for being enormous.

After his stretch working out at a Bally's Health Center in Orlando, the Kitchen was closed. Newton weighed 301 pounds and was no more than the third heaviest offensive lineman in camp. Newton, who had experienced nine years of ups and downs — not only on the scale, but in his career — had weaved another fascinating training-camp tale. It almost matched the one from his summer as a rookie free agent with the Washington Redskins, when his despair over getting released nearly cost him his life.

In 1983, the Redskins pieced together a fascinating group of rookies. They got cornerback Darrell Green in the first round, defensive end Charles Mann in the third round and Kelvin Bryant in the seventh round. They had a sixth-rounder named Babe Laufenberg, and another sixth-rounder, Wisconsin's Bob Winckler, an offensive lineman who would compete for a roster spot with a free-agent blocker from Florida A&M. "Winks, Winkles, something like that," Newton recalls. "This fat guy from Wisconsin spends the year on injured reserve, but gets a Super Bowl ring. That's what he got for beating me out."

Newton knew he'd be cut in the summer of 1983. He decided to borrow some money from his roommate, Mann, and rent a car for a drive from Washington to Pittsburgh, where he'd visit an old girlfriend. While Newton was gone, Mann got the news from Redskins personnel boss Charlie Casserly that the big kid from Florida A&M had been released. Then Mann spoke with Newton by phone.

"He didn't take it too well," Mann says. "I guess he actually got a case of beer along the way and proceeded to drink that on the drive back. About 6:30 in the morning, I got another call. It was the Fairfax County police, asking if I knew a guy named Nate Newton."

Newton was too drunk to realize he was being chased by police. For five miles. Their pursuit ended when the rental car failed to navigate a sharp turn at a high speed. Newton was thrown from the car and lifted by police out of a puddle of blood. "I think my size saved my life," says Newton, whose lack of size almost a decade later figures to save him from "dying because I've turned into a 700-pound guy."

In Japanese, "arigato" is the word for a perfunctory thank you. "Makotoni go shinsetsu de gozaimasu" is the way to say thank you if what you mean to say is "What you have done or proposed to do is truly and genuinely a kind and generous deed." By the time the Cowboys were finished with their late-July trip to Japan, they would definitely feel worthy of a "Makotoni go shinsetsu de gozaimasu" or two. And Donald Harris would definitely be ready to tell the Cowboys "No arigato."

Harris is the former Texas Tech safety who fancied himself a two-sport star. He was selected by Dallas in the twelfth round of the 1992 draft because some Cowboys officials were convinced of the same thing. On July 27, when Harris signed a contract to join the Cowboys, it was an especially intriguing story because he'd just spent twelve days playing center field for baseball's Texas Rangers. Harris could have accepted the Rangers' demotion to the Double-A Tulsa Drillers. But he was upset at being sent down, and whined to agent Jordan Woy to do something about it. Woy called Jerry Jones. Suddenly, the outfielder who couldn't hit (.143 batting average, no homers and one RBI) was being touted as a six-foot, 185-pound safety who could.

But Harris ran into a problem. Unlike in baseball, football players are tortured in training camp. They have to study. And at least in the summer of 1992, they didn't just take bus rides from Sarasota, Florida, to Port Charlotte, Florida. They had to find their way to Tokyo.

This was no pleasure cruise for any of the Cowboys. Jimmy Johnson's idea of travel is that five-block drive from his Valley Ranch house to his Valley Ranch office. He viewed the excursion as another "distraction," and clearly would refuse to enjoy himself. Going to try chopsticks, Coach? "Somehow, I expect I'll find a knife, fork and spoon somewhere," he said.

Troy Aikman, who had traveled to Tokyo a few months before on a promotional junket for this American Bowl exhibition game, testified to the problems with the sixteen-hour flight, the fourteen-hour time change, the jet lag, and the unfamiliarity with the culture, the language and the grub. "The food is different, the streets are crowded, and if you're tall and especially if you're blond, all the people stare at you like you're a freak," he said.

Offensive linemen John Gesek, Kevin Gogan and Dale Hellestrae were among the Cowboys who attempted to alter the perception of the Ugly American by serving up hamburgers from behind the counter of a Tokyo McDonald's. And defensive lineman Jimmie Jones, a six-foot-six, 280-pound black man, was among the Cowboys made to believe the perception of Americans is permanently twisted when he was approached in the lobby of Tokyo's New Otani hotel by a Japanese man who wanted his autograph. "Sir," the man asked Jones, "you are Troy Aikman?"

The Cowboys' arms had to be twisted to go to the Pacific Rim. Three times Jerry Jones heard NFL commissioner Paul Tagliabue's request to represent the league in Japan. Three times Jones politely declined. A fourth time, Tagliabue jetted to Dallas for a face-to-face session with Jones. "He explained some things to me," said Jones, who, duly persuaded, immediately ordered the Cowboys' bags packed.

But Harris couldn't pack that fast. There had been no time to get him the proper paperwork. He was hurried to Houston in order to process his passport, and then he was shipped to Japan's Narita Airport. Immigration officials are tough in every country, of course. While catching a connecting flight in Detroit on his way to Tokyo, Cowboys staffer Bruce Mays was halted by federal guards who believed that under his thick wig walked an FBI fugitive. Mays was released after showing the necessary papers. This was more than Harris could do with the Japanese immigration people, who discovered he'd arrived without a work visa. They detained him for thirty minutes and were preparing to ship him home before American Bowl officials came to the rescue.

From Narita, Harris was sent to Tokyo's Oda Field, where the Cowboys were practicing. Unfortunately, the equipment men hadn't had time to properly prepare for his arrival, either. Harris had no helmet, no shoulder pads and no practice pants. Harris, spoiled by his time getting the red-carpet treatment in his other, less demanding sport, was enraged. "What do you think I signed so fast for?" he screamed, within earshot of the equipment guys. "Do you think I came all this way to sightsee?"

By the time Harris actually got on the field, he had come close to experiencing what the Japanese call "Karoshi." It is a phenomenon that is cited as a reason for the high death rate in Japan. Karoshi means "literally killing oneself with overwork." Harris, who compounded his problems by sleeping through an August 9 team meeting, wanted no part of what real football players at training camp grow accustomed to.

The demands are such that enjoyment is squeezed from the simplest of life's experiences. In Austin, a few members of a Cowboys party settled into the pool room at Maggie Mae's to play a gambling game called "Quarters." Participants eye a stack of the coins, then place bets ($1 minimum, no maximum) on whether the next quarter will be heads or tails. The pot wasn't worth much until team vice-president Mike McCoy pulled up a chair. He threw a $100 bill on the pile, guessed "Heads" and lined his pockets with cash.

Trying to make Tokyo feel more like home, some of the losers in the Maggie Mae's game introduced "Quarters" to Aikman, Beuerlein and others during a lengthy bus ride. Naturally, no one had any quarters. Nor did they have dollar bills. Yen, they had plenty of. But without a dollar-to-yen conversion table handy, no one was certain how much they were losing. The game also had to be renamed. "Quarters" became "Flowers and Numbers" because those symbols represented the Japanese version of "heads and tails" on the available coinage.

"I'll bet 'flowers!'" Aikman would say, while dropping into the pot a yellowish piece of paper that, for all he knew, might have been worth his annual salary. Somehow — maybe because no one could handle the conversion, maybe because someone cheated, or maybe because Mike McCoy wasn't available to pump his earnings from the oil-and-gas business into the pot — the payoff funds came up short. No one griped louder than Beuerlein, who would have to make up for his losses after the 1992 season, when the quarterback played Flowers and Numbers with NFL's new system of free agency.

But none of that fit Johnson's idea of games — the sort he felt he had to play with the Cowboys' heads to steer them from the 2-3 preseason record, the travel problems, the contract disputes and the beyond-football rigors of summer.

"There is a conscious effort to bring the players together through almost working them to the edge, to where they are irritable and tired, to where they have to bond together to deal with the coaching staff and deal with me," Johnson says. "That's one of the main goals of training camp, not all the other stuff. Bringing us together as a team. If it irritates them that I've worked them harder than what they've wanted, if practices are more physical and demanding than what they've wanted, that's a positive thing."

Training camp is not automatically a sealant, however. It is not automatically "a positive thing." Certainly, for instance, the 1990 Cowboys had not bonded by the time they broke camp in Austin. Like most teams, they needed wins to heal wounds.

In the locker room following the 17-14 victory over the San Diego Chargers that opened the 1990 season, guard Crawford Ker grabbed a game ball and grabbed Johnson.

"There's been a lot of crap in the newspapers about how we don't like our coach and his staff, and about how we aren't together as a team," Ker announced. "Well, I want to put that to rest right now. Here, this is for you."

It was a lovely gesture. But Ker's words weren't as accurate as the words delivered before that September 9 game during the team's Sunday morning chapel service. The speaker was a man named Bill Glass, a former Cleveland Browns lineman. Glass was aware of the distasteful facts of the Cowboys' 1990 preseason. He and anyone else who'd paid any attention knew it had been fouled by players who didn't believe in Johnson's methods, who didn't believe in his assistants' skills, who didn't appreciate that first summer in Austin, when Johnson established Camp Cowboy as the league's most arduous.

Glass told the congregation of Cowboys players and coaches something that is applicable to any football team after any summer of two-a-days.

"After what you go through in training camp," Glass said, "anyone who comes out of it not complaining is sick."

8   IRVIN'S PAWN SHOP   ★

As the 1992 season-opening Monday night showdown with the Super Bowl champion Washington Redskins approached, Cowboys receiver Michael Irvin had his hands full of everything except footballs.

Irvin's ten fingers, to his biased way of thinking worth at least $160,000 each, were occupied by holding a microphone for "The Michael Irvin Show" on television. And by picking up chunks of brick that had been scattered about his front yard when a lightning bolt ripped into the chimney of his Carrollton home. And by being stretched out to a palm reader.

"I can say what I want about it now, because I'm set for life," Irvin says, "But I had to find a way to occupy my time, and I didn't want Jerry Jones to think I couldn't survive without football. Fact is, I don't feel comfortable in my life unless I'm catching 200 balls a day. I've caught 200 balls a day since I was knee-high to a bullfrog. When I was in my mom's stomach, I was catching stuff she was throwing down in there.

"I absolutely love to play football. And my family absolutely loves, and needs, me to play football. My family doesn't know how to be poor anymore, you know? And in my contract hassle with the Cowboys, it seemed like they were taking all that away from me because they wanted to pay me like I was an average guy."

Even in his early years with the Cowboys after being a No. 1 pick in 1988, Michael Jerome Irvin was rarely average. But his numbers were. A knee injury (he missed ten games in 1989 and four in 1990 with a torn anterior cruciate ligament) contributed to him catching just 78 passes in his first three years in Dallas. The only big number he hung up was around wife Sandy's neck: she wears a gold-and-diamond necklace that proclaims her to be better than a perfect 10. "10 1/2" her jewelry reads.

Before the start of the 1991 season, Irvin was so determined to experience a salary-drive year that he tucked into his pants a towel inscribed with the word "THINK." It meant "Think of a way to cash in," and that year, Irvin did. He topped the National Conference with 93 catches. His 1,523 yards led the NFL. He capped the comeback by catching eight passes for a Pro Bowl-record 125 yards in the all-star game in Honolulu that followed the 1991 season, winning the game's Most Valuable Player Award.

The Cowboys' negotiating argument was simple. "As good as Michael was," Jones said, "he is coming off three disappointing seasons previous to that."

Irvin's argument was more complex. He had mouths to feed. And dreams to finance. He is the third youngest in a family of the seventeen kids of Walter and Pearl Irvin. Walter, a roofer and minister, died when Michael was in high school, leaving the paternal duties to his son. Michael obeyed his father's order to watch over the brood by providing what by 1992 had become an extended family that included Pearl's thirty-five grandchildren and twelve great-grandchildren with whatever they needed financially. "That contract was the chance to set the Irvin family up for life. Getting in the million-dollar range is what allows my family security. It's what Sandy and me can retire on someday," Michael says.

Says Pearl, "It's true that if the family members need something, they try and go to him. I try to tell him he's done enough. But he's too loving a person, if there is such a thing. He was blessed from birth, and he tries to give so much back."

So Michael Irvin wanted to be, as he puts it, "a pawn shop where nobody needs any collateral" for his mom and siblings Pearl, Willie, Alice, Ray, Janet, Walter, Sheila, Renee, Vaughn, Don, Sharon, Laverne, Lisa, Pat, Brenda and Derrick.

Jones knows something about engaging in multimillion-dollar skirmishes. And of course, Irvin is a battler. In May, he'd been accused of punching a referee named Willie Summerling over a disputed call at a charity basketball game. Two years before that, despite a lack of support from teammates, he challenged the entire San Diego Chargers roster to a fight during a training-camp scrimmage.

Still, Irvin and Jones did their best to maintain gentlemanly tones in public. They had no desire to let the world know of that September 1 exchange at the team's Kickoff Luncheon at the Grand Kempinski Hotel in Addison. Irvin had been named the club's Offensive Player of the Year, and tradition held that he receive the honor at the luncheon. Cowboys management harbored some hope that Irvin might discreetly fail to show. But Irvin basked in the irony that he'd be the guest of honor at a shindig thrown by the owner who wouldn't pay him the $1.6 million a year he was seeking.

Never one to let a "photo op" slip by, Jones schemed to finalize a contract with Irvin while both were waiting in the wings at the Grand Kempinski. According to a rough version of the plan, a curtain would open to reveal the receiver and owner with pens in hand, ready to sign. But a preluncheon negotiating session involving the two men and agent Steve

Endicott produced nothing but animosity, so Irvin returned to the hotel lobby to hang with the fellas. Jones wouldn't give up. He dispatched public-relations assistant Brent Daniels to the lobby to fetch Irvin for another go-round. Irvin ping-ponged Daniels back toward Jones with a decidedly ungentlemanly reply.

The receiver's performance for his audience at the luncheon was classic Irvin. He donned sunglasses in the darkened ballroom to accept his award, made some uncharacteristically humble remarks, then bolted for his car. Cameramen and reporters sprinted in pursuit. "It was like I was President Nixon after he resigned," Irvin says. That night, after another negotiating session between Jones and Endicott proved fruitless, Irvin ran his twenty 110-yard dashes, then watched film of himself at the luncheon on three TV stations, then returned outside for his four-mile jog.

"It was all an interesting life experience for me, because here I was a kid who'd just turned twenty-six, sitting down face-to-face with this multimillionaire," Irvin says. "I'd heard a lot about how they try to demean players. But Jerry never did that with me. I did the listening when the talk was about money, but when the talk was about football, they pulled out the notepads and I was the professor.

"But you do have to pay close attention to what Jerry is saying. He goes off on, what do you call it? ... tangents. Jerry's quite a shaker now, and if you don't watch out, you'll end up paying him to play. You once in a while have to stop him and ask, 'Hey, Jerry, what does this have to do with the price of apples? Or better yet, the price of receivers?'"

What made the negotiations unusual is the frenetic, eccentric style of Irvin and Jones. At one point, the parties met at the Irving offices of Irvin's financial adviser, Dennis Carpenter.

Coach Jimmy Johnson totally loses his cool over the officiating at a 1991 game against the Giants in New York. NFL Commissioner Paul Tagliabue saw the game and generally agreed with Johnson's assessment, although it didn't do any good. The Cowboys still lost. (Jerry Hoefer, Fort Worth Star-Telegram).

Preseason drills in 1990, the Cowboys' second season under their new regime, find running back Alonzo Highsmith and offensive coordinator David Shula talking shop. Both ended up leaving the Cowboys in something less than glorious fashion. (Beatrice Terrazas, Fort Worth Star-Telegram).

Linebacker Jesse Solomon had the talent, but not much staying power. Here, he waves to the crowd while standing on the Atlanta Falcons' sideline at a preseason game after walking out of the Cowboys camp in August, 1991. (Joyce Marshall, Fort Worth Star-Telegram).

The Cowboys used up a number-one pick in taking quarterback Steve Walsh in the supplemental draft of 1989, creating a quarterback controversy because Troy Aikman had been drafted number one earlier in the regular draft. Walsh, shown here during the Cowboys' quarterback school at Valley Ranch in the summer of 1990, was eventually traded to the New Orleans Saints. (Carolyn Bauman, Fort Worth Star-Telegram).

The players' names and faces weren't the only things changing during the first few years under new owner Jerry Jones. The Dallas Cowboys cheerleaders show off new uniforms that were to be worn during parts of games. (Glen Ellman, Fort Worth Star-Telegram).

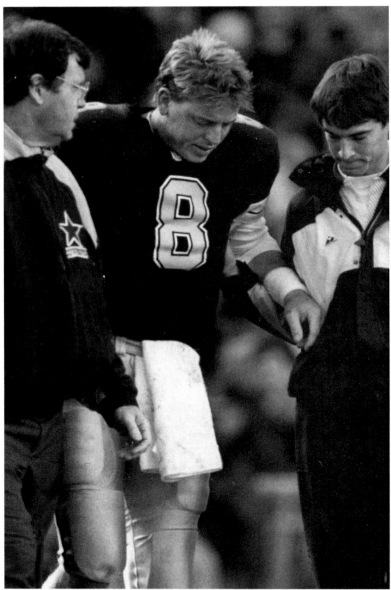

Cowboys quarterback Troy Aikman gets helped off the field at Washington's RFK Stadium during a November 1991 game against the Redskins. Aikman injured a knee and was lost for the rest of the regular season, opening the door for backup Steve Beuerlein to step in and lead the Cowboys to the playoffs. (Jerry Hoefer, Fort Worth Star-Telegram).

There was plenty to smile about after the 1991 arrival of new offensive coordinator Norv Turner, who engineered the Cowboys' dramatic turnaround on offense. Here, coach Jimmy Johnson, quarterback Troy Aikman and Turner share a funny line or two. (Milton Adams, Fort Worth Star-Telegram).

Former Cowboys star cornerback Everson Walls, now with the New York Giants, catches up on all the latest from Cowboys linebacker Ken Norton. Walls was one of the big names coach Jimmy Johnson got rid of in cleaning house over his first couple of years in Dallas. (Paul Moseley, Fort Worth Star-Telegram).

Nickel back Bill Bates, a perennial favorite among Cowboys fans and the heart of the Cowboys, celebrates his recovery of a muffed punt return. (Jerry Hoefer, Fort Worth Star-Telegram).

This was the dream deep-threat passing combination that never materialized. Quarterback Troy Aikman and rookie wide receiver Alexander Wright discuss a pass route during a 1990 practice. Wright never fulfilled his exceptional potential and was traded to the Los Angeles Raiders in 1992. (Milton Adams, Fort Worth Star-Telegram).

Cowboys rookie wide receiver Jimmy Smith meets up with Alexander Wright, now with the Raiders, after the Cowboys knocked off the Raiders in a 1992 contest. (Rodger Mallison, Fort Worth Star-Telegram).

Draft day at Valley Ranch has become a red-letter date around Dallas. This is the Cowboys' "War Room," where (right to left) coach Jimmy Johnson, owner Jerry Jones and vice-president Mike McCoy eye the television coverage of the draft proceedings in New York. This is where the "J. J. boys" did some of their best wheelin' and dealin'. (Paul Moseley, Fort Worth Star-Telegram).

Owner Jerry Jones never stops when it comes to Cowboys "bidness," even when riding around Los Angeles in his limousine the week before Super Bowl XXVII. (Jerry Hoefer, Fort Worth Star-Telegram).

This isn't a killer whale, just Cowboys defensive tackle Russell Maryland showing his exuberance after recovering a fumble. (Milton Adams, Fort Worth Star-Telegram).

Coach Jimmy Johnson looks caught somewhere between bewildered and dumb-founded, which was understandable considering that the Cowboys were losing a close game against the Redskins late in the season at Washington. This was the game after which Johnson launched into a tirade aboard the airplane flight back to Dallas. (Ron Jenkins, Fort Worth Star-Telegram).

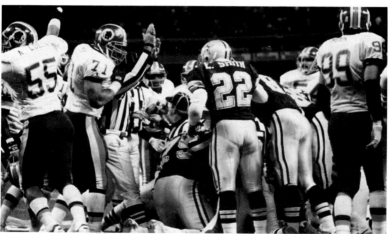

This is the end result of one of the most memorable plays of the 1992 season. After Troy Aikman fumbled in his own end zone and running back Emmitt Smith lost control of the bouncing ball while attempting a shovel pass, the Redskins recovered in the end zone for the winning touchdown. Notice the referee starting to signal the TD. (Rodger Mallison, Fort Worth Star-Telegram).

Wide Receiver Michael Irvin, the "Playmaker", always seems to find something to smile about or laugh about. (Allen Rose, Fort Worth Star-Telegram).

Running back Emmitt Smith didn't reach his goal of 2,000 yards in 1992, but he established himself as the National Football League's premier running back. (Jerry Hoefer, Fort Worth Star-Telegram).

Defensive end Charles Haley, acquired from the San Francisco 49ers in a 1992 trade, helped turn the Cowboys' defense into the best in the league. Off the field, Haley was as much an enigma as he was a terror on the field. (Jerry Hoefer, Fort Worth Star-Telegram).

Cowboys placekicker Lin Elliott could have used an aspirin after missing a field-goal try against the Philadelphia Eagles in a 1992 game. Elliott made up for this miss, later nailing two field goals helping the Cowboys to a big victory. (Paul Moseley, Fort Worth Star-Telegram).

Quarterback Troy Aikman walks onto the field at Three Rivers Stadium in Pittsburgh for a 1991 game against the Steelers. A knee injury had knocked Aikman out of the regular season. Notice the sign behind him. It says it all. (Paul Moseley, Fort Worth Star-Telegram).

Wide receiver Michael Irvin douses running back Emmitt Smith on the sideline. When you're winning, which the Cowboys did a lot of in 1992-93, a little bit of playfulness is okay. (Milton Adams, Fort Worth Star-Telegram).

Coach Jimmy Johnson and former defensive coordinator Dave Wannstedt were the closest thing to best friends on the Cowboys coaching staff. Wannstedt left the Cowboys in 1993 to replace Mike Ditka as head coach of the Chicago Bears. (Milton Adams, Fort Worth Star-Telegram).

Cowboys fans were going ape over America's Team in the week preceding Super Bowl XXVII in Los Angeles. (Rodolfo Gonzalez, Fort Worth Star-Telegram).

Coach Jimmy Johnson basks in the glory of a ticker tape parade in Dallas, celebrating the Cowboys' Super Bowl victory over the Buffalo Bills. Isolated cases of violence erupted during the victory parade, although Johnson doesn't seem to mind the setting at this particular juncture. (Ralph Lauer, Fort Worth Star-Telegram).

"I told him, 'Jerry, I'm looking at $2.3 million a year,'" Irvin says. "And he looked at me and starting talking about this little town called El Paso. He said, 'You know that town called El Paso? Well, when it comes to paying you $2.3 million a year, I'm afraid I'm going to have to 'el pass-oh.'" Man, after he left, I never laughed so hard in my life. I thought, 'This bitch is crazy!' He was so funny, I decided to drop my demands a couple of grand right there, just as a reward."

At a later point, Irvin mentioned the possibility of a trade.

Jones: "Michael, the grass isn't greener on the other side of the fence."

Irvin: "The grass is as green as I want it to be over there, as long as I fertilize it, mow it and care for it."

Jones: "Son, let me put it another way. Your story and the Cowboys' story run parallel. You and the Cowboys are like Magic Johnson and the Los Angeles Lakers. We don't know how good one would be without the other. And we ain't going to find out, because you're not going to see the grass on the other side of the fence as long as I'm alive."

A few days before, the Cowboys had signed tight end Jay Novacek to a three-year contract worth $2.7 million. Novacek, like Irvin a Pro Bowler who led all tight ends in 1991 with 59 catches, was ready to play against the Redskins in part because all summer, Troy Aikman had been faxing him the additions to the playbook. One day, Aikman sent Novacek twenty-six pages. "What a day and age we live in," Novacek marveled. So only Irvin and center Mark Stepnoski, the Pennsylvania native who was threatening to retire from football and maybe go into coal-mining or something, were left without deals.

The pressure on the Cowboys increased on August 25, when the Washington Redskins signed cornerback Darrell Green, tackle Jim Lachey and first-round receiver Desmond

Howard to contracts. The opening-day foe had all of its weapons. Troy Aikman was missing too many of his.

"I don't know for sure if we would've been able to beat Washington had we not finally signed our three guys," Aikman says. "But talent-wise, it would've made it a lot tougher on us. And I'll guarantee you this: If those guys hadn't been signed by the beginning of the season, it would have caused some anger in all the guys here. And the anger wouldn't have been directed at those players. We all felt as a team they were being fair in their demands."

Late in camp, Aikman had deliberated for days before deciding that his position on the team and his brotherhood with his unsigned offensive mates deemed a statement from him appropriate. He told a newspaper, "I know that management has a fine line to walk between winning games and making a profit. But for our offense, not having Michael, Jay and Mark here is having a major effect. There is a rhythm we're lacking because we don't have them. We keep saying, 'When we get them in here, we'll be able to do this or that.' But I'm a realist. I'll believe our offense can be strong again when I see those guys signed."

Says Aikman: "I came out and said that and went out of my way to say it because it was the truth. I'm loyal to Jerry Jones when it's not in conflict with what I believe. My loyalties, number one, are with my teammates. And then with the organization."

The organization loosened its purse strings in the final days before the September 7 opener at Texas Stadium. The trade with San Francisco for defensive end Charles Haley cost the club $1 million in base salary and $400,000 more in deferred money. Stepnoski's deal got done on September 5, when he agreed to a three-year, $1.95 million pact that featured a $50,000 bonus for participating in 50 percent of the team's plays and a

$100,000 bonus for making the Pro Bowl (he would achieve both). Irvin's contract was completed two days before, on September 3.

At 10:00 a.m. that day, Irvin told someone, "There have got to be ways to do it." At 11:00 a.m., Jones told someone, "We can be creative." By noon, the men were on the phone. Twelve hours later, Irvin was in Jones's Valley Ranch office, kissing the fountain pen he'd used to sign a three-year, $3.75 million contract. And then he smooched Jones.

"We're business partners!" shouted Irvin, who then joined the owner and others a few blocks away at the sports bar Cowboys Cafe, where the two "partners" who'd dueled viciously for months were left with nothing more to fight about than whose turn it was to buy the next round.

"I knew I'd never miss that Redskins game," Irvin says. "I'd have to have been crazy. Now, I might be crazy. But at least the day when I signed that contract I became a man who was rich and crazy."

And ready. When Irvin walked into the receivers meeting room for the first time the next morning, offensive coordinator Norv Turner immediately made adjustments in the game plan. With veteran Kelvin Martin knowingly humming "Taps" into second-year man Alvin Harper's ear, Turner made it clear that all those plays that had featured Harper as the No. 1 target would now feature Irvin.

Defensive coordinator Dave Wannstedt was fiddling with his new toy, too. Some wondered where Haley, who'd been a pass-rushing linebacker with the 49ers, would be plugged in as a Cowboy. Johnson played coy. But on the eve of the opener, Wannstedt left no doubt: "In our system, the defensive ends rush the passer. We have linebackers fill holes and make tackles. We have linemen rush upfield and wreak havoc. Bet on seeing Charles with his hand on the ground, wreaking havoc."

Twenty miles from Texas Stadium, baseball's Texas Rangers thought they held all the Labor Day drawing cards. Newly acquired legend Jose Canseco had just joined the team and taken a spot in right field. Nolan Ryan, the forty-five-year-old legend, was on the mound, opposing Boston's Roger Clemens, another legend. But the full house was in Irving for Cowboys-Redskins. "It's the two biggest dogs in the yard going at it," rookie cornerback Kevin Smith said.

Before the Redskins game, Johnson had predicted a win in front of players and coaches. He was convinced that unlike the previous meeting between the clubs, when Steve Beuerlein was the winning quarterback thanks in part to Johnson's grab-bag attack featuring onsides kicks, alley-oop passes and what-the-hell attitudes, he finally had the arsenal to play straight-up with the best team in football.

He was right. He had Emmitt Smith, the defending NFL rushing champ who ran for 140 yards against Washington. He had Haley, who earned a sack while flip-flopping back and forth from right to left end. He had Irvin, who wrapped his fingers around five passes for 89 yards. He got a blocked punt for a safety from Issiac Holt for the game's first score. He got a 79-yard punt return for a touchdown from Kelvin Martin. And with a 23-10 victory, he got Dallas off to a 1-0 start for the third straight year.

"That the loudest game we've ever played," says veteran offensive lineman Kevin Gogan. "But that's not the only reason it is the most memorable season-opening game we've ever had. Beating San Diego in 1990 felt good, but we all kind of knew down deep that ultimately, we weren't that good a team. And beating Cleveland in 1991 was great, but we still knew we weren't yet a great team. But beating Washington. ... that meant something."

The Cowboys were similarly motivated in Week Two when they traveled to New Jersey to face the Giants, the Super Bowl titlist two years before. Dallas hadn't won at Giants Stadium since 1987, had been outscored 68-27 in three previous trips, and for the first time since 1984, were actually favored to beat the Giants.

"There were just enough things going against us to make sure we didn't get too cocky," cornerback Larry Brown says. "Jim Jeffcoat, Charles Haley and Ray Horton have been through big games before. Those kind of guys kept us from celebrating too much, and we made a mental modification."

That modification lasted only until after the Cowboys' first possession of the third quarter in that September 13 game, however. The Cowboys scored in the first half on touchdowns from Emmitt Smith and Jay Novacek, a blocked punt recovered by Robert Williams and two Lin Elliott field goals.

"At halftime, we made a point to tell the guys that the first possession of the second half would be the most important one of the game," Wannstedt says.

The guys paid attention, with an Aikman-to-Irvin touchdown connection of 27 yards putting Dallas ahead 34-0 just ninety seconds after intermission. Backup quarterback Beuerlein and backup running back Curvin Richards were told to ready themselves to spell Aikman and Smith. Irvin was clowning around behind the bench, woofing at the Bronx-cheering crowd. CBS-TV switched its national audience to other games.

"Then the roof caved in," Wannstedt says.

The Giants stormed back with four second-half touchdowns. With 1:40 left in the game, Dallas needed a first down on third-and-seven. Fittingly, ex-holdout Irvin would be the hero. Fittingly, Johnson's old nemesis, Everson Walls, would be the goat. Walls was supposed to cover Irvin, but he mixed up the assignment and sent rookie safety Corey Raymond against the receiver. That simplified Aikman's decision to throw to Irvin, who slanted in for a 12-yard catch that sealed the win.

The day was flawed. What should have been a blowout win ended up being a 34-28 squeaker. What should have been a "Wow!" ended up being a "Whew!" Even the flight home was abnormal. Defensive tackle Danny Noonan, whose $615,000 base salary made him an expensive spare part, suspected correctly he was due to be cut within days. So he and his buddies transformed the plane ride into a wake.

Throughout, Wannstedt begged to be allowed to offer perspective. "Remember," he said, "a few hours ago, if you would have told us we could come in here and beat New York by a point, we would have taken it."

In a sense, the Giants did the Cowboys an immense favor. Had Dallas drubbed New York by some bloated and lopsided score, the temptation to ignore another "mental modification" would have been huge. Says Johnson: "As young as we were and because we had a home game against Phoenix coming up, I think a 34-0 win would have caused some of what we said that next week to fall on deaf ears. I don't believe there is any such thing as winning 'too much, too soon,' or whatever it is people were saying about our football team all year. But we definitely got snapped back into reality when the Giants came back. That got our players' focus back to thinking that any team was good enough to beat us if we weren't at our very best."

Except for the Phoenix Cardinals. The Cardinals were off to an 0-2 start, had lost three straight games to Dallas and had dropped a league-worst ten straight regular-season games. At the same time, the Cowboys were riding the league's longest regular-season streak with seven straight victories. Was there reason for overconfidence as the Cowboys prepared for the September 20 game at Texas Stadium?

"We've always looked at Phoenix like it meant a win, which was pretty ridiculous at one time, since we were actually the team that meant a win for whoever we were playing," Nate Newton says. "The Redskins and the Giants, those teams are easy to get up for. But you better find a way to get geeked up for the Cardinals, too."

Newton and the offensive line dominated the Cardinals, helping Dallas to a 31-20 victory. The highlight was a 19-play drive that consumed eleven minutes and eleven seconds. The work of tackles Mark Tuinei and Erik Williams, guards Newton and John Gesek and center Mark Stepnoski was almost flawless. "Everyone talks about how linemen have to be these six-foot-six, 320-pound guys who were All-Americas and first-round draft choices," says Stepnoski, a six-foot-three, 270-pound former third-rounder. "I know coaches and scouts get all caught up in wanting these blue-chip cookie-cutter guys who are just the right size and just the right everything. But I think that's how teams get into trouble, trying to judge guys by how much they weigh. We've got linemen who can play."

Irvin was spectacular, laughing off a challenge from Cardinals cornerback Lorenzo Lynch, who told Irvin before the game that he'd be "shut down cold." Irvin answered with eight catches, three for touchdowns, and 210 receiving yards. Though Dallas limited Phoenix to two-of-11 on third-down conversions, the Cardinals did manage 371 passing yards, which made the timing of the weekend's trade for holdout safety Thomas Everett from the Pittsburgh Steelers impeccable. The need for help at the position was obvious to everyone except the incumbent starters, Horton and James Washington.

"Why do you ask me? I'm just a token Indian," said an agitated Horton. "Go ask Jerry Jones, he's the chief around here."

Added Washington: "Me and Ray are going to start all sixteen games and then we'll think about next season. They can bring in Joey Browner, Ronnie Lott and Dennis Smith all in here and we shouldn't change our defense."

Dallas would have escaped unscathed, but for those bruised feelings and three extracurricular incidents: Stepnoski sustained a concussion after getting kicked in the head; Johnson suffered a split lip when an excited Irvin swung his chin strap into the coach's face; and Aikman danced out of the way of a beer can tossed toward the back judge by an angry fan.

"Winning those three NFC East games to start really got me thinking there was about to be a changing of the guard in the division," fullback Daryl Johnston says. "With the Giants, you could tell they were starting to slide. Even in 1991 we were able to beat them. We were getting to be pretty confident we could play with Philadelphia. It just seemed like we were on an upward swing, while the other teams were either regressing or staying the same. A team like the Redskins, where else was there to go for them? When we started 3-0, it was obvious we weren't staying still or regressing."

Behind the Cowboys were a summer's worth of worries over the club's lack of maturity, the five preseason games (four is standard), the travels to Tokyo and the dealing with contract disputes. Jerry Jones says maybe the Cowboys benefitted from what had been an atmosphere of uncertainty.

"There is a business term called "tolerance for ambiguity,"' Jones says. "Some salesmen can't get the work done on Monday through Thursday unless they know there is a paycheck coming on Friday. Those are the salesmen who don't work well on commission. Other salesmen like the unknown, like creating their own limitations. Maybe our team, being as young as it is, is like the salesman on commission. Maybe the younger you are, the more you can take. Maybe we had a high tolerance for ambiguity."

The Cowboys knew their theories about "tolerance of ambiguity" and "changing of the guard" would be tested on Monday, October 5, when they were to visit Philadelphia. The buildup was outrageously profuse. "That was just a fourth week of the season, and people were treating it like it was a mini-Super Bowl," Emmitt Smith says.

Those people included Jimmy Johnson. He relished the fact that the bye week added seven more days to the hype, that the game would be aired on Monday Night Football, that Philadelphia radio station WIP-AM was furiously promoting the Cowboys-Eagles matchup as if it was the Second Coming. (On the day of the game, WIP launched a fifteen-hour pregame show, which "Iggles" fans could tune in while reading the *Philadelphia Daily News'* twenty-page pullout section previewing the game.) "I think getting caught up in the hype will be good," Johnson said. "I like the buildup. I don't think you could have a bigger regular-season game."

The drama was heightened by dozens of subplots that caused coast-to-coast hyperbole hyperventilation. The Eagles and Cowboys were both undefeated. Eagles quarterback Randall Cunningham, recovered from his 1991 season-ending knee injury, was 7-0 as a starter against Dallas. Troy Aikman was 0-5 as a starter versus the Eagles. Running back Herschel Walker, who'd been bounced from Minnesota and signed off waivers by Philly, would be facing his old team for the first time. Cowboys right tackle Williams, a Philadelphia native, would line up opposite the Eagles' Reggie White, a future Hall-of-Famer. The Eagles wanted revenge after being eliminated from the 1991 play-off chase by Dallas, 25-13 winners in that December 15 meeting. The Cowboys were still licking some wounds inflicted in their 24-0 loss to Philly on September 15 of that year.

There was the city of Philadelphia's plan to charge a 6-percent tax of visiting professional athletes of income earned there. "They wanted me to pay for their potholes," Smith says.

And there were other charges, from Eagles Andre Waters and Wes Hopkins. They said they intended to punish Irvin for his "inappropriate behavior" at a June 1992 gathering of mourners of the late Jerome Brown, who died behind the wheel of a car. Their comments created a slight suspicion that the Eagles were preparing to milk the death of their defensive tackle as a motivational tool — a suspicion that would be confirmed when the two teams played for a third time, in their January 10 divisional play-off game.

In the play-offs, the Eagles turned Brown into a morbid traveling attraction, like that King Tut exhibit that displayed the old guy's dust in the back of a trailer. The Philadelphia organization boxed up Brown's old Veterans Stadium locker and transported it to game sites. It was erected in the Superdome for the Eagles' first-round victory over the New Orleans Saints, and by the time it got to Texas Stadium, Jerome Brown had been reduced to a 300-pound rabbit's foot.

"That whole thing was absolutely sick," Irvin says. "First of all, who were they to tell me what was an inappropriate way to act about a man who I was friends with before they ever heard of him? I'm not saying they didn't know Jerome. But you don't see me telling them how they should behave, and I'll guarantee you I had a friendship with him that not too many people can match. So how dare they try to insinuate I didn't know him! How dare they try to tell me how to mourn my friend!"

Brown and Irvin were close from in their days together at the University of Miami. One night in 1985, a group of Hurricanes football players, led by that pair, took an oath. They would react to the deaths of those in their group by "celebrating the time God allowed us to be on this earth," says Alfredo Roberts, the Cowboys tight end, also part of that group.

"When one of us dies," Brown said that night, "let's the rest of us throw a party. Drink a beer, have something to eat, have fun. Let's understand that God blessed us while we were here and that now he's blessing us by taking us."

Brown also instructed the buddies to ceremoniously "pour a drink down (onto the floor) for our fallen friend" as a sort of toast. Which a number of NFL names such as Irvin, Roberts, Darrell Fullington, Melvin Bratton, Brian Blades, Bennie Blades, Alonzo Highsmith, Brett Perriman, Eddie Brown, Anthony Carter and Bernard Clark did after the funeral, when the group met in a hotel lobby. It was there that the Eagles players saw Irvin laughing, kidding, bragging and pouring a drink onto the floor. It was there they got the notion that he was being disrespectful of Brown, the defensive tackle who'd been a Philadelphia team leader.

"Reggie White, Seth Joyner, Clyde Simmons, Eric Allen, Mike Golic, lots of Eagles were there," Irvin says. "All of us were talking. Everything was fine. None of this ever came up."

But it came up before that Eagles-Cowboys duel on October 5, the one that would decide which NFC East power would enter the second fourth of the 1992 season undefeated.

Understandably, Johnson was concerned that some of his players were using the off-week to turn their attentions from the Eagles to matters such as contracts, honors, personnel changes and the ongoing NFL labor dispute. That concern prompted a team meeting in which he cautioned against the evils of selfishness. "Coach Johnson wasn't exactly bawling anyone out," defensive end Tony Tolbert says. "But he had reason to be concerned that we might be ruining things by not staying focused. We didn't need stories on us about who would get what contract and who would get to go to the Pro Bowl. He cleared the air by saying that all that stuff comes after the season, but it only comes if you take care of business as a team instead of as one guy who's looking out for himself."

On the Sunday night before the game between these foes that, according to legend and the creative minds at NFL Films "hate each other," Jerry Jones was seated at a Philadelphia restaurant called Bookbinders. As he turned to look for a waiter, he recognized a face at a nearby table. It was Herschel Walker. Sitting with Randall Cunningham. To soften up the pair (or maybe to fatten them up before the anticipated kill), Jones offered to pick up their tab. They declined, deciding to wait twenty-four hours before making Jones's Cowboys pay.

Troy Aikman threw one of his three interceptions on the game's third play. Along with a fourth turnover that caromed from the hands of Johnston into the hands of guard John Gesek then into the hands of the Eagles, Dallas coughed it up four times, leading directly to three Eagles touchdowns in their 31-7 flogging of the Cowboys. Cunningham ran for one score and threw for another. Walker totaled 86 rushing yards and reached the end zone twice, once bluffing a spike in vengeful glee.

"There really were a lot of positives that came out of that game, most of all the fact that we established we could move the football against an outstanding Eagles defense," Johnson says. "The turnovers killed us. It was really the only sub-par game Troy had all year. But we did enough good things to come away with some confidence."

Also contributing to the defeat were two of the sort of go-for-it decisions that earned the Cowboys their crown four months later, but on this nippy night in Philly earned them only a dunce cap. The Cowboys opened the second quarter down just 10-7, and faced a third-and-goal from the Eagles' two-yard line. Aikman rolled right, away from the pressure. He attempted to drill a pass into a crack that really wasn't there. Philadelphia linebacker William Thomas deflected the ball away from intended receiver Roberts and into the hands of Hopkins.

At the end of the same quarter, Dallas remained behind 10-7. One minute and eight seconds remained in the half when Johnson sent his field-goal unit on the field for what seemed like a smart move: let rookie Lin Elliott try to tie the game with a 50-yard field goal. But Johnson ordered his unit into a scrimmage-play formation, with holder Beuerlein under center. Because it was fourth-and-five, Johnson hoped Beuerlein would lure the Eagles offside with a hard count. When it was clear the Eagles weren't going to jump, Johnson should've asked for a time-out, which would have salvaged a scoring chance with an Elliott kick. Instead, Dallas was penalized, losing the chance to score at all.

Waters didn't gain any revenge against Irvin, but he attempted to debilitate Emmitt Smith, bulleting helmet-first into the running back's knee at the end of a play. After the game, Beuerlein and Waters exchanged shoves.

"Hey Waters," Beuerlein said as the teams were leaving the field. "Do you ever hit anyone above the waist?"

But snappy retorts aside, Philadelphia had claimed the biggest victory. The Eagles were 4-0. The Cowboys were 3-1.

Bill Bates says of Cowboys' trips to Philly, "It's always intense, no matter what the records are. You don't know whether the fans will throw snowballs at you, or trash, or if they'll want to shoot you."

That warning was not heeded by Jimmy Johnson. On the Monday afternoon before kickoff, he was looking to swallow some time and maybe a cheesesteak sandwich. So the Cowboys coach exited the Philadelphia Hilton, drawing the stares of the hundreds of citizens who recognized him.

But unlike in his previous public appearances in the City of Brotherly Shove, no hooligans fired snowballs, trash or bullets. Johnson went unbothered as he cockily strutted down the city's famous Broad Street like he was on top of the world. He didn't suspect for a second that by the end of that night, he'd no longer even be on top of the NFC East.

9 A PAIR OF ACES ★

Bill Bates was the poster boy.

Alexander Wright was the whipping boy.

Their 1992 campaigns with the Dallas Cowboys ended prematurely, and on the same day, October 12. It took such an ironically timed coincidence for the names "Bates" and "Wright" to possibly find their way into the same headline.

"I've been making that same move for ten years, hundreds of times maybe," says Bates, recalling the moment in the second quarter of the Cowboys' 27-0 win over Seattle on October 11, when he planted his left leg onto the Texas Stadium carpet while covering a kickoff and in doing so tore the anterior cruciate, medial collateral and medial meniscus ligaments in the knee. "I was going full speed. It seems like most of the times guys normally get hurt is times they're not going full speed. I've seen the film. I don't remember falling down, but I did. I beat the guy who was supposed to block me, and I was chasing the ballcarrier. Then when I planted my leg, the guy I'd beaten chased me down and hit me in the back of my shoulder.

"I do remember looking down when it happened. For some reason, I looked down and saw my foot kind of stay in the turf.

I remember a shot of adrenaline going through my body. It all felt really weird."

Bates knows that football is too unforgiving a sport to allow all its participants to last until the final gun. And he knew that after a decade in Dallas as a too-small, too-slow, undrafted free agent from Tennessee, he'd already beaten the cutdown-day odds ten times, to the point where he's now considered too old. But as was the case even months into his post-1992 rehabilitation, this former Pro Bowler also refused to accept that the knee injury might mark the finish line to his career. In fact, there was a time in the days after the injury when Bates refused to accept the fact that he'd even been injured at all.

"Here I was walking around on it pretty good, and I got to wondering if I was even hurt," says Bates, whose one-year contract stipulated that his annual salary be sliced from $450,000 to $250,000 if he was disabled. "I was paranoid, I guess. Or maybe I was just in mental denial. I was definitely depressed. I was out there looking for some doctor, any old quack, to tell me I could play. I was telling doctors who'd spent their whole lives working on knees that they must be wrong about this one."

In his temporary dementia, it actually occurred to Bates that placing him on IR (injured reserve) was a move made by the organization not to protect his knee, but to save the company money. "I never felt they were plotting against me, because everybody in this organization is great," he says. "I trust them all. But, well, a lot of things go though your mind."

Says veteran safety Ray Horton, who signed a similar deal: "You're proud of Bill for flying around and playing the way he does. But now he's kind of getting screwed because he doesn't have anything to fall back on. (Management) wants the best of both worlds from guys like him. They say, 'Go out and give your body up, but if you get hurt, too bad.'"

The Cowboys ended up paying Bates less (the injury cost him exactly $171,875), but they still put him to work. In the Johnson era, Bates has often served as a liaison between players and management. In 1990, he became the hero to a new generation of Cowboys when he persuaded Johnson to reward the team for its Thanksgiving Day win over the Redskins by giving players three straight days off. By 1991, as he approached the twilight of his football life, he fancied himself a sort of player/coach, as mentor Tom Landry had once been as a New York Giant. On October 12, 1992, with the "player" half of the tag stolen away, he decided to salvage what he could of his dwindling duties.

"The Cowboys coaches know where I'm coming from, and I know where they're coming from," said Bates, who became an unofficial aide to special-teams coach Joe Avezzano. "There isn't the barrier, of ego or whatever, that usually comes with that boss-employee hierarchy. I'm not intimidated from going into Jimmy and speaking up. I thought I was still capable of contributing something, even if I was on crutches."

Player/coach may be a paradox. But so is Bates.

To be a coach is to have authority. A coach is sport's equivalent of the commanding officer. But to pound away as a special-team drudge, to ignominiously barrel through practices as a scout-team running back, to be a football player who truly doesn't have a football position, that is sport's equivalent of latrine duty.

Bates is a devoted Baptist, husband (to Denise) and father (to triplets Graham, Brianna and Hunter, and baby Tanner). But he is not nearly as square as his adoring public thinks. "Bill Bates is really a symbol of what football is all about," Jerry Jones says. Bates may be Mr. Cowboy. Clean-cut. Western-cut. Not getting cut. Still, when MTV quasi-celebrity Downtown Julie Brown, masquerading as a reporter, flounced around the

Cowboys' hotel at the Super Bowl, Bates was as moved as the next red-blooded male to remark on her bountiful cleavage.

"I'm a guy who has some deep feelings and beliefs that cause some people to think of me as squeaky-clean," he says. "But I'm far from perfect. I have a lot of faults. I cuss, use the wrong language, chew tobacco occasionally. I've got vices."

To be a six-foot, 200-pound brute who says he salivates at the thought of "knocking someone's head off" when he attempts a return to the field in 1993 does not jibe with Bates's habit of stuffing into notebooks items of inspirational, philosophical and motivational value. But as much as that first trait helped him survive playing football, that second trait helped him survive not playing.

"There are a million of those phrases in there, and I went back and got something out of all of them," Bates says. "I had a lot of people coming to my side. Michael Irvin and Emmitt Smith both told me I was an inspiration to them. That meant so much. Ex-players came over to the house to console me. Everyone was pulling for me and praying for me, and that kept me upbeat. But I'm glad I had that notebook. When I finally got put on IR, and I knew my season was probably over with, I sat down by myself with that notebook. I started thinking, and praying, and I took all those things that I'd clipped out or written down and decided I needed to swallow some of it as my own medicine."

What sort of messages are included in Bates's notebook?

"Dream and shoot for the stars. Even if you fall short, you'll land high."

"To try and fail is at least to learn. But to fail to try is to reach an inestimable loss of what might have been."

"Be good to the people you meet on the way up, because you're likely to see them again on the way down."

Bates shot high. He tried. And if Bates's fall came in 1992 — an unfortunate season capped in the post-Super Bowl XXVII locker room, when he discovered someone had stolen his new $1,200 leather Cowboys jacket — he was certainly good to the people he saw on the way down. His January 8, 1993, pep rally is testament to that.

"I've never witnessed anything like it," says Bates, who offered up his ranch in McKinney, Texas, as a Friday night playground for twenty thousand rain-drenched fans who refused to wait until the January 10 play-off opener against Philadelphia to scream themselves into a frenzy. "You know that scene in "Field of Dreams" where all the headlights are lined up for miles as cars are making their way to the cornfield? That's what this was like. Field of Dreams. And I was so happy to be a part of it. I cried. I've always been the type who wants to be involved 100 percent. Even though I was hurt, that pep rally was the type of thing that helped me feel I was making a contribution. Most guys, when they get hurt, seem to go into a shell."

Some guys retreat into that shell even when they're not hurt. Guys like Alexander Wright, the genuinely sweet football misfit who admits, "Maybe I sometimes put my tail between my legs."

Bates milked his limited body for every ounce of talent it contained. Wright, the team's second-round pick and twenty-sixth overall selection in 1990 and the winner of the NFL's Fastest Man Competition in 1992, couldn't even locate the udder. He milked nothing from his seemingly unlimited body, but impressive 40-yard-dash times.

In exchange for his unselfish contributions to football, fate told Bates to grab a crutch. In exchange for his maddening inability to understand true commitment and his sad inability to overcome his fear of contact, fate told Wright to grab a flight to Los Angeles, where the Raiders were willing to pay a fourth-round pick to give him a second chance.

In that one October 12 press conference, Jimmy Johnson detailed the futures of both players. And when asked about Wright's work habits, Johnson exhibited his understanding of irony.

"There is a gauge," Johnson said. "At the top is Bill Bates. ... The bottom (of the gauge) guys are no longer with this club."

Johnson tried to backpedal, saying something about Wright maybe being somewhere around the middle of the gauge. But he knew better. Over the course of more than two years, he'd given the six-foot, 190-pound sprinter too many chances. Receivers coach Hubbard Alexander tried to big-brother Wright, who'd been beaten by his alcoholic father as a child growing up in Albany, Georgia. Michael Irvin tried to boss him around in an effort to motivate Wright, who so easily became an All-America track performer at Auburn. Strength coach Mike Woicik and a few others, sympathetic to the plight of Wright, tried to embrace him.

None of it worked. It was two years before Alexander "Ace" Wright spoke up to tell anybody that he preferred to be called "Alex" rather than "Alexander" or "Ace." The meek might inherit the earth, but in pro football, all they do is get buried under it.

Says Johnson: "Any time a new player comes in, you are going to have to deal with their different characteristics. The ones who are supposed to be head cases, like Charles Haley, I can deal with, because at least he expresses himself to you. The tough ones, the ones I've never been able to make headway with, are the ones who just won't open up."

As a rookie, Wright was allowed to come along slowly in the hope that would help him feel comfortable. After all, he'd played just one year of high school football and started just one year in college after being recruited as a defensive back. "I've always been a late bloomer," he says. That approach resulted in Wright catching just 11 passes that year.

In the spring of 1991, Wright ran a 4.09-second 40, believed to be the quickest time ever recorded by an NFL player. He bench-pressed an astounding 385 pounds. But the numbers haunted Wright more than helped him. Johnson decided to elevate Wright to first-string, in the hope that would push him to make the commitment that didn't seem to be there earlier, when Wright planned to spend his off-season working in hotel management instead of in the weight room (an idea Johnson vetoed). That approach failed, too. Wright caught just 10 passes that year, all of them coming while he was a starter in the season's first eight games.

Wright reacted to failure by burrowing into his Bible. He said a prayer before every snap of the football. Even that didn't work, because the prayer in his soul was always chased by the butterflies in his stomach. Alexander Wright is a good Christian, a good person, a good sprinter. But he can't play football.

The Wright stuff? Alex doesn't have it.

"It seemed like everything that could go wrong, did," Wright says. "When it came time for the games, everything was like Freon — frozen. Look at what I did in training camps. I kicked butt in camps. I don't know why it didn't happen in games. Maybe it was because as hard as I think I worked, I didn't do the extra things. Maybe it just wasn't meant for me to be a Cowboy."

Teammates who'd spent almost three seasons guiding Wright to his proper position after breaking the huddle could have told him that. Quarterback Troy Aikman had no confidence in Wright, both because of his underdeveloped receiving skills and his lack of mastery of the playbook. None of Wright's other peers believed in him, either. Veteran Kelvin Martin, a receiving technician who produced a team-high 64 receptions when he was allowed to start in 1990, indicates the reason he never put up a fuss while the Cowboys were making a fuss over Wright is that Martin always knew coaches would end up relying on him in crunch time.

Says Irvin: "Ace isn't stupid. Far from it. And he's one of the nicest people in the world. But when he got traded, none of the reporters asked us about it. None of the players really talked about it. Everybody knew about the trade, but there wasn't any passion about it one way or the other, which kind of fits Ace. Let me tell you, this is a killer sport. This really is like a real war. Ace is a great athlete, and I still think he can be a football player. But he isn't the gladiator type."

Bates epitomizes the NFL player who is somehow able to block out the fact that his mortality could be proven at any moment. Wright epitomizes the NFL fan, who enjoys watching the game, but puts his hands over his eyes when they're about to show a replay of a gruesome collision.

In his final season in Dallas, Wright caught flak — ugly fans had gotten his home phone number and were leaving demented messages for him and wife Veerle — but he caught no passes. He made a rare and uncharacteristic peep on September 22, when he and agent Pat Dye told a newspaper they might request a trade.

The last straw came when, in Wright's final weeks in Dallas, even his confidence as a kick returner unraveled. He ran back kickoffs for touchdowns in each of his first two seasons in Dallas, so by 1992, coaches resigned themselves to thinking that while Wright might never catch a throw he would always contribute catching kicks. But he disappointed again. Wright botched three kickoff returns in the September 20 win over Phoenix. In attempting to pick up the muffed football, he reminded of Bambi trying to walk on an ice pond. After that game, Wright was ordered to "rest" a tender knee that Wright whispered really didn't feel tender at all. But as usual, he didn't argue. He kept his tail between his legs and finished 1992 by catching 12 passes for two touchdowns in L.A., where more teammates are undoubtedly posing the question less gifted Cowboys players started asking back on October 12, 1992, when Bill Bates and Alexander Wright shared a headline.

"Can you imagine," Irvin says, "what a legend you'd have if you put Bill's heart and head into Ace's body?"

Game planning to win a National Football League contest allows a tiny crack of time for brainstorming. But the rigidity of the Cowboys' in-season schedule allows no room for self-delusion, for guesswork, or for a leisure-time lifestyle that in any way resembles the American norm.

"I think I'm about the only guy on that staff who would go to Jimmy and say, 'One of my daughters has a softball game tonight, so I'm going to be leaving work early,'" says Dave Wannstedt, Johnson's longtime defensive coordinator. "I stood up to Jimmy. Not all of the guys do that. But of course, I could only do it because Jimmy trusted me to be back in the office the next morning at six to make up for it."

Work is the coaches' cure-all. Work is their antidote. Got a problem? Rub a little work on it. This is how a game plan gets done in Dallas.

"No staff of coaches works harder than we do," Johnson says. "I'm not saying we outwork everyone else. But no one outworks us. Our meetings as a staff are less structured than other times, because there is some time built in there to exchange ideas. But otherwise, there are very specific assignments that must be done in a span of time that seems very short. That's why you can pick any minute of the day, from when we start at 7:30 in the morning to when we go home at 10:30 or 11:00 at night, and I can tell you where a certain coach is. And I can tell you what film he's watching, or what drill he's running on the field. And I can tell you how soon he'll be done with that drill or with that film.

"I don't like surprises in general," Johnson says. "And I definitely don't like them when it comes to the football team."

Often, a poorly prepared football team meets the enemy on Sundays and the enemy is itself. The Cowboys start their weekly strategic preparation by making certain the problem isn't in their mirror.

"You'd better look at yourself the way your opponent is going to look at you," Cowboys offensive coordinator Norv Turner says. "You've got to play to your strengths. But you also better have a counter-move ready. This has to be done carefully because you can out-trick yourself and go away from what you do best. When you put together a game plan, you better not try to kid yourself."

By Sunday morning, when Turner tapes to the wall of his stadium box a list of his fifteen optimal plays against that afternoon's opponent, and Wannstedt tapes to the opposite wall a similar "cheat sheet" of plans, the game plan will have survived a six-day test of endurance. And the Cowboys will be ready to put on the field what they spent the week taking off film and computer printouts.

The self-scouting process requires Dallas assistant Steve Hoffman to chart the Cowboys' own tendencies to assure they don't fall into a rut of predictability. It was Hoffman who, by analyzing Cowboys plays on the computer, detected a 1991 habit of running the ball nearly 90 percent of the time fullback Johnston was offset to the right in the I-formation. In the first three games of the 1992 season, the Cowboys purposely ran from that formation 50 percent of the time, effectively throwing opponents off the scent and helping the Cowboys to a 3-0 start.

"We don't do a whole lot on gut feeling," Johnson says. "We do extensive planning and work in the off-season, in training camp and in the weeks prior to the game. On game day, it's nothing more than executing the plan. We're not afraid to make decisions that might be termed 'gambles.' But we make them based on study that shows they'll work. We plan those 'gambles.' We plan to the point where we might even be over-prepared."

Johnson is the overseer of the process. Hoffman, who handles quality control and is the kicking coach, is the 'computer nerd.' With help from staffer Neill Armstrong, Hoffman spends Monday, Tuesday and Wednesday studying film of the upcoming opponent and the Cowboys. On a computer-ready sheet, Hoffman writes everything about every play on both sides of the ball, down and distance, personnel group, field position, how many steps in the quarterback's drop, defensive line stunts, secondary coverage, offensive line blocking scheme and any other piece of minutiae.

"We start the week with tons of information," Hoffman says. "I mean, it's every single tidbit that can be dug up."

Hoffman passes his paperwork to coaching secretary Marge Anderson, who feeds it into the computer. Also on-line with the computer is video director Robert Blackwell, who assigns each play a number and assembles cut-up sequences of film. By Wednesday, a 100-page scouting report and forty-play, cut-up film are ready to be digested by the coaches, who usually work until 11:00 p.m. dissecting the information and, by combining Hoffman's study with the existing playbook, finalizing the game plan.

In 1992, Turner, Wannstedt and Avezzano were allowed a great deal of leeway in the decision-making process. Johnson considers this to be Turner's offense. So while the head coach might issue general directives as to style of play, the details are left to Turner. The same is true of Avezzano, who rewarded the

Cowboys for the freedom given him by being named Special-Teams Coach of the Year by his peers in 1991, and of Wannstedt, whose mastery of the nuances of this upfield-pressure defense designed by Johnson would help gain him the head coaching job with the Chicago Bears.

"Jimmy has a great knack for letting the coaches coach," Avezzano says. "He's got expertise in all these areas, too, but he's more than willing to hand the reins over to one of us."

Says Wannstedt: "Because the guys on the coaching staff are friends, it's a lot easier to all sit down together and lay out the options and give our opinions on what we think should happen. There is total give-and-take. Now, some guys are more reluctant than others to get in arguments with the head coach about what should be in the game plan. But if you have an idea, Jimmy wants to hear it. He just wants to make sure you've thought it out yourself before you bring it to him and tell him to make it part of the plan."

The plan worked to perfection on October 11 against Seattle, a team whose ineptitude helped Dallas rebound from the loss to the Eagles and jump to 4-1. The Seahawks weren't seaworthy and that made them exactly what the Cowboys needed.

"After losing to Philly, but knowing we got to play them again in a few weeks (on November 1), we really wanted to get on a roll," linebacker Ken Norton says. "We were looking for somebody to beat up on."

In dominating the Seahawks, the Cowboys fed off their first shutout in fourteen years, recorded seven sacks, two fumble recoveries, an interception for a touchdown, a franchise-low 62 yards allowed and halftime pep talks delivered not by coaches, but by defensive players.

"This wasn't going to be a game where the coaches were going to stand up and whip players into an emotional frenzy,"

Wannstedt said. "The rah-rah stuff wasn't going to work. Somebody in this business once said that you have maybe five games a year where emotion can be a factor and the other ten or eleven depend on how prepared and professional your players are. ... As coaches, we had to kind of stand back today and allow the players to establish a tempo and an emotional level. They did just that, too."

Norton, Jimmie Jones and Tony Casillas were among the players who climbed the halftime soapbox, inspiring the Cowboys to continue their domination. And afterward, Johnson delayed climbing a postgame podium to instead watch the finish of the Kansas City-Philadelphia game on television. "You guys aren't in a hurry, are you?" he asked the waiting media. "There are two teams up on that screen that I'm extremely interested in. I have deep feelings for both."

Johnson needed to see the Chiefs, the Cowboys' next opponent. But more, he needed to see the Chiefs win. They did, handing the Eagles their first loss, 24-17, and pulling Dallas even with Philadelphia in the NFC East. On October 18, the Cowboys beat the Chiefs, 17-10. Meanwhile, the Eagles lost to Washington, 16-12.

"You could see the Eagles had treated that (October 5) game against us like it was the end of the world, and they were having a heck of a time getting up for any other games after it," guard Nate Newton says. "Us, we treated every week the same. In our hearts, we knew divisional games had a certain value. But Kansas City or Seattle or Washington or Philly, we tried to approach every one of them the same. That was our blueprint, and that was the difference between us and Philly right there."

Coaches hoped newcomer Thomas Everett would help make a difference, too. So the former Steeler made his first start as a Cowboy against Kansas City. He contributed eight tackles in the Chiefs game, and his solid support work against the run seemed to justify the continued benching of safety Ray Horton.

The previous week against Seattle, it had been Kenny Gant in the starting lineup. Shoved to the sideline in both games was Horton, who reacted to the demotions by wavering between bitterness and bemusement.

"All I know is coach Johnson said I wouldn't be starting so I didn't," Horton said. "As far as I know, it's not permanent, but all I can do is show up to work tomorrow and do my job."

Horton's job description changed, but his aspirations did not. Horton has in a desk drawer at home something he calls a "List of Life." On it are things he hopes to accomplish before he dies. Meet the Pope. Be a character in a Clyve Custler novel. Visit Australia. Act in a Ron Howard movie. Already crossed off the List: Climb the K-2 Mountain in China (he did it). Pass the firefighting exam (he did it, twice). Bike from Seattle to Los Angeles (he did it). And play in a Super Bowl. He did that once after the 1988 season, with the Cincinnati Bengals. And now of course, the ten-year NFL veteran has done it twice.

His second visit to an NFL title game did not come easy. Horton, the very first new-regime transaction as a March 15, 1989, Plan B signee, would have to do his thing as a substitute.

He scored on the interception return in the Seattle game. And he sealed the win over the Chiefs with a game-saving interception off quarterback Dave Krieg. The win gave Dallas a 5-1 record and its first sole division lead since December 15, 1985. But in the victorious locker room, Horton was less interested in the game's historical significance than in discussing his new status as a scrub.

"I felt like a leper," said Horton, mentioning a milepost that didn't quite make his List of Life.

Wannstedt makes it clear that in his efforts to lead a defense that would finish the season as the league's top-ranked, bruised egos were predictable. "Everybody at every position wants something," he says in explanation of the many lineup changes. "Ken Norton wants to blitz more. Charles Haley wants to get to the quarterback more. My wife wants to shop more. All of these personal goals are fine, as long as they fit the team concept."

Ask the Cowboys to name one galvanizing game when they began to believe in themselves as championship contenders, and some will mention their Week Seven outing on October 25 against the Raiders in Los Angeles. An intimidatingly large audience of 91,505 packed the L.A. Coliseum to see if Dallas was for real. The Cowboys already believed the Raiders were; the teams had worked out together for three days back in Austin and the Raiders left the impression they were the more physical team.

The Los Angeles Raiders are famous for leaving impressions. First, there is their city. In a speech that would bear repeating three months later, ten-year veteran defensive lineman Jim Jeffcoat warned some young Cowboys to wear blinders to avoid the glitter of L.A. "All that glitz, it can distract you," Jeffcoat said. "You want to see if Magic (Johnson) is in the hallway. You might see James Garner on the sidelines. ... There is so much to do here, but you've got to say, 'Hey, I've got a football game to play.'"

Jeffcoat had no problem with what he focused on: the quarterback. Jeffcoat, who started 120 games for Dallas from 1984 to 1991, led the Cowboys in sacks with 10.5 despite playing only as a substitute in passing situations. The Cowboys' first-round pick in 1983, Jeffcoat has seen enough of the NFL to know how to avoid being sucked in by his surroundings. But did his teammates?

A Raiders game at the Coliseum does have atmosphere. The cheerleaders, who appear to all be patients of the same plastic surgeon, somehow look both glamorous and slutty. Their players somehow seem both glamorous and thuggish. Their home, the Coliseum, is the world's largest biker bar. But it is also as much a theme park as Disneyland, what with the themes like "The Greatness of the Raiders" and "Silver and Black" and "Just Win, Baby" and "Team of the Decades" and "Real Men Wear Black" and The Pride and Poise Boys" and "Commitment to Excellence."

Dallas boasted but one theme. A Commitment to Emmitt.

Smith scored three touchdowns and tallied 167 total yards (152 rushing), outgaining by two the entire Raiders offense. In the middle of the third quarter, he wobbled to the sidelines after sustaining a nasty blow to the back. With the Cowboys down, 13-7, somebody else needed to do something.

"I believe the coaches' confidence in me was down before that," says receiver Alvin Harper, who came into the Raiders game with eight catches in six outings, and just 21 passes thrown in his direction. "I was out there in games running patterns, listening to DBs tell me they weren't worried because they knew the ball wasn't coming to me."

But the Raiders were double-teaming Michael Irvin. And they carefully guided Smith into the hands of the Dallas's medical staff. Somebody else needed to do something. Harper did. Running a deep post pattern against the single coverage of Lionel Washington, he broke free for a career-long 52-yard reception to the Raiders' 21-yard line. "I knew they'd have to rely on me eventually," Harper says.

Two plays later, Smith begged his way back onto the field, overruling Johnson, who was preparing to finish the game without his star runner.

"Coach, I got to go back in," Smith said.

Says Johnson: "If he's ready to go, I'm ready to go with him."

Smith carried seven yards to the four-yard line before registering one of history's most spectacular four-yard runs. Smith took the handoff and followed the up-the-middle lead block of fullback Daryl Johnston, who charged toward onrushing Raiders linebacker Riki Ellison. Ellison jumped to avoid Johnston's block and aimed himself like an arrow at Smith. "I'm not used to seeing guys flying in the air straight at my eye level," said Smith, who bounced off the horizontal Ellison, lunged forward and wrestled through tackle attempts by muscular Raiders safeties Ronnie Lott and Eddie Anderson for the go-ahead score.

Smith's marvelous work (including the clinching 26-yard touchdown run with 3:26 remaining in the game) and a defense led by Jeffcoat's two sacks pushed the Cowboys to a 6-1 record. It marked the franchise's best start in nine years, and matched the Miami Dolphins and San Francisco 49ers for the league's top mark.

Haley said he wasn't certain his young teammates understood the significance of being 6-1. That record, Haley advised, "means you're sitting in the driver's seat."

Johnson shared Haley's doubts that the inexperienced Cowboys had a level of confidence that matched their position in the standings. With Dallas a week away from its November 1 rematch with the Eagles, Cowboys players braced themselves for a tension-filled, labor-intense week of practice.

Instead, they got Monday and Tuesday off. A forty-eight-hour armistice.

"I felt like we were the better team, and playing at Texas Stadium I felt like we would win the game," says Johnson, explaining his unusual generosity. "I didn't want our guys to have any negative stigma because it was Philly. I wanted them to be as confident as they should have been going into that game. So giving them two days off boiled down to two things:

One, it gave the coaches more time to be completely thorough as far as working out a game plan. Two, because we take days off so rarely, I thought it would make an impact mentally. I thought it would give them a lift. It would be making a statement to the players, that we didn't need the extra practice day because I felt we were going to kick their ass."

Johnson's attitude rubbed off. You could see that when tight end Alfredo Roberts decided to pull over his head a T-shirt that put onto 100-percent cotton what this Cowboys-Eagles game meant.

"It's Payback Time. Pound Philly," the shirt said.

The Cowboys were a game up on 5-2 Philadelphia. The Washington Redskins were also 5-2. The Cowboys were taking days off, putting boastful T-shirts on, and not worrying about the back of the NFC East bus. Said center Mark Stepnoski: "(In 1991) we spent most of the season in second place, and the theme was, 'Take care of our own business.' Well, if you think about it, it's the same no matter where you are in the standings. In second place, it's a mistake to look ahead. In first, it's a mistake to look behind you."

Stepnoski should have given that advice to Randall Cunningham, the Cowboys slayer turned Eagles bench warmer.

Coming into his appearance at Texas Stadium, Cunningham was slumping. He completed 69.6 percent of his throws in the Eagles' first four games, leading Philadelphia to a 4-0 mark highlighted by that 31-7 win over the Cowboys on October 5. But in Weeks Five through Seven, Cunningham was more problem than solution as the Eagles went 1-2. While Dallas was beating the Raiders, Cunningham was struggling to a nine-of-20, 121-yard passing day in a 7-3 win over Phoenix. Asked about the problems with his franchise offensive player, Philadelphia coach Rich Kotite shrugged his shoulders and said, "I'm not a psychologist."

Jimmy Johnson, of course, pretty much is.

"We went into that game with an attitude," Norton says. "That first Philly game was huge, but the fact we lost didn't cause us to miss a beat. Personally, all I could think about was our rematch with Philly. And when we played well enough as a defense to force them to change quarterbacks, that was a sign that our attitude was successful.

"Maybe we had approached Philly before a little fearful. But the second time, the only thing we did different in our game plan was to get rid of the fear and take everything to a higher level."

Also leveled was Cunningham, previously 8-0 as a starter against Dallas, but demoted in favor of Jim McMahon after a first half in which he completed three of eight passes for 13 yards. Dallas's offense wasn't much more successful in the first half, having built just a 3-0 lead after Lin Elliott made just one of three field-goal tries. "The thing about a kicker," says position coach Steve Hoffman, "is that you can't exactly replace him with your second-stringer."

Elliott was taken off the hook thanks to two touchdown throws by Aikman, who hadn't beaten the Eagles in six tries and therefore, said the pundits, had his "back against the wall." (In fact, Aikman's failures against the Eagles would more fairly be attributed to the frequency his back was against the turf.) Also key was a defense that suddenly found itself leapfrogging over the Eagles and on top of the NFL's statistical rankings. "We showed we can play today," middle linebacker Robert Jones said. "Maybe all those people who talked about how great Philadelphia's defense is should start talking about us."

And there was Emmitt Smith, whose 30 carries for 163 yards (the first 100-yard game allowed an individual by the Philadelphia defense in three years) was made possible by his earth-moving front line. Erik Williams, the second-year right tackle, earned national recognition for his effort. Williams won NFC Offensive Player of the Week for his handling of Reggie White, who was apparently very taken with these upstart Cowboys.

After the game, White (who would be the free-agent market's hottest commodity after the 1992 season and a Green Bay signee) sidled up to Haley and asked him to pass an unusual message to Dallas team management.

"Would you please inform Jimmy and Jerry that I'd be interested in leaving the Eagles as a free agent and finishing my career with the Cowboys?" White whispered.

At 10:20 a.m., with ten minutes to go before the Cowboys charter was to take off for Detroit on November 7, staffer Robert Blackwell marched up the aisle and into first class to report to Jimmy Johnson that one seat, 20C, was still unoccupied.

"Michael isn't here yet," Blackwell told Johnson.

With one minute to go, Blackwell made the long march again.

"Michael isn't here yet," Blackwell said.

Johnson waited exactly sixty seconds before leaning forward so the flight crew could here him order, "Shut the door!"

The Cowboys were 7-1. The Lions were 2-6. But history — dating back to 1991, when in two tries Dallas was blown out at the Silverdome by a combined 72-16 score — offered no evidence to suggest they could travel so light as to leave their 6-foot-2, 200-pound pass-catching package behind. The "Playmaker" wasn't a plane-maker. Still, when staffers were scrambling to help Irvin catch a later flight to Detroit, Johnson interrupted their efforts.

"That's not our concern," Johnson barked. "He's a big boy. Let him find his own way to Detroit."

Irvin found his way to the Auburn Hills Hilton late that night. He checked in a few hours before the arrival of Frank

Sinatra (whose attempts to buy a round for everyone in the lobby were snuffed out by the bar's midnight closing time), but far too late for Johnson, who prepared to sing for Irvin a few bars of his unique rendition of "My Way."

"We've had players miss the plane before," Johnson told Irvin as he met him in a hallway outside a meeting room. "And it was not really a concern. I give the fine and we go on about our business. But with you being one of my, quote, favorites, you set the example for the others. With you being one of the, quote, stars, and being such a visible player, you really put me in a bad position. I'm going to fine you $1,000. And I'll give it some thought before I decide if you'll play tomorrow."

"Jimmy, that's bull," said Irvin, as the coach started walking down the hallway, refusing to argue with his player.

Says Irvin: "I woke up way before the time my alarm was set for. My bags were all packed. I brought them out to the living room, sat down to watch some TV, and fell asleep in the living room. By the time I woke up, I was late."

The flight nearly had two empty seats. Emmitt Smith admitted that he, too, had alarm clock problems. A fortuitous phone call from his sister woke him up in time. Had he and Irvin been absent, "It would have been the end of the world," Smith said. "(Johnson's) hair would have been standing up on end for the first time ever."

The Cowboys won, 37-3. The No. 1-ranked defense, led by safety Thomas Everett and his two interceptions, retained the tag by allowing just 201 yards, 41 below their average. The Cowboys were so dominant that for the first time in thirty-five games, Smith didn't lead Dallas in rushing, retiring early after gaining 67 yards. Irvin was benched for the first series, then took the field to catch five passes for 114 yards and a touchdown.

"Really," said Aikman, "I don't care if Michael makes the plane or makes the meetings as long as he's there on Sundays."

Johnson hoped the Irvin incident would be the alarm clock that would wake up his players to the fact that "distractions" can be homicidal to a team's chances at a title. Could Irvin's gaffe be flip-flopped into a positive? Would everyone now make sure they are aboard the team flights? And in the team meetings? And focused on football exclusively?

Hardly. In the week that preceded his 9-1 team's November 15 game at Texas Stadium against the Los Angeles Rams, Johnson turned page after page of the clippings to see few pure football stories. After "Irvin Misses Team Plane" came "Dallas On Super Bowl Path." Then there were "Cowboys Favor AIDS Testing" and "Emmitt Smith Turns Down $5.76 Million Contract Extension" and "NFL Cites Cowboys For Sloppy Uniforms" and "Nate Newton And The 'Boys Eyeing Music Video" and "Give The Defense A Nickname." Additionally, the national media was beginning to sense the Cowboys might be something special. Thus began the onslaught of network features and magazine covers that by January were old hat, but in November were still a fresh delight.

"There were extra things going on," receiver Kelvin Martin says. "More media. More people on the bandwagon."

On Sunday arrived the ultimate distraction: a 27-23 loss to the Rams, a team that before its visit to Dallas was a fourteen-point underdog and a 3-6 loser.

Emmitt Smith blamed the loss on "lack of intensity." Tony Casillas tried "complacency."

Says Aikman: "Losing to the Rams was the low point of the year. It was a team we expected to beat. Maybe that was one of the problems, in retrospect. Plus, as poorly as we played at times, we had so many opportunities to go ahead and win it."

The final opportunity belonged to Aikman. On the game's final play, Aikman dropped back from the Rams' 14-yard line and looked toward the end zone for a chance to record the sort of dramatic rally-to-victory that Cowboys legend Roger Staubach so often engineered. He had already set the stage by driving Dallas from its 24-yard line with 1:50 remaining. One more great throw and he could overshadow the fact that the Cowboys' defense had allowed an embarrassing 367 yards. He could supplement the efforts of Irvin and Smith, who each surpassed the 1,000-yard marks as receiver and rushing, respectively. He could create his own legend.

"Ace Right, Zero-Forty-Four," called Aikman in the huddle.

With 00:01 on the clock, Aikman dropped. Alvin Harper ran from Aikman's right against Todd Lyght. Irvin ran from Aikman's left against Darryl Henley. Martin was in the slot and went straight upfield. Aikman looked toward Irvin. He wasn't open. Aikman was forced out of the pocket by Sean Gilbert. When Martin turned and couldn't locate the quarterback, he adjusted his pattern unpredictably.

"It became a crowd in the end zone," Martin says.

"The last play was a little helter-skelter," Aikman says. "Kelvin had to run his route deeper that normal. He had a step on his man, and I let it go assuming he would keep running. He lost sight of me and pulled up."

Aikman's pass thudded into the end zone. Staubach lives.

On Monday, coaches informed their players that in addition to the ending of a five-game winning streak and an eleven-game home winning streak, they tallied "mental mistakes" at a season-high rate. The resulting mood was dour. "Ideally, this should be no different than if that throw in the end zone was caught for a touchdown," Turner said.

But there was nothing ideal about this situation. The only upbeat person in the Valley Ranch dressing room was Bill

Bates, hobbling around without crutches, trying to pull his teammates out of their pouts.

"Here's one of my favorite lines," Bates says. "It describes how I try to approach things: 'Yesterday was but a vision, tomorrow is but a dream. Live so that each today will be a vision of happiness and each tomorrow a dream of hope.'"

Happiness and hope? There was a shortage. Distractions? There would be plenty to go around.

10 HEDONISM, COWBOYS-STYLE ★

It's past midnight. Do you know where your Cowboys are?

It was always easy to find Kenny Gant. He'd be at the nearest automated teller machine, withdrawing from his bank account his daily limit of $400. Then he'd be somewhere on Greenville Avenue, sipping (or often guzzling) the good life. Trying to outlast the moon.

"God, I lost a lot of money trying to impress people," says Gant, who had never ridden in a plane before coming to Dallas as a 1990 ninth-round pick out of tiny Albany (Georgia) State. "I spent a lot of money trying to be big. I always had a bunch of money in my pocket. I bought drinks for everybody. I had flashy clothes. Flashy habits."

Gant says his April 1992 marriage rescued him from a nightlife that was steadily siphoning off his salary. He says he bordered on financial trouble, especially in his rookie year, when he grossed $130,500 but estimates he "partied away" more than $20,000 in the twenty weeks he was in town during the season.

"It caught up to me, and I didn't even realize it until after the year, when I looked back and said, "Oh, damn, I just blew a lot of money,'" Gant says. "I knew I couldn't keep going like this. Because of the way I was spending — I sent money to my family back home (in Lakeland, Florida) — there were times when I had to double-check to make sure I had my rent money every month.

"The worst thing isn't the money. The worst thing is that I think back at how much better a player I could have been had I been more disciplined," says Gant, who in 1992 added to his resume as a special-teams standout by excelling as a Nickel back. "I was single, going out five times a week during the season, spending maybe $400 a night. I still came to practice every day and ran around the same, but I was always real antsy to get the day at Valley Ranch over with and see what was going on out there."

What is going on out there? Dallas is hardly a tourists' delight — the attention span of visitors is tested after they've seen the Kennedy assassination site — but it is a city lined with nightclubs and bars operated by people who know having Cowboys as regular customers is good for business. All those wet-T-shirt contests need judges, you know. All those drug dealers need clients. All those strip joints would rather seat guests who fill dancers' panties with $5 and $10 bills rather than the usual $1 bills.

Dallas is a city bloated with hoity-toity organizations whose leaders know their party won't get proper billing in society circles unless they persuade a tuxedoed Cowboy to attend. The Cowboys perform in a major metropolitan area that suffers from a massive inferiority complex that is soothed by its creation of hometown celebrities, even if their star power is artificial or imagined. It is a place where some low-profile males see a high-profile player and think "cash cow(boy)." A place where some low-neckline females see a high-profile player (who looks sexy in his tight, shiny, silver knickers) and think "husband." A place that has an insatiable hunger for its Cowboys, who are young and handsome and rich and sometimes a little gullible.

It is a place where, says one Cowboy, "The women line up like whores, actually waiting their turns in line. If one steps out of line for a minute, she loses her place and has to start all over."

This place probably caused Mike Saxon his marriage.

"Sheri couldn't take the celebrity lifestyle, and I can't say I really blame her," says the punter of the split from the woman he'd been with for ten years and been married to for three. "We walk into a restaurant in Dallas, and people are staring at us like we got a booger hanging out of our noses, or something. I still love her. I think she still loves me. We have a little girl (Erika) who means the world to us. I can see us someday, after my career is over and I'm in a less noticeable job, getting married again. But she doesn't want to be married now.

"Sheri has a lot of suspicions about what a pro football player is doing when he's out on the town, or away from his family. If you make a whole list of all the temptations that are out there for a football player, and make a whole list of the reasons why we filed for a divorce, the items on the list are pretty much the same."

Receiver Michael Irvin acknowledges his word-on-the-street reputation as a "player" — someone who feasts on nightlife. And he does come with all the trimmings and affectations, including a black Mercedes convertible, a closet full of silk shirts, gaudy gold jewelry and the perfectly-timed rap of a man looking for something exciting to do.

"I'm not a player," Irvin says. "I think it all has something to do with the Cowboys mystique. The fans? They come up to you and explain about how it was back in '69 when they played football, and how back in '29 when they were born their mamas wrapped their little newborn bodies up in Cowboys blankets.

Of all the people in all the cities in the world, no one treats their football team like our people treat us. Especially when they get two or three drinks in them.

"And the women? I know what Saxon is talking about, because I think my wife (Sandy) has it tough. But hey, I've got it tough, too. With all the women out there, it takes a good man to be faithful. And I'm a good man."

It is at clubs such as New York, New York, or Lexington, or Detour on Greenville Avenue, where the morals of these good men are subjected to blindside hits. Irvin was at Detour one night when a leak in the roof poured a steady sprinkle of water onto the dance floor. He unbuttoned his shirt, letting the rainwater spill onto his chest.

Women dumped their dance partners and came to Irvin's aid. They desired to help him dry off. One might say they used their bodies as squeegies.

A Cowboy doesn't have to be a cover boy to be a sexual magnet. In the spring of 1991, fourth-string tight end Steve Folsom — whose pasty skin and bald head make his attractiveness a matter of taste — opened a letter from a woman he'd never met who pledged to him her everlasting lust. Because he had a girlfriend, Folsom never considered calling the woman. Because of the frightening eroticism of the perfumed note, he did consider calling the police. "Hey, I've seen 'Fatal Attraction,'" Folsom said.

Says receiver Alvin Harper: "A lot of stuff comes your way because of who you are and what you do. When you go out, girls come up to you, and they only want to talk to you because you play ball. You've got to remind yourself that if you didn't play, if you didn't drive a nice car and make a lot of money, they wouldn't want to deal with you."

They all want to deal with Emmitt Smith, of course. "Oh yeah," Smith says. "People automatically assume I have an endless amount of money, and that I should spend it on them. And you know that being in the limelight and having some dollars is probably helping a lot of people find you more physically attractive."

Find your way into one of the right clubs and you'll realize that Smith is the closest thing Dallas has to a rock star. If you go to Detour as a part of Smith's entourage, you are advised to wear clothing you don't care much about. The problem is that women, in their manic efforts to "deal with" Emmitt, might mistakenly tear off a piece of your shirt instead of a piece of his, as they intended. "They want to touch you and slap you and hit you, and they hit you on your shoulders when your shoulders are hurting," Smith says.

Smith joins quarterback Troy Aikman as the Cowboys who have vaulted toward that no-turning-back station in their careers when their fame transcends their sport. Both are featured on Metroplex billboards, Aikman mugging for Kroger Foods, Smith for Starter athletic wear. The Starter ads don't bother explaining who Emmitt Smith is, or what he does. The Kroger ads don't even bother mentioning the name "Aikman." In Dallas, "Troy" says it all.

All Aikman and Smith have to do is to set one foot out of their front doors before the community commences to rolling out red carpets to meet their feet. The tearing of clothing, the pounding on car windows and the interrupting of dinners grow tiresome. Both have curtailed their carousing. Aikman now generally frequents dance clubs or restaurants where he's known by the regulars and therefore harassed less often. And his once-a-week housekeeper now cooks some dinners for him so he doesn't have to go out at all. Smith is considering following the lead of Irvin, who takes his wife to dinner at the Palm near midnight, after the restaurant is closed to the public.

"If you're one of the big spokes in the wheel, the demands can get ugly," Irvin says. "I can be sitting in a restaurant with fifty other players, and I'm the one the people come up to if they want to blame someone for a Cowboys loss."

At some nightclubs, management lets Smith and Irvin sit behind the glass walls of the DJ booth to escape the women literally climbing over one another to get closer to them. "I don't ask the clubs for special treatment, but I'll take it," Smith says. Teammates say they admire the often brusque way in which Smith deals with unwelcome demands. "Emmitt just tells people, 'Back up, leave me alone, because I'm not here to talk football and sign autographs,'" Harper says.

Gant says most players "don't want to be rude to people who, for instance, ask for an autograph while you're eating dinner, because you'll get the reputation of a bad person around the city. Why they don't wait until you're done eating, I don't know. But most of us go ahead and give them what they want, and we keep our composure.

"Now Emmitt, he doesn't have that much tolerance for people who put on that bum rush. I will never fault Emmitt for the actions he takes. People actually just try to touch him. And he can be cruel to people who do that."

Says Smith: "The worst part is that everyone hits and pulls you from different angles. Everyone wants something. 'Do this.' 'Help that.' You don't get the opportunity to enjoy all that's happening to you like a regular person might. You can't go to a party and be regular. I go to a party, and it's talking football seven days a week. Try to eat a meal, go to a movie, go bowling, go to a nightclub, all anyone wants to talk about is football. Football, football, football. Off-season and in-season: football, football, football."

But that is Texas. Football, football, football. That is why no fewer than ten members of the 1992 Cowboys organization had regular television or radio gigs. Michael Irvin had his weekly TV show. Guard Nate Newton made a weekly TV appearance and worked as an analyst for radio broadcasts of high-school football games. Tight end Jay Novacek, quarterbacks Aikman and Steve Beuerlein, Emmitt Smith, defensive tackle Tony Casillas and center Mark Stepnoski all did weekly radio segments. Owner Jerry Jones and coach Jimmy Johnson each had their own TV shows, radio shows and newspaper columns.

"Our guys have a lot of things swirling around them in Dallas," Johnson says. "Everyone wants a piece of them."

Irvin says he cannot imagine a more enjoyable life for a man who is single and smart. Tight end Alfredo Roberts says "feeling loved," as the Cowboys do even when they are mobbed in the lobbies of road hotels, "is vastly different than it was in Kansas City. The Cowboys go to a road game, the lobby is full of cheering fans. When we (the Chiefs) came to town, all that was waiting for us was the rats and the roaches."

Still, the Cowboys are surrounded by the human rats and roaches and barnacles, some with sucking power that makes them truly dangerous. Says Daryl Johnston: "You've got to find a way to be able to separate the regular people from the leeches."

Safety Darren Woodson, a rookie in 1992, wisely did just that. He says he relied on defensive end Jim Jeffcoat and safety Robert Williams to guide him. "They let me in on everything from who to hang out with to which malls to shop at," Woodson says.

There is the businessman whose unofficial affiliation with the team ended in 1992 because of his sudden disappearance. He is said to be hiding somewhere in South America now, having escaped the FBI's pursuit of him on drug-smuggling charges. There are gamblers who bill themselves as "sales representatives" and con artists who bill themselves as "financial advisors." The organization is unable to police everything and everyone (in mid-January, when Super Bowl tickets were made available to players, the Valley Ranch parking lot was crawling with scalpers whose pockets were full of $100 bills). But it tries, right down to denying dressing-room access to a persistent-but-innocuous jewelry salesman named Ron Traxler.

"Look in the players' mailboxes, you'll see them full of letters promising get-rich-quick deals and investment opportunities," Irvin says. "Look in the parking lot. You see the car dealers going right after the young guys making $78,000 a year. And a few days later that guy making $78,000 a year has bought a $78,000 car. Now, that ain't too bright, hoss."

Says Harper: "You'll get yourself in trouble out there if you don't think before you leap. Because there is a lot of trouble out there, and you'll be leaping into a big ocean."

It was on June 16, 1992, when Emmitt Smith first articulated his desire to cannonball into the biggest statistical ocean pro football can offer: a 2,000-yard season. "That's my goal," he said in a newspaper interview. "To reach 2,000 I'm going to have to take advantage of every opportunity I get, so hopefully there will be some games when I get 30 or 35 carries."

Then Smith, who in 1992 was to finish up a contract by being paid a relative-bargain rate of $465,000, steered the conversation toward other large, round numbers. "That (number of carries) will be great as long as (management) respects it and remembers it when it comes time to renegotiate. For two years I've done everything they've asked and more, and I want it to pay off at contract time. I don't want them to say, 'Well, he's this or that.' They don't get any griping from me, and I don't expect any from them when the time comes."

There would be plenty of griping, both ways, in the ensuing months. In November, after reading a story in which Smith said he wanted to be paid "Barry Sanders money" because of his conviction that he is as talented as the Detroit Lions star, management came up with "Sanders money." They proposed a three-year, $5.76 million deal (identical in value to Sanders') that would increase Smith's 1992 wages by $1.055 million. Smith and his agents, Richard Howell and Pat Dye, decided to turn down that offer. As the weeks passed — and as Smith continued to put statistical distance between himself and Sanders and the rest of the pack — Smith talked of guaranteed money and escalator clauses. He announced his desire to make "Emmitt money," to "set new standards."

"By far, I should be the highest paid back in the NFL," Smith said. "I think I deserve something special. Something that will set me apart from everybody else. ... I definitely proved myself to the Cowboys and also to the world."

"Proving himself to the world" is part of what makes Emmitt run. He is a creative runner, but when it comes to self-motivation, he is an even more creative thinker. He talks often about the satisfaction he gets from "proving the critics wrong," from "showing I belong when nobody thought I did," from "overcoming all the obstacles people set up for me." In reality, of course, Smith doesn't have many critics, has always belonged and erects his own obstacles.

"Emmitt likes to challenge himself," Aikman says. "He's so good at what he does that some people might find it easy for themselves to quit pushing, but he never quits pushing. You see that when he runs. Sometimes during games, I don't go through with my fakes as completely as I should because I'm so amazed at watching what he does. I'm behind him, so I have a vantage point to where I can see where a hole might develop. He's right in the middle of a pile of people, but somehow he can sense the same hole. We're the only two people on the planet at that moment who get to see it from that vantage point. And because it's Emmitt, I don't want to miss seeing it."

In 1992, Smith fell short of the 2,000-yard standard previously achieved by only Eric Dickerson (2,105 yards with the Los Angeles Rams in 1984) and O.J. Simpson (2,003 with the Buffalo Bills in 1973). But by voicing such a lofty ambition, Smith — who isn't always careful to measure the impact of his words — created a focal point for himself and those who serve as his guardians.

"As soon as I read that, I knew I wasn't going to get 20 carries for the whole season," jokes Johnston, who in fact managed just 17, while Smith totalled 373 regular-season carries for 1,713 yards. "It didn't strike me as selfish. Once you've done what he'd done at the time, winning a rushing title and going to two Pro Bowls, it makes sense to raise your goals a little higher than they were before."

Smith couldn't have achieved what he did without tackles Mark Tuinei and Erik Williams, guards John Gesek and Nate Newton and center Mark Stepnoski, all of whom match "Moose" Johnston in their acceptance of subordinate roles. "I've never been a guy with a big ego," says Johnston, who, fittingly, once had a summer job hauling toxic waste. "Maybe it's because I've never accomplished anything worth having a big ego about."

Before lead-blocking for a two-time rushing champion, Johnston's most publicized claim to fame was his dashing appearance. In 1991, he drew a bid of $5,200 for Cystic Fibrosis in a celebrity date auction. Johnston attracted a higher bid than heartthrob singers Michael Bolton and Clint Black. "It's a bad market," chided Stepnoski. "I could've beaten Daryl wearing a potato sack."

Stepnoski is the team pessimist, the sort of guy who wins the lottery then bitches about the taxes he'll have to pay.

"People think I'm a cynic," he says, "but I'm actually a realist." Williams is, as Aikman puts it, "part Baby Huey and part monster." Newton, a low-fat, sags-to-riches success story, alternates between his playful class-clown mode and his wisened guru-on-the-mountain-in-Tibet mode. Tuinei is the most quietly funny of the bunch, a wistful artist who fills the margins in his playbook with caricatures of teammates. Gesek is an overstuffed Everyman, a regular Joe in an irregular business whose psyche best typifies what happens at this position where humility is beaten into you for three hours every Sunday afternoon.

Tuinei wins respect for his decade-long presence as an NFL battler. Williams is considered an emerging dominator. Stepnoski and Newton capped 1992 by being selected first-time Pro Bowlers. Gesek graded out as well as any of the Dallas blockers. But his mindset seemed to leave him unwilling to accept his arrival as a top-line front-liner.

"They're going to trade me," he moaned to friends on August 23, when Jimmy Johnson's tinkering with the offensive line left unclear his future as the starting right guard. Williams had been elevated to first-team right tackle. That moved Newton to a guard, putting the status of either Kevin Gogan or Gesek in jeopardy. "It's a trade. I know it. I've had this feeling before."

The Los Angeles Raiders thought of Gesek as a journeyman. He had played at Cal-State Sacramento. He had been just a tenth-round pick. On September 3, 1990, when the Raiders decided he might not be good enough to help them and shipped him to Dallas for a fifth-rounder — confirming one of Gesek's "feelings" — his modest football resume allowed him to be hurt by the trade. The same background allowed him to wrongly suspect that he, and not Gogan (who became a valuable reserve) would be the odd-man out.

"It's been a constant struggle for John to prove himself," says his wife, Gina. "Because of his background, he feels he's had to double-prove himself. He doesn't visualize himself as a Pro Bowl-type player."

In 1992, all the six-foot-five, 280-pound Gesek needed to do was watch himself on film. He had progressed from a "grabber" (the blocking style taught in L.A.) to a "puncher" (the Cowboys' preferred technique). He had progressed from a worrier to a warrior. "In the past, I let things get to me," Gesek says. "Especially since I've never been one of their boys here."

A persecution complex? In past years, Gesek had his wife tape-record every televised game. Upon returning home, Gesek couldn't sleep until he'd reviewed the tape. Now, "He doesn't carry around the baggage week after week. He was confident he'd done the best he could," says Gina, who didn't tape games in 1992.

The Cowboys' confidence wasn't shaken by that November 15 loss to the Rams. But their arrogance was. At 8-2, Dallas approached its November 22 visit to Phoenix as a chance for redemption. "The Rams game was a turning point," Harper says. "All during the regular season, we never had a real high and we rarely had a real low. We almost always played well enough to win. The only game that I think people looked back and said, 'We lost to a team that shouldn't have beaten us' was the Rams. And because of that, people really started taking their jobs seriously. We started having our best practices. There was a lot less giggling and laughing. People locked down."

The Cowboys needed each of their available components to handle the Cardinals — in part because the running of Smith and the receiving of Irvin were controlled; in part because Charles Haley was unavailable. Haley did not make the trip to Phoenix, opting instead to remain home and prop his sore hamstring up on the ottoman. "People wondered if we should even show up without Charles," said replacement defensive end Jim Jeffcoat, who had two sacks. "I showed up."

So did Harper and tight end Jay Novacek. Harper caught five passes for 88 yards and on a third-down toss from Aikman late in the third quarter, ran 37 yards for the touchdown that gave Dallas the 16-10 victory. Novacek, facing the club that had cut him loose via Plan B three years before, was a critical factor. He'd struggled with drops and had caught just one touchdown pass before the Phoenix game. But he caught five for 50 yards and scored against his old club to ignite a late-season stretch of five games during which he contributed 25 receptions and five touchdowns.

"Jay was never in a slump," Aikman says. "He had a finger injury that people said affected him for a time. But he's one of the most reliable players in football at any position. Look at what he's done for us since he's been here. The only reason he drew any criticism was that he'd set such high expectations. He's the best tight end in football."

Novacek finished 1992 with 68 receptions, the NFL high at the position. He caught 59 passes in each of the previous two seasons since being signed by Dallas on March 5, 1990. Novacek was one of sixteen Plan B players the Cowboys signed that year, the jewel in a somewhat motley crew handed $830,000 in signing bonuses. "We took the fishing-net approach," Jones says, "and hoped there was a keeper in there."

Novacek, the one Dallas player who most closely resembles a Cowboy in real life, was the keeper. Novacek has a passion for riding cutting horses, a comfort in wearing Western apparel and a knack for handling himself like Gary Cooper in "High Noon." He kept very quiet about everything, from his experi- mentation with wearing gloves to his broken knuckle to his visualization work with trainer Mack Newton. He admits to giving humdrum answers to reporters in the hope they'll be discouraged and quit asking. (He can be as reluctant an interview subject as the eccentric Charles Haley. But where Haley strives to be a boor, Novacek strives only to be a bore.)

Novacek thinks his shyness is a result of his small-town upbringing (he played high school football in Gothenburg, Nebraska, college ball at Wyoming and met his wife Yvette at a Nebraska street dance) and his frequent changes of address during childhood. "I had trouble opening up to people I didn't know very well because we moved so often," he says. "But I don't regret it in any way. Now, I just don't feel the need to open up."

Says Aikman: "If I had a son grow up to be just like Jay, I'd be the proudest father in the world."

Like ex-Cardinal Novacek, former Arizona State star Jeffcoat played at Tempe Stadium as if he had something to prove to the home folks. But all of the Cowboys defenders performed with the knowledge that Haley was home in front of his TV set. "We're not a one-man team," said Jeffcoat in a defiant tone. "We can play just as well with Charles as without him," added safety James Washington.

Dallas allowed 149 total yards. The two Phoenix scores capped measly drives of 13 and 33 yards. Quarterback Chris Chandler was forced from the game when massive Leon Lett piled atop a Jeffcoat sack and crushed a vital organ or two. "I wanted to ask him what was wrong," said Lett, worried when he heard Chandler wheezing beneath him. "But he couldn't answer. I guess he was out of breath."

By the time coordinator Dave Wannstedt's top-ranked defense lined up against the New York Giants four days later, it was good enough to be accused of "kicking a dog when it's down." That was the allegation issued by New York defensive end Leonard Marshall at Dallas after its 30-3 drubbing of the Giants on Thanksgiving Day at Texas Stadium.

After the victory, which pushed the Cowboys to 10-2, Giants coach Ray Handley refused to shake hands with Johnson, who said later, "I was really shocked. ... when I heard some of the comments. Maybe with the Giants, it's a little bit of frustration on their part. They've had a disappointing season (Handley would be fired after New York's 6-10 finish). ... It seems to me we were up 34-0 (in the teams' September 13 meeting, a cuticle-nibbling 34-28 Dallas win), and they did score 28 points on us. ... We emptied the bench. I don't understand the controversy. We didn't do anything wrong."

Dallas did most everything right in what became a lopsided win. Emmitt Smith touchdowns from 26 and 68 yards out (the latter score following blocking on which linemen Erik Williams and John Gesek seemed to be textbook pages jumped to life) were killers. Three Lin Elliott field goals also helped. And one make from 53 yards helped Elliott's confidence. The Dallas native and undrafted rookie from Texas Tech was shocked when he heard the field-goal team ordered onto the field with 2:22 left in the first half and Dallas at the Giants' 35-yard line. "But coach, that's a 53-yarder!" Elliott told Johnson in protest. "I know," Johnson replied. "So go power the son of a bitch."

What did the Cowboys do wrong? In the Giants' view, they were attempting to pad their defensive ranking, trying to punish the Giants for past crimes committed against lousy editions of Cowboys teams, and trying to show off for CBS-TV broadcaster John Madden and his national TV audience.

The Giants objected to Aikman's fourth-down, fourth-quarter pass completion while Dallas was ahead, 23-9. They objected to Aikman's third-and-three pass from the New York four-yard line caught by Harper for another touchdown with 6:04 remaining. They objected to what they viewed as relentless blitzing from the Cowboys defense, even with 1:55 left in the game and fourth-string rookie quarterback Dave Brown taking the snaps.

"Screw 'em," Wannstedt said to his assistants when the subject was discussed the next morning. "Everybody jumped my ass the last time we played the Giants because we were in a so-called prevent. Now I pressure them, and I'm a jerk. Tell the other team to quit trying to play offense, and we might quit trying to play defense."

The Cowboys' defensive "tip sheet" was covered with 7's.

"With John Elway in there, it makes all the difference in the world," said Wannstedt, preparing his defense for a December 6 game at Denver against Elway and the Broncos. "He's got mobility, arm strength and experience. You try a lot of things against him, but he's seen them all. It's difficult to trick him. But it could be a different story if he's not in there."

The Broncos quarterback, No. 7, was hoping to play despite an injury to his right shoulder. And the Cowboys worked all week on the assumption he would play. "That's always going to be the case," Johnson says. "It's easier to prepare for an Elway then face a lesser quarterback than it is to prepare for a lesser quarterback and end up having to stop Elway."

That's why, even on the Saturday night before the game at Mile High Stadium, the Cowboys defenders were studying their tip sheet. "#7 does a good job altering cadence," the tip sheet read. "#7 will run QB draws." "#7 can scramble and still force you to defend the whole field."

Would Elway sit while youngsters Shawn Moore and Tommy Maddox rotated in and out of the game, as was being considered by Denver coach Dan Reeves? Ironically, Maddox wouldn't have even been in the league yet had it been up to Troy Aikman. After Maddox finished his 1991 season as a sophomore at UCLA, Maddox phoned ex-Bruin Aikman for some advice on whether he should turn pro. Aikman, predicting correctly that Maddox wasn't physically ready to be better than a late-first-round pick, strongly advised him to remain in school. Maddox, who would be the twenty-fifth pick in the first round and join the fired Reeves as a scapegoat in Denver's 8-8 season, hung up on Aikman.

Safety James Washington noted the Dallas defense's statistical excellence — a league-low 238.8 yards per game, a league-low 25.2-percent third-down conversion rate, no fourth-quarter points allowed in eight straight games — and said, "I don't care who we line up against. We're the No. 1 defense. They can put Buckwheat and Alfalfa in there, and we're not going to change what we do."

Buckwheat and Alfalfa, no. Shawn and Tommy, yes. Reeves did in fact play tag-team quarterbacks. And they were effective enough, heading toward 354 total yards, to put the Broncos in position to win. Reeves relied on a barrel of gimmicks, including a double-pass from rookie Maddox to rookie Arthur Marshall to rookie Cedric Tillman that resulted in an 81-yard touchdown completion that gave the Broncos a 27-24 lead with 9:04 remaining. "They couldn't beat us traditionally," says rookie cornerback Kevin Smith. "So they played trick-'em dick-'em."

Adding to the Cowboys' challenge was the aura of frosty Mile High Stadium, where orange parkas for the 76,000 sufferers of Bronc-itis are both fashionable and necessary. Denver was 6-0 at home, had won sixteen of its last seventeen at Mile High and, at 93-29, owned the NFL's top all-time home record. "Denver has snow, the altitude and those fans screaming their brains out," Gesek says.

But the 10-2 Cowboys had an implied directive from Johnson to feed off the frenzy of road crowds, to react to sensing spittle on the backs of their necks by spitting back, to be the nasty houseguests who wipe their hands on the good towels. That's how Johnson and his hip-hop renegades at the University of Miami did it, explains defensive tackle Russell Maryland. "The more (road crowds) yelled at us, spit on us and poured beer on us, the more we loved it," he says. "There's nothing like going into a team's backyard and leaving it with a win. It's an attitude we're developing here."

Says safety Kenny Gant: "It gives you a chill up your spine to hear that many people yelling for you to do bad. It's also great motivation. When you win, you just want to point out each and every one of them and say, 'I told you so.'

"A road game ... is fun and games."

But the situation facing the Cowboys in that final 9:04 took 6:18 to be fun and to win the game.

The Cowboys started at their own 23-yard line. "All of us couldn't help but flash back to that Rams game," admits guard Nate Newton, referring to a November 15 loss in which Dallas failed to forge a comeback drive in a similar circumstance. The Cowboys were lined up against a defense littered with Pro Bowl types: safeties Dennis Smith and Steve Atwater; linebackers Simon Fletcher, Karl Mecklenberg and Michael Brooks; and nose tackle Greg Kragen. And they stared through their visible breath and into that aura, that orange avalanche.

"You don't want to let yourself be intimidated, even when things start going wrong," Aikman says. "I personally had regrets about not being able to help us win the Rams game, but this was a whole different deal. The Rams didn't go through my mind. And the 'aura' of the Broncos really didn't, either. You try to block that stuff out. You fight through it. You build up an immunity against it."

The drive was Aikman at his methodical finest. This was the Henryetta Water Torture, a slow death. A six-yard toss to

Daryl Johnston on first down. A run for no gain by Emmitt Smith. A third-down pass to Jay Novacek for 11 yards. A 22-yard completion to Novacek on the next play, then a 17-yarder to the tight end on the next play. A sack by Fletcher, and a loose ball recovered by Aikman. A second-and-14 situation from the Broncos' 25, and an incompletion. Third and 14. Aikman finds a sprawling Michael Irvin for exactly 14 yards, to the Broncos' 11. A first-down pass to Johnston for five yards. A three-yard run by Smith, who takes it to the Denver two. A time-out.

"Norv talked about a couple of pass plays," Aikman says. "But he had seen on film that some teams had had success running draws in close to the goal line against Denver. He decided to go with a draw."

But before Stepnoski snapped the ball, Aikman convincingly bluffed the pass. In conjunction with the three-receiver alignment that suggested the Cowboys would throw on third-and-goal from the two, there was Aikman, theatrically waving his arms at receivers, pointing them into position, yelling last-second instructions at them. The Broncos' down-linemen dug in to rush the passer. The Broncos' defensive backs leaned toward their heels in anticipation of their backpedals. "They were yelling, 'Watch the pass, watch the pass,'" Irvin says.

Aikman took Stepnoski's snap, hesitated, and handed to Smith, who pranced untouched into the end zone. Cowboys 31, Broncos 27. Dallas was in the play-offs. Aikman — who'd been informed before the game by broadcaster Dale Hansen of a *Denver Post* article written by ex-Broncos receiver Steve Watson that misguidedly stated, "If there is a weakness in the Cowboys' offense, it's at quarterback" — was in "the zone." Aikman was seven-of-eight for 78 yards on the drive, 25-of-35 for 231 yards on the day and, for the season, was 251-of-397 for 2,883 yards, all NFC highs.

"Everyone had seen the other guy, Elway, do that so many times, they assume he's the only guy who can do it," Irvin says. "That game put Troy over the top. That game showed that he can work miracles as well as anyone there is. You let him play as long as Elway, he'll have had enough opportunities to pull off as many miracles. You let him play as long as Staubach and Montana and Bradshaw, he'll do what any of them did. He will be 'The Savior' in huge games lots of times. Denver was just the first time."

Says Aikman: "The way we won that game gave us a lot of confidence in ourselves. But deep down, there was also some frustration, because winning that game really shouldn't have been that hard. I truly believe my critics didn't accept that Denver game as proof that I could get the job done. I think anyone who didn't think I was a quality quarterback still believed it. Anyone who thought I was a quality quarterback before that game maybe believed it a little more afterwards."

Sandra Kline believed. She and her son, Aikman buddy Doug Kline, were seated in the seventh row of the Mile High stands. On Saturday, Doug had asked Aikman to give a football to Sandra. Aikman tried to comply twice. In the third quarter, after his third touchdown pass of the game, Aikman took the ball from Novacek and tossed it toward the Klines.

"People were diving everywhere for it," says Doug Kline, who played with Aikman at UCLA, but whose football talents didn't help him wrestle the prize from other souvenir hunters.

Aikman and the Klines got another chance. The quarterback was near mid-field when he knelt to take the final snap of the game. When the clock struck 0:00, Aikman wheeled and heaved the ball toward the seventh row again.

The ball landed seventy yards from where Aikman released it, and two feet in front of the Klines. Doug Kline and another man found themselves at the bottom of another pileup.

"I've got the ball," the man yelled.

"No, I've got the ball," Kline yelled back.

Responded the man: "The hell you do! You've got my head!"

Doug Kline dusted himself off and explained to the man that Aikman's bomb had been intended for Mrs. Kline. He politely handed the pigskin to Sandra Kline, who eyed Aikman seventy yards away and said, "Now I know why he's a million-dollar quarterback."

11 FIRST-CLASS TURBULENCE ★

The Dallas Cowboys' December 13 team flight was scheduled to leave Washington National Airport and fly nonstop to D/FW Airport. But Jimmy Johnson hijacked his own American Airlines charter. And he forced it to make an unscheduled landing in Hell.

"Egotistically, I'll always like to think I stayed in control," says Johnson sheepishly, "even though that night it may not have looked that way."

The single most tempestuous incident in new-regime history, the one moment that could have boiled over into a divisive, ruinous, cancerous catastrophe, would have never happened had Johnson simply kept his headphones on.

"I was in my seat on the plane, watching the replay of the game, like I normally do," says Johnson, a frown crossing his moon face at the thought of that afternoon's bizarre 20-17 loss to the Redskins. "I get immersed in watching, and in listening with the headphones on. I'm kind of not aware of what all is happening around me. But then, the game was over with. I took my headphones off."

Johnson left his customary Row 1 seat in first-class and threw open the aisle-way curtain. Guard Nate Newton says, "I tried to warn everybody. I told them, 'He's in the aisle and he's comin' our way.'" But Johnson came in too fast and too forcefully, like a headwind. It was time for the Cowboys to fasten their seatbelts and place their heads between their knees.

A man called Turbulence was about to enter coach-class.

Johnson saw offensive coordinator Norv Turner standing in the aisle. He saw two rookies, middle linebacker Robert Jones and reserve cornerback Clayton Holmes, out of their seats in order to allow teammates to play cards.

"Sit your asses down!" Johnson barked.

Says Johnson: "I don't know who was in the aisle. But whoever it was, I didn't want them there. I obviously didn't have a very pleasant look on my face. Anyway, for some reason, I then decided to head to the back of plane."

Johnson made his way, bracing himself on the headrests, then paused and looked sharply toward a window seat.

"Jesus, I thought he was staring at me," says Larry Lacewell, the team's director of college scouting. "Understand, I've known this man for decades. He was the best man at my wedding, for Christ's sake. But I saw what was in his eyes. I've seen it a few times before. I didn't know what the hell I'd done wrong. Then I realized he wasn't looking at me. I thanked God he was looking at the seat behind me."

Johnson had detected an unwelcome smile. Who the hell could be smiling after losing a game like that? he thought. We just pissed away a chance to defeat the defending Super Bowl champions on their own turf. We had a chance to do it on national TV, in a game that edged toward prime time where the world would see it, against Washington's Joe Gibbs, the coaching peer I most respect, in a game that could have given us the NFC East title!

"Frank Cornish was smiling about something," says Johnson, who ordered the backup offensive lineman to dump the grin and assume a more appropriate mood. Johnson continued down the aisle. Cornish rose from his seat, wishing to explain himself.

"Frank," urged trainer Kevin O'Neill, "leave it be. Don't mess with The Man."

Cornish ignored the advice and followed Johnson down the center of the plane.

"I wasn't smiling at anything!" Cornish said, pleading for justice.

Johnson had no intention of debating the subject. "I didn't want to stand there in the middle of the plane and have a long discussion," Johnson says. "So I told him, 'Get away from me! You go sit your ass down, too.'"

Cowboys charter flights after road trips in 1992 were usually festive. Part of that can be credited to the team's 8-2 record (including postseason games) away from home. But part of it is "The 24-Hour Rule," a mantra that indicates Johnson's willingness to let his players pop their celebratory corks until the following day, when preparation for the next week's game begins.

"On the way up to a road game, it's a business trip," Emmitt Smith says. "There's no clowning around. We're wearing suits and ties. We're studying and talking quietly. On the way back, if we win, we loosen up and let our hair down."

Newton, usually the toastmaster on such return flights, says, "Coach Johnson made it clear to us when he first came here that if we win, the plane is ours. I mean, as long as we win, and we don't hurt anybody or break any laws, we can tear the mother down. We can do anything except get buck-naked."

There was none of that on this flight. Some blackjack, some story-telling, maybe an involuntary smile or two. None of what

Johnson calls "cuttin' up." Still, the coach was unconvinced that his team was suffering as he was. To him, this defeat ranked with losing the national championship in 1986 at the University of Miami, when a club he "honestly felt was the best college football that ever played the game" was downed by Penn State in the Fiesta Bowl. And now this, a loss to the Redskins that tormented him to the point that he couldn't stand for more than a terse ninety-second postmortem press conference back at RFK Stadium.

Even thirteen hours after the plane ride, when he addressed his team, he was still crushed. "This is by far the hardest loss we've had here," Johnson told them. "To me, this was as big a game as a play-off game. We let it slip through our fingers, and we can't get it back."

Even on Tuesday, he hadn't recovered. In a riveting, emotional speech that was clearly cathartic for him and bordered on being an apology, Johnson expressed why he was still grieving forty-eight hours after the result of a silly game of football had been determined.

Said Johnson: "We're starting to be good here. When you give your heart and soul to something that you're striving for, and you lose it, it hurts. Anybody who has been around me understands that I have a difficult time losing something I have my heart set on. It's not that I have difficulty losing. I golf in the summer, lose all the time and it doesn't bother me a bit. I pay my (bet) and go on.

"Some people approach everything with a forty-hour work week effort. 'Give me my check, I'll do my job.' I don't approach coaching the Cowboys that way. If I ever get to the point that I do approach coaching the Cowboys in that manner, I shouldn't be coaching the Cowboys. ... I don't want players on our football team that it doesn't hurt them to lose. If they don't get that sick feeling when they come up short, then the next time, it'll be, 'So what?' Then you'll put a token effort into it and be like a lot of other folks. And I don't want to be like a lot of other folks."

As Johnson spun around in the aisle and balanced himself back toward first-class, his mind raced. The end-zone debacle. The Aikman-Smith fumble, or sack, or incompletion, or whatever the hell it was. All he had to do was remind himself of that grotesque double-fumble, and he found himself tensely smacking his lips in anger.

Dallas, which had lost an NFL-low three fumbles all year long, suffered four mishandled footballs on three consecutive possessions in one heinous nine-minute, sixteen-second span of the final period in Washington. Three fumbles occurred within 159 seconds. Two were burped up on one single play that twisted what had been a four-point Cowboys' lead with three minutes remaining into a devastating 20-17 loss.

On second-and-seven from their own five-yard line, Norv Turner called what he describes as "a safe play," a quick-strike option pass from Aikman to either Alvin Harper, Jay Novacek or Daryl Johnston. As Aikman backpedaled, Redskins defensive lineman Jason Buck bull-rushed center Mark Stepnoski and caused a pass-pocket pileup (Stepnoski's stubbornness was more to blame than his blocking; he was in the game when he should've been visiting with doctors who later found he'd sustained a hip pointer minutes earlier). Buck, Stepnoski and Aikman became entangled near the goal line. The ball came loose. Emmitt Smith fell on top of it, but unwisely opted to not accept what would have been a safety for the Redskins. "I tried to throw it out of there, I think," said Smith, whose underhanded, left-handed pitch kept the odd play alive. "I saw Alfredo (Roberts) and I tried to toss it to him."

The ball was available again. Bodies flew everywhere. The ball became wedged against the red-painted mud of the RFK

Stadium end zone underneath the thigh of Cowboys lineman Erik Williams. Redskins safety Danny Copeland tugged at the ball, cradled it, and — after what seemed like hours of official hand-wringing — was awarded the game-winning touchdown.

Was Aikman's arm going forward when he was hit by Buck, which would have meant the officials should rule the play an incomplete pass? Did Smith really try to throw it forward, in which case his attempt should have been ruled incomplete? Or was Smith touched down while his knee was on the ground, meaning a safety?

An on-site NFL observer judging the work of referee Bob McElwee's crew scribbled exclamation marks and question marks into his grade book, and made a note that in his view, Smith should have been ruled down in the end zone on the play that will top Cowboys-Redskins lore.

Johnson was not pacified later in the week, when the NFL admitted its error. So Johnson certainly hadn't cooled by the time he returned to his first-class seat in Row 1. Instead, he wondered: Are my players letting the nauseating memory of this failure fade too quickly?

"I'm not saying they weren't hurting," Johnson says. "I wasn't mad or disappointed at their effort in the game. I was frustrated, because I felt we should've won the ball game. I guess, however bad they hurt, I wanted them to hurt more. I didn't want the players to accept defeat, to give themselves excuses. I didn't want them to be saying, 'Well, we really won the game but we got screwed out of it.' To me, it didn't make any difference how that game was lost, because the fact is, we came up short. I just didn't want anyone feeling maybe it was acceptable to have lost to the Washington Redskins."

Johnson saw the flight attendants preparing to move through the plane to offer after-dinner drinks and desserts. He leaned forward toward the flight attendants' station and instructed them that there would be no passengers in need of after-dinner drinks or desserts.

"Y'all can sit down, too," he told the women.

Did Johnson lose his cool? Temporarily, yes.

Did he lose some of his players? Temporarily, yes.

Johnson does not pretend to believe the incident had any positive effect. Nor do those closest to him. On Monday, Wannstedt suggested his friend had made a mistake, and persuaded him to phone the head flight attendant to seek her forgiveness. Says Lacewell: "Was it the right thing to do? I don't think so. But as usual, he did things his own damn way."

Says Irvin: "Pipes get enough pressure in them, they bust. Jimmy busted. And for one of the rare times, he was wrong. Dead wrong."

From Newton: "He just lives to win football games. If a man is a bricklayer, and all he wants to do is lay bricks all day, go home, sleep, and then lay bricks again the next day, and this is seven days a week, thirty days a month, 365 days a year, you know where he's coming from. All he wants to do is lay bricks. Well, that's Jimmy. All he wants to do is win football games. So you should know how losing affects him.

"However," Newton says, "he didn't handle it the way the guys wished he would have. I think coach Johnson learned something and the players learned something. It opened some eyes. But it also really hurt some of the young guys."

Says broadcaster Dale Hansen, a passenger on that flight: "Jimmy crossed the line. By the time we landed, players were madder about the flight than they were about losing the game."

All too aware of Johnson's lingering malaise, the players were bothered by his violation of his own "24-Hour Rule" in reverse. Johnson, so concerned with avoiding outside "distractions," had himself become an inside distraction.

Players complained to each other, some in mutinous tones.

"Our concern got to the point where it wasn't losing the game, but Jimmy's reaction," linebacker Ken Norton says. "Losing games, that's going to happen. But Jimmy is what everyone was buzzing about. We got together as a group. It was another growing time for us."

Aikman, Irvin, Norton and other veterans took it upon themselves to counsel teammates, going locker stall to locker stall to spread an unusual message: For the time being, ignore the coach. That's just Jimmy, they said. We don't play this game for the coach. Since when have we told each other, "Let's win one for Jimmy?" We play for ourselves. We play for our families. So don't let Jimmy's mood drag us down. Let him worry about pulling himself up in time for the Atlanta game. We've got to worry about each other.

Says center Mark Stepnoski: "Some of those young guys who got fronted on the plane needed to be told not to get bent out of shape over what Jimmy did. I'll guarantee you, if I was a rookie and got fronted like that, I'd go into the tank. Nobody wanted to see that happen to our younger guys."

In a move privately applauded by Cowboys players in need of a voice, Aikman went public with a sterilized version of the overriding sentiment.

"The longer we sit here crying about losing to Washington, the harder it's going to be to get ready for Atlanta," Aikman said. "I see (Johnson's) pain. I see my pain. I see everybody's pain. It's not fun losing. Fortunately, we're 11-3. I'm not going to let this loss distract from what we can accomplish."

But Dallas, which hadn't won a division title since 1985, was in charge of the NFC East. The Cowboys held a two-game lead over the Redskins and Eagles, and needed just one victory or an Eagles loss to clinch the division. On Sunday, December 20, the Cowboys were in their hotel rooms at the Atlanta

Airport Hilton, crossing their fingers while watching the Eagles-Redskins game. When a last-second end-zone pass from Washington's Mark Rypien was slapped away by Philadelphia cornerback Eric Allen to preserve an Eagles victory, there were actually mixed emotions at the Atlanta Hilton.

"That was fine with us," Aikman says. "We believed we deserved to win the NFC East. We had played everybody we had to play and beaten them all. We didn't want people talking like we had backed in, which you know would have been the case had an Eagles' loss clinched it for us. So we were glad they won on Sunday. And we were very confident we were the better team going into Monday."

A glance at the standings, which showed the Atlanta Falcons at 6-8, made that obvious. So did a look at the NFL's stats, which ranked Atlanta twenty-seventh on run offense, twenty-seventh on run defense, and twenty-fourth on pass defense. Still, a late-season Falcons-Cowboys game with play-off implications had become a recent tradition. On December 30, 1990, Babe Laufenberg quarterbacked Dallas to a 26-7 loss at old Fulton-County Stadium that effectively ruined the Cowboys' play-off hopes. On December 22, 1991, at Texas Stadium, a 31-27 Cowboys victory prevented the Falcons from winning the NFC West. Besides, it was Monday Night Football, starring the Falcons' sharp new Georgia Dome, weird Falcons coach Jerry Glanville, spectacular Falcons cornerback/receiver/kick returner Deion Sanders and flashy Falcons Run-and-Shoot offense.

But it was all Cowboys.

Before the game, Johnson promised his players that if they kept the pressure on the erratic Falcons, the home team would eventually fold. He was correct. In a precursor to the sort of success Dallas would have in its "must-win" spots in the postseason, the Cowboys executed almost perfectly on their way to the most dominating win of the regular season. Aikman missed on his first and 15th passes. But he completed all 13 in between on his way to a career-best half: 15-of-17, 196 yards and two touchdowns. He finished the night 18-of-21 for 239 yards and three scores, and his completion percentage (60.34 career) moved him into the top three positions on the NFL's all-time accuracy charts.

Emmitt Smith contributed two 29-yard touchdown runs, and after campaigning to stay in the game late, totalled 174 yards. That left him five yards behind Pittsburgh's Barry Foster in the chase for the league rushing title. Defensively, Dallas stole a fumble on the game's first play. And the Cowboys swiped two more the first two times Atlanta touched the ball in the second half.

But there was no coronation. The Cowboys did not "tear down" the plane, as Nate Newton says they had permission to do after road victories. "We came into the season with three big goals," Aikman says. "Number one was to make the play-offs. Number two was to win the NFC East. Now comes Number three. We want to get into the Super Bowl."

The Cowboys players were buoyed by both the Christmas spirit and the championship spirit. When two buses pulled up to Valley Ranch to take players on a tour of three Metroplex children's hospitals, the buses were jammed with willing spreaders of cheer. When various Cowboys announced plans to host Christmas parties, players excitedly RSVP'ed — and hoped Ebeneezer Johnson wasn't also on the guest list.

"I've made the mistake of letting people get the idea that I don't appreciate Christmas as a religious holiday and that's wrong," Johnson says. "It's a great holiday. It's the commercialization of it that I don't get into."

Johnson's low tolerance for "commercialization" was tested when he permitted girlfriend Rhonda Rookmaaker to put up a decorated tree in his living room — the first time in twenty years the Johnson house has been so adorned. He even let her play hostess for a party for coaches' wives at his home.

"She was excited about it, so I went along with it," Johnson says. "I thought it was a nice idea, to have the party. The only thing that was a negative about it was the tree. I sure wasn't going to help put it up. It had a lot of balls and peppermint sticks and things on it. And then, it would have taken me half the day to take the tree down. But I went along with it all because they all took the tree down, too."

On Christmas Eve, three days before the Cowboys' December 27 regular-season finale against the Chicago Bears, Johnson attended a Christmas party at Norv Turner's house. Johnson greeted one staffer with some cuttingly demeaning words that caused the employee to leave the party less than five minutes after he'd arrived.

"Oh, that was just laughin' and cuttin' up," Johnson says. "I actually thought I was in a pretty good mood that night, considering I really don't like social gatherings like that. Hey, I was in such a good mood, I even gave a present. You know that thing, 'The Wizard' (a crystal ball that makes predictions)? The guy who owns that company sent me some, so I took one over to Norv's and gave it to the kids. At Norv's parties, he always has everybody's kids over. They were lining up to play with it. So no, I thought I was okay that night."

But down deep, was Johnson — "a very bad loser," Jerry Jones says — still haunted by the Ghost of Losses Past?

In the time it took Johnson to leave Turner's party and arrive uninvited at another gathering in another suburban neighborhood, did he come to the realization that his dark side was casting too ominous a shadow over the rest of the Cowboys and their accomplishments? That it was bad enough that one loss two weeks before engulfed and swallowed Johnson without dragging sixty or so more men into the same black hole?

"My door swings open," says tight end Alfredo Roberts, who was hosting a party for about twenty Cowboys at his house, "and Jimmy pops in. The coach crashed my party."

Says Johnson: "A few guys, (Steve) Beuerlein, Kelvin (Martin), Ax (receivers coach Hubbard Alexander) said they were heading over to Alfredo's (Alexander was invited because players were presenting him with a Rolex gold presidential watch). I thought all the players, knowing the way I am about Christmas and parties, would get a big kick out of seeing me there."

The party screeched to a stop. Roberts cringed, knowing what emotional havoc the man was capable of. With one below-the-belt dig, Johnson had just shifted Turner's party into a lower gear; it was safe to assume that Johnson was about to tear through Roberts's Christmas party like a twister ripping through a trailer park.

But players who wanted to drop into hiding behind furniture instead felt their jaws drop. Jimmy Johnson was jovial. He even. ... apologized?

"Well, kind of," Irvin says. "Jimmy apologized in his way. You're not going to get him to stand up in the middle of a room and out-and-out say, 'I'm sorry.' But he admitted he gets very ugly when he's not winning, and that he's not a 'let's-get-them-next-time' guy. He explained how bad losing hurt him, especially the way that Washington game blew up in his face. I think he realized that a team that lost three games all year didn't need to be slapped that hard."

Says Roberts: "I know he'll say it was just an off-the-cuff thing, him coming by. But he came to check the morale of the team. And also, he wanted everyone to know he was alright."

The Cowboys beat the Bears in their regular-season finale, 27-14, crowding the left side of the won-lost ledger with a franchise-record thirteenth victory. But more crowded was the postgame locker room at Texas Stadium. Who were all those people, and why were they acting so important?

No matter how bad the new-regime Cowboys were, they always attracted visiting dignitaries. And no matter how hard they try, the new-regime Cowboys often deal with visiting dignitaries with something less than aplomb. Not that allowing purple-eyed acting legend Elizabeth Taylor to participate in the September 24, 1989, home-opening, pregame coin flip was a bad idea; but when Liz called "heads" on behalf of the Cowboys, it seemed to rile up the Washington Redskins. Hey, visiting teams are supposed to call the flip, reminded the Redskins throughout their 30-7 pounding of Dallas.

It was at the 1989 training camp in Thousand Oaks, California, when the organization's all-thumbs handling of guest celebrities first became a running inside joke.

A tall, stringy-haired man in a motorcycle jacket was spotted on the sidelines of a Cowboys practice that summer. He was inside the ropes, well beyond where spectators are allowed to roam.

"Can I help you?" said offensive coordinator Dave Shula, preparing to run the interloper off.

Says Babe Laufenberg, a quarterback on that team: "We're sitting back, laughing our asses off. 'Shoe' must've been the only guy in the place who didn't recognize the guy. So we all said, 'Aw, let's let "Shoe" hang himself.'"

The stringy-haired biker was actor Gary Busey. "David, I know you're wrapped up in football," Laufenberg told his coach, "but you need to get out a little more often. Go see a movie once in a while, will you?"

Ever since that time, Laufenberg says, "If somebody important showed up at practice, we made sure everyone knows who they are. We didn't want Shula running Bill Clinton out of practice. We made sure to tell him, 'No, no, "Shoe," that's Jerry Jones. He's the owner. Don't chase him off, too.'"

Shula's value to the Cowboys would have reached an all-time peak had he been policing that December 27 locker room. As Johnson points out, "It's funny how athletes look up to movie stars and entertainers, but movie stars and entertainers look up to athletes."

After the Cowboys beat Chicago, they were on a pedestal of sorts. Dallas finished the regular season with a 13-3 record, would rest for two weeks before a divisional play-off game, and was basking in the defense's No. 1 ranking in the league (based on yards allowed per game). The Cowboys allowed Chicago just 92 total yards, 28 rushing yards and nine pass completions while stealing a fumble and three interceptions. Defensive tackle Russell Maryland, a Chicago native, rumbled 26 yards with a loose ball for a touchdown, then mimicked the "Shark" dance popularized by teammate Kenny Gant by naming his end-zone belly flop the "Killer Whale."

The Cowboys joined the 1983 Cincinnati Bengals as the only teams to lead the NFL in defense yet go unrepresented in the Pro Bowl. "We decided to use that as a rallying point," Wannstedt says. "We wanted to make the vote look silly." Dallas did have six of its offensive starters named to the Pro Bowl. Rushing champion Emmitt Smith, who ran for 131 yards against the Bears to reach 1,713 and edge Pittsburgh's Barry Foster by 23 yards, would be joined in Hawaii by tight end Jay Novacek, quarterback Troy Aikman, receiver Michael Irvin, center Mark Stepnoski and guard Nate Newton.

The star power of two entertainment galaxies made for an overflowing locker room. One section of the place looked like a backstage gathering at a "Hee Haw" taping. Country-music singers Brooks & Dunn milled about. So did singer Gary Morris. Musicians Hank Williams, Jr. and the guys from Shenandoah had become locker-room fixtures. Golfer Fred Couples was in there, as was (attention, Dave Shula!) Gary Busey.

Sometimes, these celebrities take a little, then give a little. Aikman says one of the most enjoyable days of his life was January 10, 1993, and not just because that was the day his Cowboys advanced to the NFC Championship Game with a 34-10 victory over the Eagles. That night, singer Hank Williams, Jr., invited Aikman to a private jam session in Williams' suite at the Loews Anatole Hotel in Dallas. (Williams says Aikman knows the words to his songs better than the singer himself does; one of Aikman's locker-room monikers at UCLA was "Bocephus," Williams' nickname.) And Aikman is personally responsible for the presence of members of Shenandoah, who bunk at his house when they're in town.

But after the win over the Bears, most of these luminaries were taking. Taking up space.

Cowboys-Bears served as a valedictory event for Chicago linebacker Mike Singletary, who was retiring; for Bears coach Mike Ditka, who had a feeling he was about to be ousted; and for Dave Wannstedt, who, as fate would have it, would be Ditka's replacement as Chicago's head coach.

But it was also the game that bid adieu to running back Curvin Richards — and, if Johnson gets a vote, to his locker room being taken over by nonfootball people.

In his two years with the club serving as Emmitt Smith's caddie, Richards had always been a sort of team mascot. He was the puppy dog that you tell your parents "Followed me home, so can we keep him?" When Richards scored his first NFL touchdown to give Dallas a 27-0 lead over Chicago, and was met with a warm sideline handshake from his coach, all indications were Johnson intended to keep his puppy dog.

But then Richards engaged in a fourth-quarter shoving match with Bears defensive lineman Chris Zorich, and when he came to the bench this time, Johnson screamed in his face. Richards completed the final quarter of the game by double dribbling two fumbles that contributed greatly to the Bears' comeback attempt.

"There was more than just the fumbles taking place," position coach Joe Brodsky says. "There were times when I wanted to kill Curvin. He danced to a different beat." Richards' study habits were pitiful. He often chose not to take notes in meetings. Before the Bears game, the running backs were given an optional pop quiz. Curvin opted out.

The examples of the carefree Richards's irresponsibilities are many. It might have been funny when as a rookie in 1991 he refused to shower, fearing he'd wash away his strength. It wasn't funny when he missed the team flight to Cleveland for the September 1, 1991, season opener. It wasn't funny on July 25, 1992, when the buses pulled away from team headquarters at St. Edward's University for a scrimmage in San Antonio, and Richards wasn't aboard (fullback Tommie Agee compassionately persuaded the driver to wait while he located his teammate). It wasn't funny on September 1, 1992, when Richards was supposed to be at the Grand Kempinski Hotel in Addison for the Kickoff Luncheon, but was the only one of the forty-seven team members who didn't make it. Richards had planned to hitch a ride with injured teammate Ricky Blake; Blake, not a part of the forty-seven-man roster, wasn't going to the Luncheon.

After the debacle against Chicago, Johnson huddled with assistants into the night in a Texas Stadium luxury box, weighing the possible effects of canning Richards on the spot. The next day, Johnson announced his decision to release the running back.

"It just got to the point where the concerns built up and I said, 'I've had enough.' I want players I can count on for the play-offs," Johnson said.

Johnson closed his Monday press conference with a cryptic, unprompted remark.

"I had two matters I wanted to take care of," Johnson said. "Curvin was one. The other. ... Well, I shouldn't have even brought it up."

It turns out Johnson's other "matter" was the suffocating presence in the postgame locker room of Prince Bandar of Saudi Arabia's entourage. The Prince is another of the millions who describe themselves as "World's Biggest Cowboys Fan." (He is indisputably the "World's Wealthiest Cowboys Fan" and the point man of the "World's Biggest Group of People Pushing Their Way Through A Locker Room In Which They Don't Belong.") So in addition to Couples and Brooks & Dunn and Morris and Busey and the rest, there was Bandar and nineteen of his bodyguards and cronies.

Had Johnson opted to fully explain his dual concerns as the Cowboys were about to embark on the postseason, it would have been quite obvious right then and there that Dallas was ordained to breeze past the Philadelphia Eagles, San Francisco 49ers and Buffalo Bills on its way to a Super Bowl title.

Because if the magnitude of Johnson's "two matters I wanted taken care of" were cutting Curvin and banning Bandar, the man didn't have a real worry in the world.

12 BYE-BYE BUFFER   ★

Dave Wannstedt sat behind the desk next to sports anchor Jon Kelley on the set of Chicago's WMAQ-TV News. It was January 19, 1993. Wannstedt had just been named head coach of the Chicago Bears, and with the cameras rolling, Kelley had a surprise for him. Wannstedt, appearing on live television, was told to look at the monitor and respond to what he saw and heard.

Cue tape.

"Our relationship would have deteriorated if he remained in this division," Wannstedt saw close friend and boss Jimmy Johnson saying.

Cue tears.

Wannstedt's eyes widened, then moistened. He stammered into his microphone something that indicated his shock, hesitated, then finally gathered himself.

"I tried to make a joke out of it," Wannstedt says. "I mean, I had the whole population of Chicago watching, right? After I got back on the plane later that day to come to Dallas, I gave it some thought. Now I knew that by taking the Chicago job, the competition wouldn't be there as much between Dallas and myself had it would have been in New York (the Giants play in the NFC East, as do Johnson's Cowboys). But 'deteriorated?' I never looked at it as it would have deteriorated. Those words. ... that was rash.

"If a family member leaves home, maybe you lose some contact with him. But does the relationship 'deteriorate'? That's not the way I think. That's why it hurt."

Wannstedt says Johnson's press-conference remarks seem less unfeeling in context — his point was that competing for the same division crown year after year would prevent the two men from openly exchanging ideas, and would therefore shred their ties — but Wannstedt was stunned by what he heard.

After all, Johnson had not only seemed supportive of whatever direction Wannstedt's ambitions took him; Johnson had orchestrated much of Wannstedt's accelerated ascent. In February of 1992, it was Johnson who pushed hard for the Pittsburgh Steelers to hire Wannstedt as their head coach. He finished second in the running for the job in his native city, to another Pittsburgher, Bill Cowher. But throughout, Wannstedt pursued his first head coaching position by conducting himself Johnson's way. When he sat down in meetings with Steelers president Dan Rooney and director of football operations Tom Donahoe, Wannstedt buried them with mountains of detailed plans and demands. Flow charts. Budgets. Scouting information. It was all mapped out. And it was all too much.

"I had a definite idea of how I thought things should be run, having learned a way to win from Jimmy for fourteen or fifteen years," Wannstedt says. "Maybe I came on too strong. But I was convinced that the ways we'd done things at Miami, and then in Dallas, were going to have a lot of impact on the ways I was going to do things wherever I became a head coach."

There are a lot of facets in Wannstedt's life that mirror nothing in Johnson's. Wannstedt wears his emotions on his sleeve. He has no gift for deceptive conversation. He attended church twice a week during his time in Dallas, and in the spring in 1993, when his family was in Dallas while he was in Chicago, he attended mass every morning. He tries not to miss a school event involving his teenage daughters Keri and Jami. He considers Jan an equal partner in everything he does.

"For me, it's important to spend time outside of football," Wannstedt says. "Everyone's different. I need to have balance. I have other interests. Jimmy is one of the greatest influences in my life, but I don't necessarily want to be like him."

But he does want to coach like him. In late 1992, Johnson helped Wannstedt to another shot at realizing that aspiration. Johnson in effect was Wannstedt's agent as he fielded the first phone call from University of Pittsburgh athletic director Oval Jaynes, and then handled some negotiations with boosters and other representatives of Pitt who had targeted Wannstedt, a Pitt alum, as a replacement for outgoing coach Paul Hackett.

"Pitt would have been great," Wannstedt says. "My family is there. Jan's family is there. We're both from there. There are just so many ties that would have made it a great situation for us."

Through Johnson, Pitt offered Wannstedt a five-year guaranteed contract worth $1.5 million. There was one proviso: Wannstedt would have to relocate in Pittsburgh by December 30, in order to begin the recruiting process.

"We'd gone back and forth on some numbers, and there was a point when we talked to them about a ten-year contract, basically a lifetime contract, something that would give my family security," Wannstedt says. "They had some people talking to Jimmy, and I was talking through Jimmy. The toughest part was having to leave the Cowboys by December 30. It made sense for Pitt — that's really the only way I could get a jump on doing a good job there — but that would've been right before our first play-off game. That didn't seem real fair to the Cowboys. It didn't feel right."

On the December 5 airplane ride to Denver, where the Cowboys were to play the Broncos, Wannstedt and Johnson exchanged opinions on the Pitt offer.

"Dave, we'll make the necessary adjustments," Johnson told him. "You do what you have to do for your future and your family."

Wannstedt did just that. He stayed.

What Jan Wannstedt calls "one of the toughest decisions we've ever made in our lives" became the most fruitful decision of their lives by January, when four National Football League teams began clamoring for Wannstedt's favor.

The New York Giants attempted to display the same respect for protocol exhibited by the Steelers a year earlier, when they waited until 8:00 a.m. on January 6 to call Wannstedt, whose season with the Cowboys had ended on January 5 with the play-off loss in Detroit. But the Giants began to scramble when the Bears and New England Patriots joined the Wannstedt sweepstakes while the Cowboys remained alive in the play-offs.

On January 9, Patriots chief executive officer Sam Jankovich resigned his position over a dispute with new owner James Orthwein ignited by Jankovich's plan to fly to Dallas to interview Wannstedt. Orthwein, who probably intended to dismiss Jankovich anyway, told his CEO he was "moving too fast," then forced him out of a job.

When Johnson openly invited teams to interview Wannstedt — an announcement timed to cement Wannstedt's future before it became a Super Bowl distraction, and one that made Wannstedt the first man to be publicly introduced as a coach of one team while working in the Super Bowl for another — everyone started moving fast. Wannstedt's office phone rang off the hook; one night when he escaped to his home, there were twenty-one messages from reporters on his answering machine.

His first call came from the Giants, with general manager George Young working his way through the proper channels to arrange an interview while part-owner Robert Tisch assured Jerry Jones his club's sincere interest in Wannstedt would do nothing to disrupt the Cowboys' postseason run. Then Bears president Mike McCaskey and Denver Broncos general manager John Beake called on the same day. Wannstedt suspected all along Denver's interest was token. But he was intrigued by the contact from the Bears and McCaskey.

"One of the things I liked about the Steelers the year before is that they looked like they had the ability to be a play-off team," Wannstedt says. "They didn't look like they were that far away. And it turns out, they weren't (Pittsburgh lost to Buffalo in the divisional round of the AFC play-offs). The Bears seemed like they had some of the same things. Another thing was the Bears were willing to give me the authority I think is absolutely necessary if a coach is going to make it. The coach is the guy who is sticking his neck out there every day on the field with the players, so it should be the coach who has a major, major voice in choosing those players. Plus, there were the relationship things. Mike McCaskey and I hit it off, for instance."

"The relationship things" were many. The Johnson-Wannstedt affiliation was primary, of course. "He understands me better than most people, better sometimes than I know myself," Johnson said in that same tear-evoking press conference. "And I knew our relationship would be better if he was with the Bears." Indeed, Johnson and Wannstedt talked by phone almost daily in the months after Wannstedt left Dallas for good after the Super Bowl. Wannstedt had two striking offers on the table at once. Chicago and New York both presented similar five-year, $3 million proposals. Says Jerry Jones of Wannstedt's decision to accept the Bears' deal: "This way, there can still be that interplay, that exchange of information."

Wannstedt felt comfortable with Bears player personnel director Bill Tobin after he learned of their common ground: Tobin had coached Cowboys secondary coach Dave Campo when Campo was a player at Central Connecticut State. He even felt secure with the legendary former coach occupying a desk in another office down the corridor from Wannstedt's digs at Halas Hall. Ex-coach Mike Ditka, like Wannstedt a Pittsburgher who starred for the hometown college team, remained on the Bears' payroll as a consultant. One of Wannstedt's first acts as Bears coach was to consult with his predecessor and boyhood idol.

(It says here the city of Chicago will embrace Wannstedt, who at six-foot-five, 220 pounds, has Ditka's physically imposing frame, his gravely Easterner voice, his scraggly moustache, even his slight limp, but not his self-destructive temper. Wannstedt is Ditka Lite.)

"Dave will need to learn to be less open about his emotions, he'll need to learn to be more under control," Johnson says. "He'll have to learn how to deal with the media, how to deal with the ownership people above him. But he can motivate. He can teach. He knows football. He's been trained pretty well, you know."

There was still that matter of which Dallas assistants would depart with Wannstedt. He had been given permission by McCaskey to assemble his own group of aides. The hangup came back in Dallas, where Johnson was reluctant to allow the NFL's most harmonious staff to be stripped.

No pro staff spent more time together, liked one another more, or rooted harder for one another than Johnson's "gang."

Their noontime jogs have become a ritual. So have their almost-annual spring vacations to the Bahamas, where Johnson transports his coaches and their wives for some sun, surf and gambling. (They'd go to Las Vegas if the NFL didn't frown so on wagering.) Everything is paid for and arranged by Johnson, who can be expected to casually approach a staffer and flip him a $5,000 chip. "I've seen him do it for years," says one of Johnson's benefactors. "He always gives the chips to guys who couldn't afford to spend that kind of money themselves. It's Jimmy's way of helping guys out who could use the help." Johnson makes the offering with the instructions to split the winnings with another aide. As is the case when he's discussing a football game, Johnson doesn't bother specifying what should be done in the event there are no winnings.

Says Dave Wannstedt: "I've been going to the Bahamas most years with Jimmy since after the 1978 season. The first staff we took down there, it was eight guys. All stag. Jimmy got us one room and two beds, and we slept four to a bed.

"To tell you how things change, last year in the Bahamas, he rented us the whole floor. He took twenty-six couples. Instead of eating at either McDonalds or off the free hors d'oeuvre tray at happy hour between 4:00 and 6:00 p.m., we had room service whenever we wanted. God's been good to us."

In May of 1992, the coaches endured a seven-week diet. Each man bet $500 on his ability to lose twenty pounds. All succeeded, though chubby offensive line coach Tony Wise was encouraged to perform jumping jacks in the sauna to beat the scale on weigh-in day. Each of the coaches' Sansabelts fit more loosely, but their chests puffed out in unison.

Wise is one of a kind. He is a connoisseur of fine cars, fine films and lousy cigars. Defensive line coach Butch Davis insists Wise has written out all the words to his favorite movie, "It's A Wonderful Life," and recites them back at the TV screen every

Christmas when the Frank Capra classic is shown. "Not true," Wise says. "I just do that with my favorite parts." Wise brings an odd dynamic to coaching: though he was a letterman at Ithaca College in football, lacrosse and hockey, he is no Bruce Jenner or Bo Jackson. He understands his limitations to the point where he almost assumes a figuratively subordinate role to the players he coaches, not unlike he had to in a literal way when he worked as a waiter at Elmer's Place by night, cleaning up after the same offensive linemen he coached by day at Central Connecticut State. Wise lived in Campo's basement one year when they coached at Washington State, and slept on a couch on the stadium office at Pitt another year.

A "ball guy." In the vernacular of the Cowboys' coaches, the phrase is used to describe a person who in school was more interested in scouting reports than in report cards, a person who loves his football and lives his life with a minimum of frills. That's what Johnson admiringly calls Wise. A ball guy.

Characters dot this staff. Running backs coach Joe Brodsky considered a career as a bail bondsman. Special-teams coach Joe Avezzano sells jewelry out of his home and yearns to be a country-western crooner. Wise dreamed of gaining employment as head of the lacrosse program at Rensselaer Poly. Kicking coach Steve Hoffman coached football in the Italian League. Offensive coordinator Norv Turner pokes self-effacing fun at his playing career as a backup quarterback for the University of Oregon Fighting Ducks.

Twenty-five years of connections bind this staff. Brodsky, whose avuncular style has motivated athletes for four decades, was a legendary Florida high school coach who counted Avezzano as one of his pupils. Avezzano was on the same Iowa State staff with Johnson in 1969 and was Wannstedt's line coach at Pitt. Avezzano was the head coach at Oregon State at the same time Robert Ford, Dallas's tight ends coach, was there.

Campo was at Oregon State when Avezzano was there and at Albany State, Bridgeport, Washington State and Syracuse when Wise was at those schools. Strength coach Mike Woicik was a member of the same Syracuse staff. Offensive coordinator Norv Turner worked with Wannstedt at Southern Cal. Defensive assistant Bob Slowik was a Baldwin (Pennsylvania) High School teammate of Wannstedt's. Receivers coach Hubbard Alexander preceeded Johnson at Miami, as did Brodsky, and they were retained. Davis was hired by Johnson at Oklahoma State in 1979. Hoffman joined Johnson in Miami in 1985.

Johnson surrounded himself with both leaders and followers, with assistants like Davis, who is fueled by ambition, and assistants like Wise, who professes to want nothing more than to be a good line coach. There are designated "yes" men, and designated "no" men. There are coaches who are X-and-O strategists and there are coaches who even the players joke seem to be the ones being coached. There are men who might contribute little were they to change teams, but who contribute mightily in Dallas, and there are coaches who are one break from running their own teams.

"I've seen so many situations where good assistant coaches haven't been allowed to develop fully, and they end up wasting away as career assistants who just punch in the clock then bide their time before it's time to punch out again," Johnson says. "The way we do it, a coach like Dave or Butch or Bobby Slowik has all the opportunity in the world to move to the top of the profession, if that's what he wants to do. ... Some blossom. Some do well. Few falter."

Says Brodsky: "Jimmy Johnson is a master of knowing people, of knowing who fits and how they fit. He understands chemistry. Now chemistry among people isn't worth a damn if the people can't coach. But you've got something special if the guy can coach the player and get along with the other coaches.

We've got that. Our guys are friends. We jog together. We have a drink together. We work so damn much together, it makes more sense if we somehow get along."

It is trite to call it a "family," but it is unavoidable. The feelings extend beyond the members of the staff. For instance, Johnson is like a relative to Wannstedt's kids. They cherish the fish tank he gave them as a present a couple of years back. "It's a gift that, to me, shows another side of Jimmy, to how he feels about Dave and people he's close to Jan Wannstedt says. "They're all like brothers. Sometimes, Jimmy is the big brother. Sometimes, Dave is his big brother. When you get inside the group, you see what sort of a person Jimmy really is, and what sort of relationship he's truly capable of. I mean, you should see him with our daughters. They really love him."

It was a foregone conclusion that Johnson would allow Wannstedt to take Wise to Chicago. Wise spends his Christmases with the Wannstedt family, considers Dave and Jan to be two of his closest friends, and would be a steadying influence for Wannstedt as he sought equilibrium in a new city. The assumption that Wise is a Bears coach because of his friendship with Wannstedt — a coattail concept that causes Wise to stew — is inaccurate, though. "The reason I needed Tony to come with me," Wannstedt says, "is because he's the best. The best." Best friend? Or best line coach? Wannstedt means both.

Wannstedt also wanted to bring a Dallas staffer with him to help on the defensive side of the ball. Johnson said, "Anyone who leaves will be at my choice. Dave and I are close enough that that's the way it would be."

On January 19, 1993, Johnson and Wannstedt had all but settled on which assistant might be permitted to join Wannstedt and Wise in Chicago. Johnson had not decided what resulting changes he'd make in the Cowboys staff. In part because the Cowboys had thirteen days before they were to face the Buffalo

Bills in Super Bowl XXVII, the subject was a hot topic of conversation among coaches at Valley Ranch.

It became hotter when Johnson overheard one particular conversation.

Johnson turned up a hallway and noticed that a meeting room door was closed. He opened the door and heard his aides casually discussing which of them might end up with promotions and which might end up in Chicago. They froze when they realized Johnson had come within earshot.

"All of you can go to Chicago right now, if that's what you want!" Johnson screamed. "I'll coach the damn Super Bowl by myself!"

Wannstedt assumed the blame for the incident. He thought Johnson's outburst was directed at him, and thought Johnson was in effect accusing him of drawing the staff's attention away from its work. Says Jan Wannstedt: "That crushed Dave. It was natural that during an off moment, the guys might talk about Chicago and the staff changes. He couldn't believe Jimmy not only didn't understand that, but that he would blame Dave for it. It took Dave some time to regain his composure and remember that, well, that's just Jimmy."

After the Super Bowl, Johnson and Wannstedt jointly made their decision public. It would be Slowik who would be Chicago's defensive coordinator. Davis would be elevated to defensive coordinator in Dallas. Turner assumed the extra title "assistant head coach," as Wannstedt had the year before after the Steelers job fell through. Jerry Jones would distribute staff-wide raises and contract extensions. Hudson Houck, an old friend of Turner's, would be hired to coach the offensive line. Jim Eddy and John Blake were added to the defensive staff.

It is Johnson's contention that he's weathered staff changes before — "I'll be going into my fifteenth year (in 1993) as a head coach, and in fourteen of those I've had to make changes," he notes — and that he'll weather this one. It is the hazard of success, this process in which the ripest fruits from the strongest trees get plucked. It will happen to Johnson on offense sometime soon, when coordinator Norv Turner is stolen away. Turner's players say he is ready now. Turner thinks the same thing. "I'd like to do that at some point," he says. "I'm never going to go out searching around, because that takes too much away from what I'm doing here. And what I'm doing with the Cowboys is something I can be happy with for a long, long time."

But it probably won't come to that. Turner will leave, just as Wannstedt did. And to some degree, the old psych major Johnson is doing a psych job on himself if he believes Wannstedt's absence won't have a negative impact, at least temporarily.

A mentor needs a protege.

In 1978, Wannstedt was a twenty-six-year-old tight ends coach on Johnny Majors' University of Pittsburgh staff. Johnson was the defensive coordinator. In 1979, Johnson moved to the head coaching job at Oklahoma State University. He asked Wannstedt to join him — as a defensive line coach.

"Jimmy, I can't coach D-line," said Wannstedt, who'd been an offensive lineman at Pitt. "I've never coached defensive line in my life."

In 1986, Johnson won the head coaching job at the University of Miami. He called Wannstedt, who'd departed OSU for a job on the Southern Cal staff. Johnson asked Wannstedt to be his Miami defensive coordinator.

"Jimmy, I don't know," said Wannstedt, who'd served just one year as the OSU defensive coordinator. "I don't have much experience there."

Johnson replied, "You'll learn."

By February 1989, when Johnson moved to the Cowboys, Wannstedt (who a month before had joined the Miami Dolphins as a linebackers coach) did not dispute his boss' high opinion of him. There wasn't much debate when Johnson promised Wannstedt he'd learn to excel as an NFL defensive coordinator in Dallas.

As usual, the mentor was right. In Wannstedt's four years in Dallas, he pushed the Cowboys defense from laughable to laudable.

"We have an excellent defensive scheme," says Johnson of the Cowboys' 4-3, upfield-charging philosophy that relies on athletic quickness to apply pressure. "But our greatest strength is that our coaches are so indoctrinated in this and believe in it so much, we know every in and out."

Wannstedt knew enough about the talent level of the 1992 Cowboys defense, statistically the NFL's best, that he was not surprised when none of his charges made the Pro Bowl. But he was also convinced he had players who could fit into the Cowboys system. Like defensive tackle Tony Casillas.

"I want to be an actor," Casillas said one day. "The Hispanic Terminator." Before 1991, the only thing Casillas came close to terminating was his pro football career. A first-round pick of the Atlanta Falcons in 1986, Casillas bordered on stardom in his early years there, twice earning an alternate Pro Bowl berth. Then new coach Jerry Glanville came to town, and Casillas's game went south.

"Blame Glanville for everything, for every problem that team has," Casillas says. "He's a horse's ass, he really is." Casillas forced a July 22, 1991, trade to Dallas (the Cowboys gave up just picks in the second and eighth rounds) by threatening to retire from football. With Dallas, he was the foundation upon which was built the deepest defensive line in pro football. Flashy, he wasn't. When he pulled down 49ers quarterback Steve Young three times in the NFC Championship Game, he matched his sack total for the entire 1992 regular season. But flashy will come when he starts that movie career. "Compared to me," says Casillas, "guys like Brian Bosworth (another footballer-turned-thespian) can't act their way out of a paper bag."

More typical of the members of the Dallas defense are linebacker Vinson Smith and safety James Washington — typical because management is always striving to replace them. "I've been in the league six years, and I wasn't even supposed to be in the league one year," says Smith, who bounced from Atlanta to Pittsburgh to Dallas after not being taken in the 1988 draft. "It doesn't matter that I bench 400 pounds, squat 600 pounds, jump thirty-three inches, cover tight ends and don't miss tackles. The Cowboys have always tried to replace me with somebody. In '91, they drafted Godfrey Myles and Dixon Edwards to replace me. But when the season starts, I'm on the field."

Washington was also made to feel unwanted after being trashed by management in a training-camp contract dispute. For much of the season, he flip-flopped from strong safety to free safety as coaches experimented with contenders to supplant him as a starter. Washington gained a troublemaker's brand before leaving the Los Angeles Rams for Dallas on March 3, 1990, via Plan B, and in 1992, his teammates were shocked that he wasn't squawking about being "disrespected." His teammates didn't know that two factors prevented Washington from mouthing off.

First, a clause in the contract he signed in August stipulated that he be on his best behavior at all times. No bad-mouthing teammates. No second-guessing coaches. The "Jesse Solomon Clause," management named it, recalling its 1991 troubles with the difficult-to-control linebacker. "Bite my tongue, I get my money," says Washington, who earned his dough by finishing third on the club in tackles, and totalling a team-high five interceptions over the course of the regular season and postseason.

Second, he strived so diligently for inner peace that external situations were secondary. Growing up in the troubled Watts section of Los Angeles, Washington was introduced to adversity at an early age. He never knew his father. His mother chose booze over her son when he was four. He lost some of the people closest to him: his father figure, grandfather Eddie Alexander; his idol, former UCLA and Cleveland Browns safety Don Rogers; Al Wilson, another teammate at UCLA and the best man at Washington's wedding. "I cope," Washington says, "because when people close to me pass away, I use their energy. I suck in their energy." After the Super Bowl, Washington returned to strife-torn South Central L.A. with plans to open a homeless shelter. Says Henry Washington, the coach at Jordan High School who served as a mentor to this self-described "bad, violent" product of a bad, violent neighborhood: "He's a peculiar kid. But he's a lovely kid."

Another son of Watts is Ken Norton, Jr. He's also the son of the former heavyweight boxing champion, whose 1992 estrangement from his father made his return to southern California for Super Bowl XXVII a painful one.

Norton's parents divorced before he was two years old. His father, then a struggling boxer who hadn't yet received his huge paydays for his series of early-1970s fights with Muhammad Ali, raised Ken Jr., without the benefit of a second parent or a spare bite to eat. "We had some difficult times," the son says. "It wasn't exactly a silver-spoons setup." The father was so protective of the son that Ken Jr., was not allowed to play football until his junior year in high school, and never saw his father box.

"I did watch boxing movies, though," says Norton, who lists "Raging Bull" as his all-time favorite. "You can't keep a kid from going to the movies, right? Sometimes I go to the movies and get chills, because there are certain scenes when a person is down and he fights to come back. That's what gives me chills."

Fighting to come back must be a Norton family trait. The elder Norton had to after February 23, 1986, when his car veered off the Santa Monica Freeway and into a tree. The accident robbed him of his speech, his motor skills, his memory. "I was just a college kid, into football and school and growing up, into my own little things," the son says. "But that accident made me realize what comes first in life. I was always close with my father, and when he needed me, it was a wake-up call. It put everything else in my life on hold."

Seven years later, with much help from his son, the father is nearly recovered. But then came a falling out. The two men who had always relied on each other suddenly separated. The father objected to the son's February 1992 plans to wed Angela, who is white. Norton says the dispute goes deeper than just the interracial marriage, says there are more principals involved than just his wife, his father and himself, and says it's too complex to be repaired by a simple conversation — which father and son haven't had since that February wedding.

"People stop me in the streets and say, 'C'mon, why don't you and your dad just make up?'" Norton says. "They don't understand. You can't understand someone else's situation unless you're in the middle of it."

There was a time when Norton felt in conflict with his own team and the family name was among the reasons. As a rookie second-round pick in 1988, Norton missed thirteen games with a thumb injury. Because he was a high-priced high pick who was contributing so little to a 3-13 club — and because of his lineage — he feels he was a target of abuse from media, fans, teammates, everyone. "I was down like a dog, and they were kicking me," Norton says. "I used it as fuel, as motivation. I think it contributed to me eventually having the success I've had. But I didn't feel my own team was even supporting me much."

When Johnson took over in Norton's second year, 1989, the linebacker received a fresh and healthy start. But he became the pea in a shell game that had him trying all three linebacking positions. As the team's leading tackler at weak-side linebacker in 1992, Norton found prosperity. Still, there were times when he joined other Cowboys defenders in feeling resentment toward the attention given "The System," believing it steals credit from the players. Says former Dallas middle linebacker Eugene Lockhart: "If those coaches had Lawrence Taylor at linebacker, they wouldn't let him rush the passer. Because that's just not what linebackers do in that scheme."

"We really never did get our due," Norton says. "That's not the fault of the coaches. It's outside people who really don't realize that we have good players here. Haley is given his credit. But Tony Tolbert, Jeffcoat, myself, Robert Jones, Thomas Everett, Kevin Smith. ... that's a lot of talent. People started noticing us in the play-offs. But nobody still was in the Pro Bowl. You can't say we've had our due until the 1993 season starts, and we see how people take us on, how the press takes us on, who gives us respect. It seems like we took everybody by surprise."

The surprise was a result of the unusual method used to assemble this group. History's best defensive units have been anchored by can't-miss stars who develop a kinship over the course of five or six seasons. The Cowboys are thin on can't-missers — even defensive tackle Russell Maryland, the top overall pick in the 1991 draft, has enough physical flaws to have "missed" — and the only defenders on the 1992 payroll who were in town before Johnson arrived are Jeffcoat, Bates and Norton.

Their newness contributed to their identity crisis. So did the rapid-transit pattern of mass substitution that prevented the naked eye from discerning that the starting line of ends Haley and Tolbert and tackles Casillas and Maryland was replaced on passing downs by a line of Jeffcoat, Jimmie Jones, Leon Lett and Haley. Observers had to pay attention when the trio of strong-side linebacker Vinson Smith, middle man Robert Jones and Norton was pulled in certain situations in favor of a combination of Norton flanked by safety Kenny Gant and linebacker Godfrey Myles, or Norton teamming with safety Darren Woodson. Defensive backs rotated for reasons of playing time and game situation, with Kevin Smith and Larry Brown getting the bulk of the action at cornerback and James Washington and Thomas Everett emerging as the starting safeties. But Issiac Holt, Ray Horton, Robert Williams and others participated in enough Nickel packages here and there to befuddle even their boss.

"Sometimes I don't even know who's in there," Johnson says. "I just count heads to see if it adds up to eleven."

Players tried to overcome their lack of recognition in a season in which they permitted just fifteen points per game and led the NFL in preventing third-down conversions and yards. But their efforts to gain acclaim were substantially less organized than their on-field work. "Lynch Mob" was one of the nicknames experimented with; but when defensive lineman Jim Jeffcoat showed up at the Super Bowl with a ballcap that read "Lench Mob," it was clear these guys would never agree on a moniker if they couldn't even agree on spelling.

Says Norton: "Some guys liked "Lynch Mob," and that was a pretty good one for a while. We tried "DWA" (Defense With an Attitude), and some guys had towels made up that they wore in the Super Bowl, but that never caught on. Some guys liked "The Posse." The old Cowboys defense was called "Doomsday," and I heard some people saying we were "Dooms Deja Vu.' But maybe that was too awkward."

But as Norton said of the Cowboys defense in the days before the Super Bowl, "We're getting famous for not being famous."

Andre Waters's head wasn't empty. But his threats were.

The Philadelphia Eagles had won their first road play-off game since 1949 by defeating the New Orleans Saints, 36-20, in a wild wild-card duel, setting up a January 10 postseason rubber match in Dallas. In preparing for the first play-off game at Texas Stadium in ten years, the visiting Eagles grasped at motivational straws.

The martyred Jerome Brown would be called upon. So would the hollow guarantees of victory issued by Eagles Keith Byars and Fred Barnett. And naturally, Philadelphia would attempt to extract all it could from the contrived "rivalry" between Andre Waters and Emmitt Smith.

"I don't think there has been a lot of trash talk, not anything above and beyond what you might expect in any game," Jimmy Johnson said before kickoff. "Maybe from my background (at jive-talkin' Miami), I'm accustomed to more. ... The rivalry is already as intense as you'd want to have it. There will be the same intensity Sunday afternoon. Early on, we really didn't have much of a rivalry because we didn't hold up our end of the bargain. There is more of a rivalry now, even though there is less talk back and forth."

There was some residual bitterness from the teams' regular-season meetings, a 31-7 Eagles win and a 20-10 Cowboys victory. Most of it was propelled by the words and actions of

Waters, the Eagles safety generally recognized as a reasonably talented but insanely dirty player. During and after the Eagles' win over Dallas on October 5, various Cowboys denounced Waters for his style of play. Said Emmitt Smith: "He was going for the knee. He was spearing. Andre Waters is a cheap-shot artist. The rest of their defense is pretty solid, but he's always talking, telling you he's going to get your knees. He's not a real man. ... He'll get his someday. If I don't give it to him, somebody else will. If he doesn't get it in this lifetime, somebody is still going to get him."

Coincidentally, Waters sustained a broken leg on October 18, and missed the November 1 rematch as well as the rest of the Eagles' games before the November 10 play-off in Dallas. He said his hopes of returning to the active roster were stoked by his wish to retaliate. "Two of us are going to walk on the field," Waters said, "but only one of us is going to walk off. They're going to have to carry him off."

Waters said more. "I think Emmitt Smith will accept the challenge that I'm playing. I'm like this: If you talk the talk, you better be able to walk the walk. If he's the man I think he is, he'll walk the walk. It will be a personal challenge to him as well as a personal challenge to me."

There was a problem with Waters's side of the challenge. As of a few days before kickoff, he remained on injured reserve. When he was finally activated, he clearly wasn't healthy enough to contribute much beyond pep talking and trash talking. In the visitors' locker room at Texas Stadium before the game, Waters found a black marker and penned the phrase "PSALM 70" onto a strip of athletic tape, which he adhered to his forehead. Excerpt from that biblical psalm include: "Make haste oh God to deliver me. Make haste to help me oh Lord. Them that seek after my soul, let them be turned backward and put them to confusion that desire my hurt. Let them be turned back for a reward of shame that say 'Ah ha, Ah ha.' ... They are after my life and delight in hurting me. ... I am in deep trouble."

Once the game began, Waters supplemented his religious zeal with an expressed desire to maim a Cowboy or two. "Hold him up, I want a shot at him!" screamed Waters while Smith was being tackled. "I want to see him hurt! I want to break his leg! I want to see him go down!"

But Smith, who gained 114 yards and walked on Waters for a 23-yard scoring scoot, went down rarely. The Eagles were "in deep trouble." The Cowboys, 34-10 winners, were one step deeper into the play-offs.

Wannstedt's waves of personnel created four fumbles, permitted Eagles season lows in all yardage categories and held Philadelphia from the end zone until the game's final minute. Byars, Barnett and Waters were hardly factors. Same with Herschel Walker, who carried six times for 29 yards, and Heath Sherman, who finished with six for 12. With three minutes left in what would be the most lopsided postseason loss in the Eagles' history, quarterback Randall Cunningham had managed only 90 yards passing, had been sacked five times and was trailing 34-3.

"We were electrified into an unconscious state," Norton says. "And we had Randall flustered."

Troy Aikman completed just three of his first 10 passes, but overcame the jitters of his first postseason start by totalling 15-of-25 for 200 yards and no interceptions. With fifty-five seconds left in the first half, he found Alvin Harper on a "Nine Pump" — a pump fake and deep throw — for a 41-yard gain to the Eagles' 14. (The six-foot-three Harper made life tough for five-foot-seven Eagles corner Mark McMillian, whose green uniform and diminutive frame prompted Dallas's Issiac Holt to chide from the sideline, "Hey No. 29, time to get back on that Lucky Charms box!") Two plays later, Aikman hit Jay Novacek for a six-yard touchdown. Forty-seven seconds later, Lin Elliott followed up a fumble recovery by the Dallas kickoff unit with a field goal that put the Cowboys up 17-3 at the half. "We all knew with our defense, that would be enough," says rookie cornerback Kevin Smith. "We had a fourteen-point lead. We had the better team. It was over."

In the second half, Emmitt Smith escaped to the sanctuary of the bench, where Waters couldn't find his valuable legs. His sub, Derrick Gainer, who'd been activated to replace the exiled Curvin Richards, plunged in from a yard out in the second half. Elliott added another field goal.

"People were saying, 'Uh-oh, here come the Eagles,'" guard Nate Newton says. "They should've been saying, 'Uh-oh, here come the Cowboys.'"

None of this was a surprise to Johnson, who says his confidence level was so high that after watching the 49ers' 20-13 victory over Washington on Saturday, he immediately ordered the sprinklers turned on the Valley Ranch practice fields so that after they beat Philly, the Cowboys could simulate the muddy grounds they'd encounter at San Francisco's Candlestick Park in the following week's NFC title game. (Scoffed center Mark Stepnoski: "What are we going to do, practice slipping down?")

Johnson's speeches to his squad echoed with cocksureness. Early in the week, he announced it was "time to have fun." Throughout the week, he told his team, "In the past year, we beat the Eagles with Steve Beuerlein at quarterback, and we beat them with Troy Aikman at quarterback. We beat them at Veterans Stadium, and we beat them at Texas Stadium. We beat them under every circumstance. We'll beat them again."

Tight end Derek Tennell was even a scheduled part of the plan. Signed on December 29 as an emergency backup because of an injury to Alfredo Roberts, the Eagles could not have suspected he would account for the game's opening score. Tennell, after all, had been dropped by three teams in four seasons before coming to Dallas.

But on Dallas's first possession of the game, Tennell's number was called. On second-and-goal from the Eagles' one-yard line, Dallas came out in a three-tight end formation usually used for power runs. Novacek and reserve lineman Kevin Gogan were the eligible receivers on the left side of the formation. The 270-pound Tennell was eligible to the right, which is where Aikman rolled after faking a give to Smith up the middle. The pass floated toward Tennell, who knew the entire tone of the game was resting on his broad shoulders and untested hands. What was he thinking about when he saw Aikman's throw was directed toward him?

"I was thinking, 'Don't drop the son of a bitch,'" Tennell answered.

A Super Bowl, and Dave Wannstedt's final game with Dallas, was one win away. The Cowboys were going to play the San Francisco 49ers in the NFC Championship Game. They couldn't have gotten there without Wannstedt. But he's certain they will get there again without him. He's certain that one unofficial position they didn't fill — Johnson's confidant — is no longer necessary.

"You know why I won't be missed there? First of all, Butch and the coaches they have there will do an exceptional job," Wannstedt says. "We've all been schooled in the same things. We're all capable.

"And the other thing, that stuff about me and Jimmy? Hey, Jimmy doesn't need a buffer anymore. You know what made him need a buffer? Moving to the NFL for the first time out of college in 1989. Going 1-15 that first year and having people tell us we didn't know what we were doing, questioning every move. Going through his divorce from Linda Kay. You need a buffer for those times.

"Our relationship is just like a marriage in the sense that to make any marriage really have a strong foundation, you need a little tough times. Well, with the Cowboys in those early years, we had tough times. That's what made me and Jimmy's relationship. But he doesn't need a buffer anymore. Because Dallas's tough times are over with."

13 BURYING THE HATCHET ★

"Love your enemies," Jimmy Johnson is fond of saying. "It'll drive them crazy."

Troy Aikman rarely felt the love. He sometimes felt like the enemy. And he often felt like he'd been driven crazy. All of which meant that any event, no matter how seemingly innocuous or even seemingly positive, could trigger his feelings of rancor toward Johnson. Even the 1989 Herschel Walker trade, when the Minnesota Vikings got trinkets and the Dallas Cowboys got Manhattan.

After he was drafted by the Cowboys as the top overall pick in the 1989 draft, it made sense for Aikman to always tell questioners that as a kid growing up in Henryetta, Oklahoma, his athletic idol was Cowboys quarterback Roger Staubach. But there was an inconsistency in that idyllic tale: Aikman is on record as saying he never really followed pro football until he entered high school. Staubach retired after the 1979 season — when Aikman was a thirteen-year-old junior-high student.

The true identity of Aikman's high school idol? Would you believe Herschel Walker?

"When I was in high school, just about when I was getting serious about football, I read every story I could find about Herschel," Aikman says. "Once in *Sports Illustrated*, when he was at the University of Georgia, they came out with a story that said he liked to write poetry. I've never talked to him about this, but I kind of took up writing poetry for a few years after that because I'd found out he did it."

A few years later, when Aikman and Walker became team-mates, they became pals. Aikman acknowledges that though they had plenty in common, beginning with their stature as the wealthiest and most gifted players on the NFL's poorest team, such close friendships between "franchise players" are uncommon.

"Sometimes in those situations, the two players don't allow themselves to be friends, because they are sort of in competition," Aikman says. "But from Day One, Herschel was good to me. On his days off when he was out running errands, he'd stop by my apartment unannounced, just to see how I was doing or to take me to lunch. It was unbelievable. Sometimes, I've been hesitant to meet face-to-face with people who I look up to because I'm afraid they won't live up to the image I had of them. Herschel far exceeded the image I had, and that is saying something."

Then Johnson traded Walker. And Aikman discovered one more reason to feel rubbed wrong by his coach.

"What I thought about that trade at the time was that it was taking away the one proven touchdown scorer we had," Aikman says. "My thinking at the time was that I didn't want to see us going 1-15, and without Herschel, that's about the caliber of team we became. I wanted to win right away. I was thinking short-term, not long-term."

Once upon a time, Johnson and Aikman seemed to invent reasons to not co-exist. The Walker trade wasn't even the start of it. Aikman's uneasiness with his coach was initiated shortly after Aikman was selected in the draft and worsened that summer, when the Cowboys added to their stable of rookie millionaire quarterbacks by using a No. 1 pick in the supplemental draft on Steve Walsh.

Some in Aikman's circle of friends remain convinced that Johnson drafted both quarterbacks because he wasn't certain which of them was superior. As with Johnson's alleged 1990 characterization of Aikman as "a loser," the unlikelihood of such thinking was overshadowed by Aikman's belief in its validity.

In retrospect, no living human being will concede that in 1989, he advised the Cowboys to take Michigan State offensive tackle Tony Mandarich with the first overall pick in the regular draft, then grab Walsh in the supplemental. Little wonder, considering that Walsh finished the 1992 season as the New Orleans Saints' third-stringer, and Mandarich, taken by the Green Bay Packers with the second overall pick, finished 1992 out of football. But such opinion holders existed in great numbers. Notre Dame coach Lou Holtz was enamored with Walsh after watching him almost single-handedly steal a win away from the Irish. On October 15, 1988, Notre Dame defeated Miami 31-30 despite Walsh's 31 completions, 424 yards and four touchdowns. Holtz was among those to offer that Mandarich-Walsh pairing to Cowboys owner Jerry Jones.

Also plentiful now are those claiming to be the driving force behind the selection of Aikman, a group headed by Gil Brandt, the former Dallas scouting director who has reminded acquaintances of his "master stroke."

"There was never any question in our mind," Johnson says. "Troy was our guy. The first thing I told our people after seeing him work out before the draft was that he was the best I'd ever seen. And he is now the best quarterback I've ever been associated with, which is saying something with the quarter-backs we had at Miami.

"The only thing was, we did try to be coy about our plans with Troy. For instance, because it was my first year in the league, I wanted to see what kind of offers we could get for the top pick just to see the value of that pick. We didn't get any solid offers. People talked in circles, which was fine, because Aikman was what we wanted."

Johnson says he was intrigued by the talents of Alabama linebacker Derrick Thomas and Florida State cornerback Deion Sanders. But not as the top overall pick. They would have been options had Dallas traded down.

"John Wooten (Dallas's former personnel director) was talking Mandarich), but he was about the only one within the organization," Johnson says. "Gil might have been saying Aikman. But that wasn't an earth-shaking statement. Gil, Tex, Jerry, me, we all wanted Aikman. So did Barbara (Goodman, the head coach's secretary).

"We needed to build our team with an outstanding quarter-back and then good defensive linemen. I know at least a half-dozen teams that would have taken Mandarich. But not us. If everyone out there outside the organization is telling you they didn't like Mandarich or some other options, well, some people have short memories."

When it comes to his feelings for Johnson, Aikman seems to have a long memory. Aikman had stored in his mind the Mandarich thing, the Walsh thing, the Walker thing. He has been bothered by the "loser" thing, and by that two-month period during the 1990 season when he and his coach did not communicate, two events that caused him to tell Johnson of his wish to be traded. He has held it against Johnson for when he felt his friend Babe Laufenberg had been made a scapegoat for the 1990 failure to make the play-offs, and thought Laufenberg was lied to when he was invited to the 1991 training camp and then released without receiving a shot at making the team. He stewed over the way he felt jerked around by Johnson at the close of the 1991 season, when Johnson first told Aikman he'd be back in the lineup when his knee made him able, then reneged on the promise.

All the while, Johnson seemed to go out of his way to avoid praising his quarterback. When Johnson cited individuals for their performances, Aikman's name was often conspicuously absent. Says one of Aikman's teammates: "I don't think Jimmy gave Troy more than one or two game balls (awarded for individual excellence after a victory) in the first three years. Some of us thought then it meant Jimmy didn't like him. But in reality, it was probably one of Jimmy's grand psychological schemes."

Adds center Mark Stepnoski: "I'm sure for some people, Jimmy's methods have the desired effect. For some players, that psychological approach works, for some it doesn't. Most of the solid group of talented guys on this team could be successful just about anywhere, regardless of the approach the head coach takes in motivating. Most of us are self-motivated. We're twenty-five, twenty-six years old. We don't rely on the head coach to get us in the state of mind to play every Sunday. That's our job."

Johnson has two favorite psychological tenets. "Love your enemies. It'll drive them crazy" runs neck-and-neck with "Treat a person as what he is, and he'll remain that way. Treat him as what he could be or should be, and he'll become that."

How did the coach apply those philosophies to his franchise player? It was Johnson's intention to "Treat Aikman as what he could be," which meant not allowing him to accept anything less than greatness. But that demand-the-moon scheme seemed to have backfired after three seasons, when both Aikman and Johnson let fester adversarial feelings toward one another. "We have had our differences," says Johnson, acknowledging their "strained relationship."

Says offensive coordinator Norv Turner, who has served as a conduit between the two: "When I came in here (in 1991), people said different things about Jimmy and Troy's relationship. ... If there was ever a real problem, no one would have ever said anything about it had they won more games in their first two years together."

It was with winning games in mind that on July 14, 1992, Johnson and Aikman finally found a reason to get along.

What happened that night changed everything. Now, says Johnson, "things are to where I challenge you to find a coach and a quarterback who have a better working relationship." There would be no more back-biting or back-stabbing between these two men who are among the most pivotal personalities on their team and in the league. In 1992, Aikman and Johnson actually had casual, friendly conversations for almost the first time in their years in Dallas. Sometimes, their exchanges were of critical importance, involving play calling and personnel. Sometimes, they were relatively trivial, involving the distribution of Super Bowl tickets to team members or the reluctance of players to attend the pep rally at Texas Stadium before the NFC Championship Game. Sometimes, they were so inconsequential that neither man remembers the subjects. Inconsequential talks between Aikman and Johnson? They were almost unprecedented before July 14, 1992.

The event was the Cowboys' Pick-A-Ticket Night at Texas Stadium. After the team's practice, players showered and retired to the press box, where the organization presented awards for the club's outstanding performers in the off-season weight-and-conditioning program.

After a time, Aikman was preparing to leave the party, but couldn't locate his duffel bag. He was told Johnson had swiped it as a prank.

"Coach, can you give me my bag back? I need to get going," Aikman said.

"Troy, I didn't take your bag," insisted Johnson, who finally smiled and produced Aikman's paycheck, which had been inside the bag.

"That got us started," says Aikman, whose analysis of the reason for the incident ignores the fact that Johnson does nothing unplanned and has no interest in pranks. "I don't think it was anything planned. It was just a playful thing. But it was a little joke that turned into kind of a turning point."

The cease-fire summit meeting between Johnson and Aikman moved from the location of Aikman's duffel bag to a discourse on the talent level of the 1992 edition of the Cowboys. They ended up talking about how it was up to the two of them to guide that talent in a way that would allow it to be fulfilled.

"Jimmy and I were the last two to leave the party," Aikman says. "We talked over a couple of beers all night, about everything. We talked about what needed to be done by both of us, and what we needed from each other, if we were going to have a successful season. Essentially, we agreed to bury the hatchet."

Well after midnight on July 14, 1992, Aikman got his bag back. And Johnson got his quarterback.

"'The Catch'? God, I got sick of hearing about 'The Catch,'" says Cowboys receiver Alvin Harper. "I was what, fourteen, when Dwight Clark did it? It kills me that people made such a big deal about us getting revenge for what the 49ers did to the Cowboys before. When I was eight years old, I wasn't even thinking two cents about pro football or pro anything. I was just running around playing, like kids do."

In relative terms, Harper and most of his Cowboys teammates were still infants on January 17, when they prepared to
muddy their uniforms in the National Football Conference
Championship Game. The opponent was the San Francisco
49ers, the site was Candlestick Park, and the sense that the
young Cowboys might achieve symmetry was as steady as the
pregame rain. On January 10, 1982, the 49ers had defeated
Dallas 28-27 thanks to "The Catch," an improbable touchdown
completion that inaugurated San Francisco's decade of domi-
nance and Dallas's decade of demise.

Fifty-eight seconds remained in that game when quarterback Joe Montana listened to coach Bill Walsh's sideline instructions. "Sprint Right Motion" was Walsh's play-call for the
third-and-three situation from the six-yard line. As legend has
it, Walsh then said, "Look for Freddie (Solomon). If he's not
open, throw it high so either Dwight will get it or it will be
thrown away."

Cowboys fans are excused for doubting the veracity of that
part of the legend, because Walsh could not possibly have
counted on the improvisational skills of Montana and Clark to
produce one of the most memorable and important moments
in NFL history. Indeed, as Montana says, the pass "was supposed to be high, but not that high."

Walsh could not possibly have counted on Solomon slipping out of his break, or on Clark being well-covered by both
Everson Walls and Michael Downs, or on Ed "Too Tall" Jones
and D. D. Lewis converging on the backpedaling Montana just
a nanosecond before he unloaded a pass that seemed to be
directed toward Berkeley. Or on the six-foot-four Clark stretching higher than a human really can, catching a haunting pass
that was finally due to be exorcised eleven years later.

Cowboys middle linebacker Robert Jones, a lifelong Dallas
rooter, met Clark when the 49ers great, now the team's player

personnel administrator, made a scouting trip to see Jones at East Carolina.

"I got in his face and asked him why he had to catch that ball," Jones says. "He said he was just doing his job. I don't care what his reasons are. I just know I've cursed that man a thousand times and I still do whenever they show that highlight."

Emmitt Smith cursed the highlight for another reason. "I'm sick of the Dwight Clark catch, of the 49er dynasty and all that stuff," Smith said. "All that old stuff is irrelevant right now."

"The Catch" was irrelevant to most Cowboys because, like Smith and Harper, they didn't know anything about it. Their immediate concern was the pigsty at Candlestick. By the Thursday before the game, Johnson — who to his dismay was the one who alerted his players to the concerns about the oatmeal-like grounds in the first place — ordered a moratorium on turf talk. "It doesn't matter if we play the 49ers on asphalt or in a mudpile, we'll be ready to play," Johnson told his team just before that afternoon's workout. He then turned to assistant equipment manager Mike McCord, who'd arranged to make a prepractice announcement.

"Make sure you let me know which cleats you want me to bring to San Francisco," McCord said.

That night, twenty or so Cowboys were arm-twisted into driving to Texas Stadium for a pep rally. Most thought the idea "high-schoolish." Most wondered why they weren't being paid for the appearance. All were glad they were in the house that roared thanks to the send-off given the Cowboys by 67,900 fans. "Nobody really wanted to be there," receiver Michael Irvin says, "until they got there. Traffic getting into the stadium was a nightmare. But once we were in there, it was an incredible boost." Only Johnson didn't enjoy the festivities. He was something just short of churlish in a live TV interview with

KDFW-Channel 4's Clarice Tinsley, who he blew off after she served up a patty-cake question intended to draw Johnson into being charming for the home viewers.

Smith is right when he says, "People make too much out of all the trivial stuff that really doesn't have to do with the actual game. 'The Catch' was in the past. Anything that happened eleven years ago should be a dead issue. This is a totally different team. Different guys, different coaches. It's just like the muddy field, Charles (Haley) going back to San Francisco, our team's inexperience, anything you want to throw at us. None of it really mattered."

What mattered was that the NFC Championship Game pitted the two teams with the best records — and arguably the best organizations — against one another.

Unlike many pro sports franchises, the organizational charts of these two clubs are easily legible. The Cowboys, following the advice of longtime NFL coach Chuck Knox, make sure the two decision-makers are on the same page when it comes time to share credit or blame. "When we make a draft pick, I like to get the team owner and the general manager in the room with me," Knox advised Jones and Johnson when they were building their Cowboys front office. "We get out a sheet of paper, and we all sign it and put it in the file. That way, two or three years down the line, nobody can say they disagreed with someone else for making what turned out to be a bad decision."

In San Francisco, it is almost as simple. Owner Eddie DeBartolo oversees coach George Seifert, who runs the football side, and team president Carmen Policy, a lawyer who supervises the business side.

Both organizations also invite accusations of arrogance, exhibit the willingness to be patient, and have depth on the players roster, the coaching staff and the front office.

There are style differences, of course. Jerry Jones plows into crowds of Cowboys fans to exchange pleasantries; the 49ers send beefy security guards after inquisitive kids who try to peer over the walls that surround the club's Santa Clara, California, practice fields. The 49ers serve incredibly lavish meals on their team flights. As he proved on December 13 after the loss in Washington, Johnson can order flight attendants to cease service altogether.

And then there is the style difference named Charles Haley. As Haley says, the 49ers viewed him as "a lunatic." The Cowboys were thinking something more along the lines of "savior." When before the 1992 season opener the 49ers tired of his antics and dealt him to Dallas, Jones was so revved up he decided to make Haley feel welcome by personally picking him up at D/FW Airport. During their twenty-minute drive back to Valley Ranch, Jones attempted to make witty small talk.

"Charles," Jones asked, "are you leaving youre heart in San Francisco?"

"I didn't leave anything in San Francisco," growled Haley, apparently forgetting about that urine sample he deposited on Tim Harris' car.

After the Cowboys beat Philadelphia to advance to the NFC title game in the city where Haley was as much star-crossed as he was a star, he said, "It will close a chapter of my life. I'm glad we finish this way. It will get a lot of pressure off my mind and a lot of things off my chest. I don't know if I should take it as a big thrill or just that I'm going back there. For me, it's going to be a little different."

Would Haley be able to offer game-plan insight as the Cowboys prepared? "He's got a lot of information," Johnson said. "But we might have to censor it a little bit."

Because of the work of 49ers offensive tackle Steve Wallace, Haley (no sacks, one tackle) was about as much of a factor in the game as the Friday night earthquake that measured 5.1 on the Richter Scale, the week-long flood warnings, and the quagmire field that had been miraculously repaired by "Sod God" George Toma. Armed with 23,000 square feet of Bermuda grass and fourteen tons of clay and crushed ceramic, the NFL's grounds-keeping wizard transformed the rained-soaked Field of Streams into a very playable surface. Too playable, say the 49ers who'd counted on Mother Nature as an ally. "I think putting that sod in was the worst thing we could have done," Wallace says. "It gave Emmitt Smith perfect footing."

Smith danced to 173 yards of total offense. But with just three carries in Dallas's first fifteen snaps, it was obvious he would have to be patient. As a concession to what Johnson assumed would be a steadily worsening track, the Cowboys coach arose from a light sleep in his San Francisco Marriott suite for a 4:00 a.m. revision of the game plan. He recalled something Cowboys staffer Neill Armstrong, a former Bears head coach and ex-Minnesota Vikings assistant under Bud Grant, told him about starting fast on a bad-weather day. "Neill said Bud Grant beat the Rams one time by throwing early, before all the rain they had ended up chewing up the field," Johnson says. "We were going to be aggressive offensively, anyway, because we thought we could throw on them. But the weather I anticipated changed a few things."

By 8:00 a.m., Johnson had assembled his coaches, who implemented the alterations that were designed to put Dallas ahead before a mudslide or flood or earthquake sent rickety Candlestick crumbling or skidding into the Bay.

This NFC title game had no "The Catch," no single high-light that will be engraved in memories above all others. This game had bunches of catches. A first-quarter, fumbled punt — one-handed by Daryl Johnston — set up Lin Elliott's 20-yard field goal that put Dallas up 3-0. A second-quarter fumble recovery by Cowboys cornerback Kevin Smith, and a weird, drive-preserving defensive holding call against 49ers lineman Pierce Holt, allowed Emmitt Smith's four-yard touchdown run, a score that put Dallas up 10-7. A third-quarter lob snared in gymnastic fashion by Harper for a 38-yard gain that triggered Johnson's three-yard score and the 17-13 advantage Dallas rode into the final quarter.

"On that one, all I know is I somehow caught it over (49ers cornerback Eric Davis's) head," says Harper. "I didn't really know how I caught that one then — I saw the ball and I saw him put his hands up, but I just wanted to put my hands in there to prevent the interception — and when I look at tape now, I still say, 'Man, I don't know how I caught that pass.'"

In the fourth quarter, Smith culminated a brilliant Aikman-engineered drive with a 16-yard touchdown reception. The Cowboys had chomped exactly nine minutes off the clock on that 14-play, 79-yard possession, converting on all four of their third-down tries. They were up 24-13. Just twelve minutes stood between them and the Super Bowl.

The seconds would have ticked away more quickly had a non-textbook gamble by Johnson worked. With seven minutes left and Dallas facing a fourth-and-one from the San Francisco seven-yard line, a chip-shot field goal would have put the Cowboys up by fourteen points. All that "Love, American Style" smooching that took place after the game — the meaningful peck exchanged by Jones and Johnson, the almost lustful one passed from Johnson to comely CBS-TV reporter Lesley Visser — could have instead been an on-field puckerfest right then and there. "You don't always do things by the book," Aikman says. "At least we don't around here. Sometimes, maybe you feel you have the talent to beat the percentages. Sometimes you just try to beat the percentages because of the tone it sets."

Johnson's gamble failed when Smith couldn't get the needed thirty-six inches. The 49ers answered, pushing 93 yards downfield for a short Steve Young-to-Jerry Rice touchdown pass that closed the Cowboys' lead to four points.

"Never a doubt," rookie cornerback Kevin Smith says of his belief he could stick with Rice, the greatest wide receiver who ever lived. "Before you watch film of somebody, you let their reputation get to you. Then you watch film and you see them do some amazing things, then that gets to you. But when you get on the field, you realize he's just flesh and blood, just like you. He had some numbers (eight catches, 123 yards), and he got that one touchdown, but we really didn't let him do any damage. And I told him so. All game, I just kept calling him, 'No. 80,' like I wouldn't let him know I even knew what his name was. He never did respond until the very end. When he gave me the finger."

At the very end, Dallas did all the right things necessary to come a step closer to gracing their fingers with a ring. In the fourth quarter, the Cowboys got interceptions by Ken Norton and James Washington. And a third sack by Tony Casillas. And the 70-yard pass to Harper that, as he says, "broke the whole thing open. It was a great thrown pass. All my job was to catch it and do whatever. When I caught it and cut away from (Don Griffin), I saw I had some open field. It got to the point where I was running out of wind. Even though I was getting closer and closer to the end zone, it felt like it was getting farther and farther away. Eventually, I was wishing they would just hurry up and tackle me, because I knew the game was over with.

"Hey," Harper says, "you think maybe now they'll talk about my catch as 'The Catch?'"

The pattern, a "Skinny Post 8 Route," was called with Michael Irvin in mind. He was supposed to be lined up on Aikman's left. Harper was supposed to be on the right side of the line of scrimmage and was to run a curl. But Irvin's recollection that earlier in the game the curl pattern had produced a big play for Harper, caused him to order Harper to swap spots.

"I got greedy," Irvin says.

"Maybe Michael learned a lesson," offensive coordinator Norv Turner jokes. "He should line up where he's supposed to line up, and that would've been him making that play."

Three plays later, Aikman bulleted a six-yard touchdown pass to Kelvin Martin, and the Cowboys had finally sealed their 30-20 victory and a berth in Super Bowl XXVII, an achievement that once seemed as improbable as the laudatory words that flowed from Johnson toward his quarterback at the postgame press conference.

"When you're the first pick in the entire draft, and especially when you're a quarterback, the Super Bowl is what's expected of you," says Aikman, who, all modesty aside, has always envisioned himself as a budding Super Bowl quarterback. So did most of the rest of the free world. In October 1992, coach Bill Parcells presented Aikman with a gift. It was a poster of Parcells being carried off the field after one of his two Super Bowl victories with the New York Giants. Aikman considered what Parcells had written on the poster — "Troy. Hope you get a ride like this someday. Bill Parcells" — a very logical possibility.

Did Johnson believe with the same conviction Parcells and all the others did? Did Aikman's own coach number among the few doubters? Aikman still wondered in the days before the Cowboys' win over the Eagles, until he scanned a newspaper story in which Johnson effusively raved about his quarterback's excellence.

"He's the type of quarterback who fits my personality perfectly," Johnson had said. "A quarterback who stays in control can be an asset for me because I can be, well, emotional, etcetera. ... The more I'm around Troy, the more I respect his ability to keep things on an even keel and stay focused. He's accustomed to handling big games, to handling the media, to whatever the situation is. He's been tremendous. ... Anyone who thinks Troy Aikman might be intimidated is proving they don't know Troy Aikman. ... Troy's been as good as any coach could ask for."

Aikman doesn't usually read the papers. But this was enough to cause him to consider a lifetime subscription. "Did he really say those things?" Aikman asked. "That's some of the nicest things he's ever said about me."

Johnson said more after the 49ers game. After repeating that irritating "How 'Bout Them Cowboys!" rallying cry he'd chanted over and over in the locker room (did Johnson know he was in effect creating titles for at least two Cowboys-chronicling books that would be published after the season?), he directed his remarks toward Aikman, who'd just completed 24 of 34 passes for a season-high 322 yards, two scores and no interceptions.

Johnson nodded to his right, where Aikman was waiting to take his turn behind the podium. "It was Troy's game," said Johnson, who, just before embracing his former "enemy" added humbly, "Troy has come a long way. And he's brought me with him."

14 SUPERSTAR-GAZING ★

"You know what struck me the most about that Darryl Talley fight?" receiver Kelvin Martin says. "Once it started, none of Talley's teammates stepped in to help him. I couldn't believe that. Their team must be a lot different than we were. If that would've been one of our guys involved, it would have been one of the most massive brawls of all time. Because every single Cowboy in that joint would've jumped on the pile."

As it was, says Magic Johnson, "Nobody wanted anything to happen, because it would come out like it was bigger than the game."

Well, not exactly. It came out innocuously enough. In the *Fort Worth Star-Telegram*'s January 27 edition, it came out exactly like this:

Magic's Guard Keeps Bills At Bay

SANTA MONICA, Calif. — Retired basketball star Earvin "Magic" Johnson, his bodyguard and Buffalo Bills stars Jim Kelly and Darryl Talley engaged in a Sunday-evening shouting and shoving match at a Los Angeles nightclub that resulted in the bodyguard punching Talley in the face, according to witnesses who saw what might be described as the first unofficial contact drills of Super Bowl XXVII."

Every year at the Super Bowl, like party goers waiting for an unsuspecting guest to sit on a whoopie cushion, the public waits for a game participant to do something stupid. The media's frenzied hunger for anything interesting to write about can balloon any compelling little story into a cause célébre. Jam some big-name football players into a glitzy nightclub called Roxbury (waiving the $10 cover charge, of course), add a luminary like Magic Johnson and a slab of flesh like his bodyguard, Big Anthony, stir in an excess of alcohol and machismo, and you have the makings of both a fistfight and a compelling tale.

Really, the fact that something like this happened a week before the Dallas Cowboys were to play the Buffalo Bills in Super Bowl XXVII is hardly astonishing. What is astonishing — and what caused Magic Johnson's concerns about the Super Bowl Week focus being misdirected to be realized — is that the situation was worsened by the Bills' clownish handling of it. After all, with three straight trips to the Super Bowl, all marked by the Bills' inability to handle opponents and whoopie cushions, Buffalo should have the depth of experience necessary to know how to deal with the ramifications of its own shenanigans.

In Super Bowl appearances in the previous two seasons, the AFC champion Bills had lost two games and an immeasurable amount of composure. Running back Thurman Thomas failed to start a Super Bowl because he'd misplaced his helmet. Thomas and quarterback Jim Kelly debated publicly over which of them was "the Michael Jordan of the offense."

Defensive end Bruce Smith railed on about racism in Buffalo. Coach Marv Levy skipped a mandatory press conference.

In 1992, they accomplished much on the field: an 11-5 record and a wild-card play-off berth; a 41-38 win play-off win over the Houston Oilers in which they overcame a 35-3 deficit with the greatest comeback in NFL history; and back-to-back road wins over division champions Pittsburgh and Miami for the AFC title.

But they sensed that their misadventures might overshadow their achievements. If the Bills beat the Cowboys, Thomas predicted, "the headline will probably be, 'Bills Win Super Bowl; Thurman Thomas Finds Helmet.'"

Some combination of truth and humor would have been the way to defuse the Talley bomb. Instead, Talley, Levy and general manager Bill Polian issued hollow denials and false accusations. Buffalo kept shooting itself in the foot, then sticking the bloody foot in its mouth. An unseemly sight it was.

Probably, Levy should have told the whole truth at press conferences on Thursday and Friday, as he told the whole truth to pool reporter Mickey Spagnola on Wednesday, when Spagnola asked the supposedly scholarly coach what he knew about the *Star-Telegram* story.

"Nothing," Levy said. "I haven't heard anything about that."

Probably, Talley should have used truth and humor and come clean. Yes, he was at Roxbury, the hot L.A. nightclub situated in a tony stretch of Sunset Boulevard. Yes, there were more than a dozen football players there, from the Cowboys and Bills and other teams. Yes, there was drinking, and Talley and Kelly probably did imbibe too much and go too far when they teased Magic Johnson. About Johnson's nightclubbing habits, which seem to contradict his public persona as a faithful and repentant husband and father, who has tested positive for the HIV virus that causes AIDs. Whatever, the jibes were delivered in a manner Big Anthony found objectionable.

Big Anthony told Bruce Smith to instruct his friends, especially Talley, to control themselves. "Cool him down," the gigantic bodyguard said, "or I'll cool him down my way."

"A man thing," Johnson calls it.

Says Michael Irvin: "You've got to understand something about Darryl. He likes to drink some. That's what caused it. Going over to the Pro Bowl (after the 1991 season), Talley was so drunk on the airplane, they had to get a wheelchair for him. He was too drunk to even walk through an airport! So at (Roxbury), when I realized there was some trouble involving the Bills, I immediately thought, 'God, I bet it was Talley.'"

It was. Big Anthony collided with Talley. He shoved his hand into Talley's face, flipping the linebacker to the floor of the crowded nightclub, and said, "Let's stop it here."

Says Cowboys guard Nate Newton: "Everybody in there was feeling so good. There was some drinking, women flirting, you know. It was crowded. I'm surprised the fire marshall didn't come and close the place down. It happened so quick that not everyone saw what happened — whether it was a punch or a push or whatever — but we all saw Darryl Talley getting up off the ground. Some guys thought they saw some blood, some didn't."

Says Dallas linebacker Vinson Smith: "This bodyguard was huge, so the whole thing could have been worse. But it got settled down pretty quick. He punched Darryl in the face, Darryl went down, he got back up and it was over."

Over? Not yet.

On Monday morning, retelling the story of the fight was the rage at the Cowboys' breakfast table. "The surprising thing is it took so long for this to come out," says Dallas line coach Tony Wise. "All our players were talking about it Monday." (Sorry we couldn't get it to you faster, coach.) Magic Johnson placed a phone call to Bruce Smith to apologize for the incident. On Tuesday, when Johnson met with Troy Aikman, Emmitt Smith and Irvin to conduct a round table discussion as part of NBC's pregame show, the subject of the Talley fight was broached during the commercial breaks.

"One of us brought it up," Emmitt Smith says. "Magic said it wasn't really much of a fight, because if his bodyguard had really wanted to get to Talley, Talley wouldn't have played on Sunday."

By Tuesday afternoon, news of the altercation filtered down to the *Star-Telegram*. Interviews with four players and two other witnesses not affiliated with either team helped produce the story that ran on Wednesday.

By Thursday, the Bills had the look and feel of a naughty boy trying to talk his way out of a spanking. "There was no fight," declared Talley, attempting to semantically tap dance his way out from the middle of a hundred microphones and notepads at a Thursday press conference.

He was asked if there was pushing and shoving.

"You're in a nightclub and there's a lot of people in the nightclub," Talley answered. "Now how are you supposed to distinguish?"

He was asked if harsh words were exchanged.

"No more than you would normally think," Talley said.

He was asked about Johnson's testimony that there was indeed a scuffle of some sort.

"He wasn't there," Talley said. "How could he be there? I'm telling you there wasn't anything."

He was asked if drinking was involved.

"What would you do in a bar?" Talley answered.

He was asked if he wished he'd conducted himself differently that night.

"I wish I'd gone outside and picked flowers," Talley said. "Why am I being persecuted?"

"Persecuted" is too strong. "Interrogated" is about right, and the reason is because Talley was involved in a newsmaking event, and then lied about it.

Then came Levy's meeting with the press. In an exercise borrowed straight from a high school debate class, Levy buffoonishly attempted to accuse the accuser. His statements at a Thursday media session were stunningly preposterous.

"The report is untrue. It didn't happen," Levy asserted. "Here's a story that runs in the Fort Worth paper, quoting anonymous Cowboys players about something Bills players who are supposedly not available for comment did in some bar. ... But I just have to say, happening this late in the week, considering the source, coming from a paper in that area, 'Nice but clumsy try, folks.'"

At one point, Levy wailed, "It's a lie! It's a lie!"

Polian's hands were literally shaking as he issued his bizarre denial: "The whole thing is untrue. They were never in a bar."

By Friday, Levy had lost touch with reality. KVIL-FM broadcaster Brad Sham, the Cowboys' play-by-play man, tried to help him regain his sense of reality in the middle of a massive press conference. Levy's thoughtless assertion that the *Star-Telegram* fabricated the story then published it because it was in cahoots with the home-town Cowboys was, as Sham recognized, an insult to both the Cowboy organization as well as every working journalist.

Sham: "Coach Levy, is it your contention the the *Fort Worth Star-Telegram* intentionally fabricated the Talley story to somehow give Dallas an edge?"

Levy: "No."

Sham: "Can you then explain what you meant by, 'Nice, clumsy try?'"

Levy: "It was a story that appeared on Wednesday, only in one paper, quoting an unnamed Dallas player about specific Buffalo Bills players."

Sham: "Is it your contention that they did (fabricate)?"

Levy: "I never said that. What made you ask that?"

Sham: "Because I didn't quite understand your quote, Coach, about 'nice, clumsy try.'"

It is ironic that Levy would accuse the *Star-Telegram* of unethical story-telling while himself playing so loosely with the facts. The original story did not "quote one unnamed Dallas player"; it quoted several witnesses, not all of them identified as "Cowboys," because not all of them were. The fact the story appeared in one paper makes it no less credible; does the fact that it appeared in a thousand papers by Thursday suddenly persuade Levy of its accuracy? And finally, by Friday morning, the *New York Times, Sports Illustrated*, the *Star-Telegram* and any other outlet covering the Super Bowl that recognized its responsibility to its customers had drawn out witnesses to attest on the record to the occurrence of an incident involving Talley.

When the teams arrived in the Los Angeles area on Sunday, January 24, Levy tried to incite his own controversy by staking a claim to the Cowboys' "America's Team" tag. "'America's Team' sometimes is what somebody names themselves," said Levy, adding that the club's comeback win over Houston in the play-offs drew "an outpouring of letters telling us we are 'America's Team.' I told our players, "You know who's going to be wearing red, white and blue when we play the game. You are 'America's Team.'"

While Levy was waxing patriotic before his players, Johnson was warning his. Warning them about just the sort of dangers they might encounter at a place like Roxbury.

"When you lay down a two-by-four board in the middle of a room, most everybody can get on that board and walk across it and not fall," Johnson told the Cowboys before letting them hit the streets. "Now take that board up ten stories high between two buildings. Some of the people aren't going to make it across that same board because they let themselves get distracted.

"If you let it overwhelm you that this is going to be the single most-watched sporting event in the entire world this year, if it overwhelms you that there are three thousand media people here, if it overwhelms you because of how much money is involved, it will be a distraction.

"Don't be distracted by the fact that there are other things going on here besides football this week."

A few hours later, many of Johnson's Cowboys witnessed that initial distraction. And Talley felt that distraction bust him across the nose.

The day after the Cowboys defeated the 49ers for the right to represent the National Conference in the Super Bowl, Johnson phoned Joe Gibbs and Bill Parcells, who combined to direct four of the previous six Super Bowl winners, for advice on how to structure the team's time. Both the Washington Redskins' Gibbs and former New York Giants coach Parcells were loaded with similar suggestions: install the game plan early; strip the players of as much responsibility to family and friends as possible; move to an unpublicized destination the night before the game; assume a relaxed mood in public, but an all-business attitude at practices.

Back in Dallas, the Cowboys had been deluged by calls from well-wishers and favor-wanters. Many players quit answering their phones. Newton's answering machine said: "If I didn't offer you any tickets for the regular season, I sure ain't going to offer you any Super Bowl tickets."

One phone call came into Johnson from Camp David. It was George Bush, the president. On the extension was a Camp David guest, George Strait, the singer. No, they didn't want tickets.

"I did have a very interesting phone call from President Bush congratulating us on the win (in the NFC title game)," Johnson says. "He made mention that he watched the game with George Strait and with Barbara. Then George Strait got on the phone. I did relate to him that I knew we had some players who are big fans of his. Of course, we're all big fans of President Bush."

The Cowboys' escape from Dallas also served as a break for the players from their families. Before leaving for the Super Bowl, Cowboys players took a team vote to determine whether they should bring wives into Southern California immediately, or wait until late in the week. No one raised their hand in favor of early arrival.

"One player told his wife that the reason she wasn't coming (on Sunday, the same day as the team) was that everyone voted it down," defensive end Tony Tolbert says. "She told all the other wives, so by Thursday, there were some pissed-off women coming into L.A. And did you notice that it was around Thursday when some of the guys started getting a little uptight?"

The Wednesday of Super Bowl Week was the last night of no curfew. It was also the last night of no wives. Some Cowboys took advantage of both. Over four nights, one player paraded thirteen different females to his hotel room. But most used the extra freedom to introduce themselves — to their own teammates.

"I saw guys hanging together that usually don't hang together," Newton says, "and that was the beauty of most of us deciding to not have the wives come out until Thursday. It wasn't necessarily so all the guys could go out and party, though a few guys did that. It was so guys could spend time together, get to know each other, and relish this situation we were in. I saw people spending time with each other, talking with each other, who never had really talked before.

"There were guys I'd misjudged because even though we are teammates, I hadn't gotten to know them. Jim Jeffcoat. Me and him talked a little, talked about how we deal with some financial things, and found out we had a little bit in common that I never knew before. Larry Brown. I found out Larry Brown is a decent guy.

"It was a time," Newton says, "to get to enjoy each other as Cowboys, and find out we have more in common with each other than just knocking heads."

The Cowboys should have sensed fate was leaning their way when they checked into their hotel. While the Bills were lodging downtown at the Hyatt Regency, amidst the noise and smog and honking horns of Los Angeles, the Cowboys roomed at the luxurious Loews Santa Monica Beach Hotel. It is within walking distance of the Pacific Ocean, the Santa Monica Pier, numerous trendy nightspots and Venice Beach. It was the site of bikini-model photo shoots and definitely a prominent place to see and be seen. To the Cowboys, who are usually restrained by Johnson's short leash, it was the Nirvana Inn.

Johnson eyed the locale and shook his head as bellhops dutifully grabbed his and owner Jerry Jones's luggage. "Jerry," Johnson moaned in mock disgust, "did you pick this hotel out?"

Jones, in fact, was surprised himself, especially when he was ushered into the hotel's presidential suite. Robert Tisch, a part-owner of the Giants and the owner of Loews Hotels, usually bunks in that suite.

Swarming about the hotel were the usual autograph hounds, groupies and riffraff. The unfortunate Aikmaniac named Charles, who appears to be either retarded or deranged or drugged-out, or all three, was a lobby fixture, weaving obscure-but-true facts about Aikman's personal life with Charles's own fantasies about his friendship with his old UCLA weightlifting partner. (Aikman says Charles once phoned Aikman's mother to inform her that Troy had hired him to work as his personal valet, and was wondering when they were bringing him to Dallas to start the job.) And while the floors of the players' rooms were off-limits to the general public, some hassles could not be detoured. On Tuesday, Aikman's telephone rang, waking him as the sun came up.

"Mr. Aikman," said the guy on the line, "can you tell me what time practice begins today?"

Aikman asked the caller to identify himself. The caller said he's an avid Cowboys fan.

"I'm not sure when practice starts," Aikman said. "Why don't you call Jimmy Johnson's room and ask him?"

Still, this was a special atmosphere. In the vicinity of the Cowboys on any given day or night were entertainers such as Arsenio Hall, Gene Hackman, Dennis Quaid, Tom Berenger, Kate Jackson and Whoopi Goldberg. They worked out in the weight room, drank in the lobby bar, swam in the hotel pool, a few feet from where the Dallas/Fort Worth TV news shows were broadcasting live nightly. MTV temptress Downtown Julie Brown also cavorted about by the pool, and wherever else Cowboys and cameras converged. At Tuesday's Media Day, she purred things to Jimmy Johnson that turned Dodger Stadium into one big erogenous zone.

"What's your name?" quizzed Johnson, eyeing the woman in the black leather bra and black fishnet stockings.

"My name is Downtown Julie Brown," she said in that perky British accent. Later, she asked Johnson, "What's the one rule of thumb you've given to the players?"

"Don't kiss Julie Brown," Johnson replied before pecking her on the right cheek.

Country-music stars are old (ten-gallon) hat to this team, but in L.A., the Cowboys were permitted to rub elbows with the likes of pop singers Michael Jackson and Bobby Brown.

"Bobby Brown came up to me one night while I was in a club," Emmitt Smith says. "He asked me, 'Aren't you Emmitt Smith?' Then he said, 'You're a baaaaad boy. You're good.' Bobby and I carried on a conversation. He told me he had money bet on the game. I ain't going to tell you how much."

Smith says "it was sweet" to be a guest on the "Arsenio Hall Show." But he was disappointed that it was defensive back Kenny Gant who was anointed to shake the glove of Michael Jackson at a Tuesday press session designed to promote Jackson's scheduled performance at halftime of the game. "Man, the 'King of Pop,' that's who I wanted to meet," Smith says.

Maybe Jackson was destined to be with Gant because of the latter's attempts to promote a dance craze. Jackson has the "Moonwalk." Gant has the "Shark." Early in the 1992 season, the rookie cornerback proudly displayed his array of dance-floor moves to his teammates in practice. Gant, placing his hand on his head and thrusting his elbow skyward to form a fin, stole one of the gyrations. "Kevin did it first, it was his idea, but I was the one who wasn't afraid to do it in front of sixty thousand people," says Gant, who by the Super Bowl was acknowledging fans who called out, "Hey, Shark" and were wearing T-shirts bearing his likeness.

The Cowboys may not have followed the lead of Johnson, who says he never stayed out past 10:00 p.m. and whose most eventful outing came on Thursday evening, when he dined at a place called Jimmy's with former Cowboys boss Tex Schramm and former NFL commissioner Pete Rozelle. Until Wednesday, many players came far closer to crawling into their rooms at 10:00 a.m. than p.m. But, says receiver Alvin Harper, "We realized how hard it is to get to a Super Bowl. And while we wanted to enjoy every minute of it, because it might never happen again, we didn't want to ruin it by having fun in the wrong way."

There was a logical theory that had the Cowboys crumbling under the weight of their own inexperience. "We were too young and naive, and things were happening too fast, to take the time to analyze that theory," says Michael Irvin. Indeed, their week was a blur. A sample:

There was a party hosted by Los Angeles Clippers basketball star Ron Harper. "A Who's Who of football showed up," Newton says. "I've seen a lot of those parties where everyone thinks they're big, where some of my players turn into asses and guys on other teams turn into asses. This was nothing like that. Very mellow, very nice." Adds defensive tackle Russell Maryland: "Maybe some people wised up. Nobody had any fights."

Says Martin: "Man, there were some great celebrity parties. We went to one party put on by (rapper) Baby Face one night and the next night it was a party by Heavy D (yes, another rapper). That was cool."

At Media Day, every player was in demand. Some of the Cowboys were too inexperienced to know they were supposed to wear their game jerseys for the session so they could be identified; rookies Robert Jones, Kevin Smith, Darren Woodson and others avoided some of the questions because many reporters never figured out who they are. But one rookie, fighter pilot/defensive lineman Chad Hennings, was cornered. He offered that he is "opposed to homosexuals in the military."

Daryl Johnston, Kevin Gogan and Alan Veingrad took turns behind the wheel of a Hummer, the half-tank, half-car military vehicle used by U.S. troops in the Gulf War. "Doesn't handle well," Veingrad reported. Tony Casillas had dinner with Brian Bosworth, the former Oklahoma teammate once labeled by Casillas as "a fraud." Surly Charles Haley accepted free beers from the hotel bartender, but wouldn't return the favor of autographing the barkeep's hat. Bills owner Ralph Wilson proudly ordered a press release stating the Bills will play Super Bowl host to Virginia Kelley, President Clinton's mother. "What's the big deal?" countered Jerry Jones. "We're inviting her son."

Johnson was asked about his inflexible hair. "It just so happens that this is the way I like my hair," he said. "But I do have a touch of spray on it. Hey, it's true. Just a touch. I'm not lying to you. I'm not a closet sprayer." Michael Irvin said he had cut charity-benefitting deals with two of the sponsors of his television show. If the Cowboys lose to the Bills, "I'll be sacking groceries at Kroger's, and I'll be throwing luggage at Love Field for Southwest Airlines," he said. "Both of those are good jobs, don't get me wrong. But it will be enough to make me try and help us win, believe me."

Johnson claimed his IQ is 162. Nobody argued.

Newton said he wanted to thank the media "for the good times. I want to beat the hell out of y'all for the bad times. Most of all, y'all take care of yourselves. I hope y'all get one of them Pulitzers one day in your life. I don't know what a Pulitzer is. I just heard somebody say something about it."

Johnson said he'd seen two films in a theater in the last twelve years. "Just excellent," he said of the one he recalled,

'Silence of the Lambs.' "And (the murderous character Hannibal) Lecter, he was neat. I mean, he's somebody I'd like to study."

On Thursday evening, TV anchorpeople were agog with the news that Aikman was preparing to dine that night with Jim Kelly. Meanwhile, Aikman was at Gladstone's in Malibu, carving into a steak as thick as a fist and discussing the reasons he wouldn't "do L.A." with Kelly.

"The problem with Jim," Aikman said, "is that he's so competitive, he'll try to take advantage of me if we go out. He'll get me drunk then ask me for information. Or else he'll push me in front of a car. I'll go out with him at the Pro Bowl, maybe."

Happy thirtieth wedding anniversary, Gene and Jerry Jones. Plans were made for the Jones family to meet at Chenois Restaurant for Oriental food at 6:30 p.m. Jerry Jones arrived at 9:30, and didn't stay long. "We spent thirty minutes to commemorate thirty years," says Gene, who must be a very tolerant woman.

Jones was so busy, he didn't even find time to rediscover his roots. Early in the week, he made plans to locate the Southern California house he was born in. "I know it's in El Segundo," Jones says, "but I never made it out there. I'm not even sure if it's still standing."

Players read about a man named David Bridges, twenty-four, who was arrested by Grapevine, Texas, police for twice burglarizing a home. Bridges first broke into a residence to steal a TV set. He was apprehended later when he returned to the residence to swipe the remote control. Meanwhile, KVIL-FM Radio could not find its rental van. Had David Bridges taken it? No. Kevin Gogan had. "Oh, c'mon, I turned it in that same night," Gogan says. "Late that night. Really late. But there was a cellular phone in there, and we did keep that for the week."

Some Cowboys stayed in the slow lane. Aikman visited his old UCLA stomping grounds, scarfed down some lasagna in the student cafeteria, escorted some friends through Pauley Pavilion, and exchanged greetings with the guys in the trainers room. He did go out, once with actress Janine Turner, but more frequently he retired to his room to play with his "Big Mac." That would be his Macintosh Apple PowerBook 160 computer, the one with the programmed sound effects. "Listen to this," said Aikman, punching a series of keys that produce the moo of a cow, the stutter of cartoon character Elmer Fudd and the laugh of sidekick Ed McMahon. "I hope people don't think I'm turning into a computer nerd."

Tolbert hooked up with Willie Broughton, the former Cowboy who now plays for the Raiders. Their highlight was a tour of the Raiders offices, which is somehow fitting for Tolbert, the defensive end who may have been the most consistent player on the Cowboys defense and was certainly among its most consistently ignored. He had 8.5 sacks despite playing almost exclusively on running downs, led the defensive linemen in tackles, tied for the team high with three forced fumbles and never went public with his feeling that he might have doubled some of those stats had he not rotated out to give Jim Jeffcoat playing time.

"I don't think I did anything really fun the whole week," Tolbert says. "I've got friends on the team who like to party who I don't hang out with much anymore just because I've never been into that. So you can understand that me and a place like L.A. really don't agree with each other."

Then there was Tony Casillas, who asked Maryland to join him for a visit to another sort of attraction.

"I didn't know any of the specifics of what we were doing," says Maryland, who is still amazed at the memory of strolling into Hugh Hefner's Playboy Mansion. Miss May 1990 was their gracious guide. Miss January 1993 seemed nice, too. Hef entered one of the cavernous rooms to greet his guests. "All that stuff we did that night is Tony's speed, not mine. You know, that Hollywood Boulevard stuff. So I probably would've never gone there if he hadn't asked me.

"Still," says Maryland shyly, "I wouldn't mind going again."

Do the Bills feel the same way about Super Bowls? There were indications beyond their fumbling of the Talley situation that the AFC champs' jock straps were too tight. On Monday, Levy practiced his players in jerseys with no numbers on them, better to confuse the imagined spies. At the next practice, on Wednesday, Polian ordered security to investigate a pair of binoculars poking from a fifteenth-floor window overlooking the Bills' workouts at USC. On Thursday, the organization ordered campus police to confiscate film belonging to an *Associated Press* photographer. The man had taken pictures of some kids trying to peek into practice.

On Friday, when the Super Bowl coaches' traditional pose for photos with the Vince Lombardi Trophy, Levy tried to beg out. Levy finally touched the trophy as if it was a cactus.

And the Cowboys? "As the week went on, you could feel coach Johnson had a little sense of uptightness," Maryland says. "He didn't show it to the public. But there was a little urgency."

Over at UCLA's Spaulding Field on Wednesday, a trio of binocular owners were removed from the roof of the Engineering Building, about 500 yards from where the Cowboys practiced. That was nothing compared to what happened Friday, when Jones escorted some business associates, including legendary Cowboy Lee Roy Jordan, onto the practice-field sidelines.

"I thought he was there to give us a pep talk or something," center Mark Stepnoski says. "It would have been appropriate, since he played in Super Bowls for Dallas. It was kind of funny to see Jimmy kick him out. Now that was a bold move."

Johnson said the expulsion of the businessmen, including Jordan (one of just seven men to be inducted into the Cowboys' Ring of Honor) was necessary because "this is for the Super Bowl. People want to be in the know. They might see a play, brag to someone, and then that guy will tell someone else, and before you know it, someone on the other team hears what you're doing."

Says Maryland: "I'm not surprised he gave (Jordan) the boot. When coach Johnson gets serious about something, he's serious with few exceptions. If President Clinton would've come, coach Johnson might have let him look for five minutes before politely escorting him out."

Irvin agrees, saying Johnson and his team were in a workout groove that could not be interrupted.

"I've never seen any team have better practices," Irvin says. "Troy had the best practices of his life. We were so quick on the field. Jimmy lined up against me like a defensive back in 'team takeoff' (a sprint drill) and said, 'Michael, you are so much faster than back when you were in college.'

"I thought he was just getting old in the head and soft in the body," Irvin says. "But maybe he was right. Maybe we were all quicker."

On Saturday, the Cowboys were whisked away to a top-secret destination for their final night of pregame preparation. It did not take much reportorial digging to learn the team's new temporary headquarters was the Beverly Garland Hotel in North Hollywood — the same hotel where Parcells started the tradition of hiding away back in 1987's Super Bowl XXI. There was even a smattering of fans at the new hotel waiting to greet the Cowboys' buses as they pulled up.

"It was on Saturday night when it really hit us that it was

going to be our last hurrah," says Johnson, referring to the impending departure to the Chicago Bears of defensive coordinator Dave Wannstedt, offensive line coach Tony Wise and defensive assistant Bob Slowik. "For the previous few weeks, I hadn't jogged with my old group. It was just my personality. I knew I might get emotional, and I never wanted my emotions to affect in a negative way or distract anybody from what they had to do. Really, for a time there I didn't jog with them, didn't go to our regular Friday night get-togethers at On The Border for nachos and beers, didn't do any of those things."

Johnson was so intent on maintaining his distance that he was not among the Cowboys staffers who met that night to reminisce. Wannstedt, Wise, Butch Davis, Neill Armstrong, Cowboys chaplain John Weber and Father Leo Armbrust, Johnson's "lucky charm" who presided over pregame chapel services at the University of Miami and was brought to the Super Bowl to do the same for the Cowboys, did gather in a hotel suite to share memories. "We all thought it was ironic that we'd spent four years getting to that point, and that point would be the end of us together," Davis says. "It was a touching thing, really."

On Sunday morning, Johnson finally joined those closest to him for a final jog together around North Hollywood.

"That was a little emotional for all of us," Johnson says. "We got up early that morning, had a very relaxed time, very upbeat and positive. Nobody really said much about it, but we all knew it was the last time around with my old crew."

Cowboys coaches did not overtly use the breakup of the staff as a motivational tool for players. "They didn't need to," linebacker Ken Norton says. "It's the Super Bowl, so if you really need a pep talk, you shouldn't be playing. Besides, we all knew what winning would mean to everybody, including Dave Wannstedt. As a defensive unit, we wanted to make our final game with him a tribute to him."

Johnson's Saturday night address to the team at the Beverly Garland Hotel featured lots of what he calls "planting the seed." "I told them I wanted our best game to come in our last game," Johnson says. "That was a theme I used often. I planted that seed all year long."

Says Irvin: "Jimmy had said that so often, it was engraved on our foreheads."

Johnson's only concession to his own feelings about separating from his friends came when he concluded his speech this way: "I know we have people who would like to play well to please certain individuals. But the thing you've got to understand is, this is something that will last you the rest of your life. Play this game for yourself. Because the best way for all of us to remember each other by is to be able to go out with a Super Bowl ring on our fingers."

He calls it "planting the seed."

15 DALLAS IN WONDERLAND ★

Before Super Bowl XXVII, the only Cowboys who'd experienced the championship game of professional football from the inside were ex-49er Charles Haley and ex-Bengal Ray Horton. The other members of the Cowboys family had spent lifetimes viewing the Super Bowl from widely different, and usually distant, perspectives.

Before Jimmy Johnson became coach of the Cowboys, the Super Bowl once took a backseat to winning five bucks. Before Jerry Jones became the owner of the Cowboys, it once meant a way to increase his millions of bucks. Before Geneva Jones's boy, defensive tackle Jimmie, played in one, a Super Bowl was certainly no reason to take her first airplane ride in all of her sixty-plus years.

Back on January 15, 1967, two Wichita State assistant coaches were snowed in while traveling through Chicago. The men were bored out of their minds, so they created little competitions to get them through the morning until this strange new pro football event kicked off on TV. One bet the other five dollars he couldn't run across the snow-covered hotel patio without falling into the pool.

"Jimmy won the bet," says Larry Lacewell, now Dallas's college scouting director. "I still don't know how he did it."

Later that day, the Green Bay Packers won the strange new pro football event, beating the American Football League-champion Kansas City Chiefs in what would later be remembered as the first Super Bowl.

Jerry Jones has attended thirteen Super Bowls. For four of those trips, he's been Jerral Wayne Jones, owner and general manager of the Dallas Cowboys. But nine times before that, Jones was a Super Bowl ticket-holder. He attended the "Big One" in those days as an oil-and-gas magnate who wanted to rub elbows and reward employees.

"Back then, we used attending the Super Bowl as incentive to employees," Jones says. "The setting is perfect for that. Professional football is a game that honors meeting challenges, giving extra effort, and working together toward a goal. Now, I've gotten a look at the Super Bowl from another perspective. It is certainly one of the most awesome promotional events in the world. But really, it is all about winning."

Geneva Jones had no idea what it was all about. Driving to see the games played by her son was easy in his college days. The drive from Okeechobee, Florida, to the University of Miami is a comfortable one. But Geneva had never flown to Dallas to see Jimmie play professionally. She chickened out on Jimmie's invitation to bring her to town for the play-off opener against Philadelphia.

"Mom, I'm arranging the tickets," Jimmie told her. "You get a ride from Okeechobee to West Palm, that's about sixty-three miles, get on the plane, and in three hours you'll see us play the Eagles."

"No, baby, I ain't coming," Geneva answered. "Mama can't make it. But I'll come to the Super Bowl."

Jimmie Jones tried to explain to her that the Super Bowl wasn't that automatic, that the Cowboys would have to win two games to get there.

"In that case," Geneva said, "you better win two games."

A few weeks later, Geneva Jones, Jimmy Johnson, Jerry Jones and the rest became a part of this country's celebration of its secular religion, the American Bacchanalia, the Super Bowl.

"A perfect day," Troy Aikman says. "It's impossible to imagine the scene at that Super Bowl unless you were actually there. It was just a perfect day. Perfect weather. Limousines everywhere, stretched bumper-to-bumper for what seemed like miles. Blimps all over the place. Those jet fighters flying overhead just before the start. Something like a hundred thousand people. And then Garth (Brooks) to sing the National Anthem. Perfect."

Somewhere beyond the limousines and the jet fighters and the 98,374 people in the Rose Bowl and the 133.4 million people in front of TV sets and the palm trees and San Gabriel mountains and the pro beach volleyball game in the parking lot and the blimps and the fireworks and the parties and Roxbury and the Playboy Mansion and the celebrities and the Bills' ineptitude and the Cowboys' precociousness and the leaky water pipe in Dallas's pregame locker room and the absence of toilet paper in Buffalo's pregame locker room and the pomp and the circumstance and the sensory overload, there was a football game. A game that at its core was not that much different than the two full-scale scrimmages, the five exhibition games, the sixteen regular-season games and the two play-off games the Cowboys endured to reach the Rose Bowl in Pasadena on January 31, 1993.

It was a football game that could have turned on the most elementary of mistakes. The Cowboys gained one yard on three plays on their first possession of the game. On fourth down from the Dallas 16-yard line, rookie Robert Jones forgot to block anybody. Buffalo special-team ace Steve Tasker took advantage, stuffing a Mike Saxon punt and giving the Bills the football 10 yards from the Cowboys' end zone. Five plays (and a Kelly fumble forced by Haley but recovered by the quarterback) later, Thurman Thomas scored from two yards out for Buffalo's 7-0 lead.

There was concern on the Dallas sideline. Defensive line coach Butch Davis tried to give instructions to his unit, but frustration caused some of them to snap at him. Haley interceded. "Hey, hey, everyone listen one minute," Haley told his mates. "Butch is over here trying to help us. We have to communicate with each other and not get excited. Let's not get excited."

Charles Haley as a calming influence? "Does it surprise you to learn I contribute positives?" Haley asks. Notes Johnson: "For whatever flaws you want to hang on Charles, the younger (defensive linemen) listen to him. They follow him like puppies."

When Kenny Gant's blitz of Kelly forced a bad throw intercepted by safety James Washington, the game's tone suggested the public might finally get its elusive "classic Super Bowl." That turnover — a definitive sign of things to come — led to the Aikman-to-Jay Novacek touchdown pass of 23 yards that tied the score.

But fifteen seconds later, on the Bills' first play after their kickoff return started them at the 10-yard line, Haley forced another Kelly fumble. And by finishing the first of three sequences when Dallas scored a pair of touchdowns within a minute of each other, Jimmie Jones almost made his Saturday night vision come true.

"I lined up anticipating a double-team," says Jones, a backup taking his turn as part of the Cowboys' rotation scheme.

"But when the ball was snapped and I got off the ball pretty good, I was one-on-one with the guy. I 'swimmed' him outside, and when I got around him, I saw the ball coming right into my arms."

Haley had switched from right end to left, and used an outside rush to whip around Buffalo tackle Howard Ballard. Haley popped Kelly as the quarterback was cocking his arm. The ball caromed off Cowboys lineman Leon Lett and toward Jones.

"I grabbed it with an arm, then put it in my hands," says Jones, who was two yards from the end zone when he got a grip. "And by that time, Kelly was the only guy in my way, and he was on the ground. All I did was try to go airborne. One-step, two-step, jump, like that.

"It was a little déjà vu, because that whole week I was preparing myself, thinking in my mind, visualizing myself scoring a touchdown in the Super Bowl. The night before the game, I was in my hotel room with my eyes closed, picturing a fumble, picturing me picking it up, then running it in and doing my touchdown dance. Defensive players don't get many chances to score, so it's a good idea to plan in advance. But my touchdown happened so quick, and I was so numb when I got in there, I couldn't do my dance.

"The way I visualized it," Jones said, "it was supposed to be a long, long run, so I could have time to get my celebration ready."

Maybe Jones unknowingly lost half of his visualization when it seeped telepathically into Leon Lett's brain. Jones got the early defensive touchdown from close in. Another backup defensive lineman, Lett, got the lengthy run. But he also suffered humiliation of celebrating his good fortune three yards too quickly.

"I sprinted 64 yards for nothing," says the massive Lett, who scooped up a fumble by Bills quarterback Frank Reich and headed toward the glory of a late-game touchdown that would have allowed the Dallas defense to outscore the Bills offense 21-17. "The little guy (Bills receiver Don Beebe) knocked it out of my hands. I couldn't believe that. The score was 52-17. It would have been like kicking sand in their faces, so it really didn't matter. But it mattered to me. I wanted it so bad. I shouldn't have done that."

Says Jimmie Jones: "He should have learned a lesson by watching me. You've got to cross the white marker first, then you celebrate. Ever since that, we rag on him. He'll be watching Monday Night Football someday, and they'll do that 'You Make The Call' commercial. And 'Big Cat' (Lett) is going to know the answer before everybody because it's going to be him on the screen."

But most everything the Cowboys did after the Saxon blocked punt and before Leon's Lett-down helped complete Aikman's idea of "a perfect day."

Johnson had preached that turnovers would be the key to the Super Bowl. "Fellas," he said in the days leading up to the game, "Buffalo will put the ball on the ground. They will turn the ball over."

Dallas pilfered a Super Bowl-record nine footballs. The fumble recoveries came from Jimmie Jones (who had two), Lett, Clayton Holmes and Ken Norton, who dribbled his gift nine yards for the touchdown that gave Dallas fifty-two points. "I hope I set my VCR right at home," Norton said. The interceptions came from Washington, Larry Brown, and safety Thomas Everett, who contributed two picks. One of those capped a goal-line stand that came with the Bills one yard away from tying the score at 14-all.

The Cowboys had prepared extensively on goal-line defense. In the second quarter, two Buffalo drives reached the one-yard line. The Bills got just three points out of the trips. "All day," says Everett, "we knew what they were going to do."

On first-and-goal from the four, Carwell Gardner pushed the Bills to the one. On second down, linebacker Vinson Smith corralled Thurman Thomas for no gain. On third down, Norton crashed into Kenneth Davis inches from the end zone and drove him back. "Face-to-face, chin-to-chin," Norton says. "I couldn't give ground."

Levy decided he might have better luck throwing for it on fourth down. Wannstedt guessed as much, so after considering sending in his short-yardage personnel and instructions to play man-to-man in the secondary, he kept in his standard unit and zone coverage. Levy saw Dallas's personnel, thought about calling a timeout, but didn't. He instead allowed Kelly to go with a play that asked him to throw a pass against a defense primed for it.

"Originally we were thinking they'd run," Wannstedt says. "But we eventually decided to get the people out there who could help us defend whatever they called."

One of those people was Everett. The Pittsburgh Steelers thought Everett was greedy, and in a sense, they were correct. On September 19, 1992, they still hadn't resolved their contract dispute with the Daingerfield, Texas, native and erased their problem by virtually giving him to the Cowboys. Dallas had been interested in Everett all summer, since being told of his availability in a casual conversation with San Diego Chargers general manager Bobby Beathard. Johnson's initial inquiries found the Steelers asking for a No. 2 pick; the eventual price, discovered by Jerry Jones when he was shooting the bull with Steelers officials at an owners meeting at the D/FW Airport, was a No. 5.

Is Everett greedy? His two interceptions in the Super Bowl say it is so.

Says Maryland: "We worked for days and days on their goal-line offense, on how they might throw in that situation. We worked on their running plays in close. We knew they liked to pull the guard on the outside on the run. On that third-down run, they pulled that guard, and Ken Norton read it like a book. On the pass, Everett read it the same way."

The Cowboys thought Thomas capable of beating them, especially as a screen-pass receiver. But they believed a harassed Kelly was a worthless Kelly. Gant's pressure caused that Washington interception; Kelly tried to force a timing pass, which is a tough way for a quarterback to make a living.

"We wanted to see Kelly make plays," end Tony Tolbert says. "From an athletic standpoint, we weren't worried about him like a Steve Young or a Randall Cunningham. If he was going to beat us, he'd have to throw (as receivers made their breaks). Because we had pressure on him, he couldn't even do that."

On this fourth-down play, Tolbert applied the pressure. Following the Cowboys' thinking, Kelly forced the pass into traffic. Gardner and tight end Pete Metzelaars were in the neighborhood of the throw, but Everett rose above both to steal the pass and avert one of the few Bills' challenges.

Kelly wasn't a factor. Norton knocked him out of the game midway through the second period on one of the Cowboys' featured inside blitzes. Thomas wasn't a factor, managing just 19 rushing yards before tipping his hat (he had no trouble locating it this time) to Emmitt Smith as the superior runner. Not even the high-speed tempo of the Bills' no-huddle offense made a difference. In practice, the Cowboys used two rotating offenses to rapid-fire plays at their defense. While the first group ran a play, the second group huddled and waited its turn. After that play concluded, the second group sprinted on the field to run its play. Normally, that's not enough to combat a Bills attack that prohibits defenses from making situational substitutions, thereby exposing defenses' lack of depth.

It had the converse effect on the Cowboys. It revealed their excess of depth.

"What about that no-huddle?" Washington says. "We proved that any eleven people we had on the field were versatile enough to stay on the field, if we had to. And we just made our substitutions during the natural breaks in the game, so people got to see what (Lett and Jimmie Jones and other backups) could do.

"The only hurry-up offense we saw was them hurrying up to get to the sideline when they gave us the ball."

Meanwhile, the Cowboys offense was hurrying to put the ball in the end zone. First came the fourteen points within fifteen seconds. Then, with two minutes left before intermission came fourteen more points in eighteen seconds, all scored by Michael Irvin.

"We thought they'd spend the day coming up to take away the run, with a nine-man front," Irvin says. "Instead, they were in a 'Cover-2' (with the safeties helping the cornerbacks to double-cover the wideouts), so that was our first miscalculation. I was praying I'd see some man coverage all day, then finally, I saw it. And so did Troy. I was telling guys on the sideline that if they ever tried to get me one-on-one, it'd be a joke. It was."

Irvin worked against Bills right corner Nate Odomes for a 19-yard touchdown. Dallas was up 21-10, Buffalo had the ball, and Irvin was certain he was done working against man coverage.

"But no," he says. "We get the ball back (on a fumble forced by Lett and recovered by Jones) at the 18-yard line, and I see it again. My eyes got big as saucers."

This time, Irvin was opposed alone by the left corner, James Williams. Irvin hung in the air and wrapped himself around the Aikman bullet a few yards short of the end zone, then stretched in for the 28-10 halftime edge.

Johnson danced off the Rose Bowl field with his fists in the air, as if the game was over. It was, and he told his Cowboys that once they shut the locker room door.

"Remember what Buffalo did to Houston!" players reminded one another, recalling that the Bills had staged a miracle comeback in the first round of the AFC play-offs to overcome a thirty-two-point deficit to win. "Remember Houston!"

Johnson let the players have their say, then seized the motivational moment.

"Screw Houston!" he barked. "We ain't Houston! We're the Dallas Cowboys!"

Says center Mark Stepnoski: "When we first got into the play-offs, Jimmy told us, 'Let's go 2-0 and see what happens in the Super Bowl from there.' But there was also that theme of his about making our last game our best game, so the idea that we'd go to and win the Super Bowl was built in, too. Once we were there, and in a position to win the thing, Jimmy and all the coaches did a good job emphasizing that we could win by just playing to our abilities and not making mistakes.

"He told the guys to not try and be superhuman. Except maybe for Troy, Michael and Emmitt, who seem to be able to do things that are normal to them but extraordinary to everybody else."

The heavenly status that had always been afforded the Cowboys in the Metroplex was about to go world-wide.

Stepnoski traveled all the way to Germany for an off-season vacation and was still recognized by other tourists. Throughout the Cowboys basketball team's off-season tour of Texas, it was greeted "by limousines, police escorts and bottles of Dom Perignon at every stop," Irvin says. Female membership at The Fellowship of Las Colinas reportedly increased substantially; The Fellowship of Las Colinas is Aikman's church.

In Waco, kicker Lin Elliott "noticed kids looking at me big-eyed." In Hawaii, tackle Mark Tuinei was an idol to the homefolks, who approached him on the streets and begged him not to retire. "I've been in the league ten years, and after every one I sit down with my wife (Pono) and assess my future," he says. "Because of that, everyone thought I might retire. They were all patting me on the back, telling me I can't retire now because we're going to win another Super Bowl this year. Like it's that easy."

In Cincinnati, backup linebacker Dixon Edwards — a bit player whose only substantial time in 1992 came in the Super Bowl when Godfrey Myles's knee injury created a Nickel vacancy — was given the key to the city. "Can you believe it? They had a Dixon Edwards Day for a guy who doesn't even get on the field much," Edwards marvels.

Smith and Irvin were each behind the wheels of their Mercedes convertibles one spring day when they looked behind them down Interstate-635 and realized they were the lead cars in an impromptu parade.

"People were trying to catch us to see if that was really Emmitt Smith and Michael Irvin," Irvin says.

"Next time," Smith says, "if we want to sneak around, we better drive our pickup trucks."

Oddly, the most trying post-Super Bowl event came in the city of Dallas itself, which offered its unique contribution to the festive mood on February 9, 1993, when it attempted to honor its heroes by holding a victory parade. It didn't draw the 20,000 people who visited Bill Bates's ranch for a pep rally before the Eagles play-off game, or the 67,900 who jammed Texas Stadium for a similar celebration before the 49ers NFC Championship Game. An estimated 400,000 people jammed downtown Dallas for the parade and a rally at City Hall Plaza. Planners unwisely allowed the Cowboys to ride in convertibles rather than high on flatbed trucks. The crush of overexuberant fans who swarmed the parade route and tried to touch the players and their wives and children made it a frightening experience for all. The scene was worsened by hooligans who committed more than seventy-five major crimes, injured fifty people and sent twenty-one people to the hospital. Most reports indicated many of the conflicts were racially motivated.

That night, Irvin hurriedly altered the message on his answering machine. "I tried to get him to take it off of there," says Irvin's wife, Sandy. "I thought it sounded flip."

Irvin's voice on the answering machine mimicked the voice of Rodney King, the alleged victim of Los Angeles police brutality whose case created a riot in L.A. a year before. "Peace," said Irvin's machine. "Can't we all just get along?"

Irvin was at D/FW Airport in March attempting to coordinate the Cowboys' basketball team's travel plans when he began berating his assistant and friend, Anthony Montoya. Montoya was to blame for a travel glitch, and Irvin loudly let his displeasure be known.

A woman tapped Irvin on the shoulder and said, "Mr. Irvin, my son idolizes you. You are his role model. He loves you. And I'm sure glad he wasn't here to see this."

"Lady," Irvin said, "sit down here and let me explain something to you. Some people are football players. Some people are businessmen. I happen to be both. If you and your

son can't separate Michael Irvin the football player who per-
forms on Sundays from Michael Irvin the businessman who is
responsible for transporting this basketball team around the
state, that's your problem. Because it's not my full-time job to
be your son's role model. If you think it is, then you should be
paying my black ass to be his nanny."

Aikman's similar reluctance to "always be on" is what
caused him and Hawaii to find one another unpleasant. Two
days before the parade back in Dallas, Aikman ditched Honolulu and the Pro Bowl in the game's third quarter. "I would
have rather not had the Pro Bowl thing happen," agent Leigh
Steinberg says. "It was not exactly part of what you lay out
when you're trying to create a plan to market the Super Bowl
MVP. But the way things happened is a part of who Troy is. He
tolerates people's bull for about two seconds. I mean, you
aren't going to get him to do a 'Rocky' movie dressed in a
caveman suit. That's part of Troy Aikman's charm."

A week later, Aikman was summoned to New York to meet
with NFL commissioner Paul Tagliabue, who would assess the
quarterback a $10,000 fine for going AWOL in Honolulu. After
the meeting, Aikman bumped into Dallas broadcaster Brad
Sham and his wife, Peggy. The trio agreed to share a quiet, low-
key dinner somewhere. Aikman suggested they convene at his
upper-crust Manhattan hotel, the Michaelangelo. Sham laughed
and suggested they meet at his quarters, the Boxtree Hotel,
which was far more suited to "quiet and low-key." Sham
explained to Aikman that any time the Super Bowl MVP
quarterback of the Dallas Cowboys wished to avoid being
mobbed, he should avoid high-profile venues like the
Michaelangelo.

"Naw," Aikman said. "Not in New York. They don't care
about that here, do they?"

"You just don't get the magnitude of all this, do you?" Sham said.

"I guess I don't," replied Aikman, grinning that crooked grin.

There are 615,000 words in the English language[1], 200,000 of which are commonly used by most of us. The other 415,000? They are busy being used by the 1992 Cowboys in their attempts to capture the almost indescribably sublime feeling of winning a Super Bowl.

Newton: "I am so filled with joy. ... If I could explode, I would. But I can't, because my insurance ain't paid up."

Emmitt Smith: "The greatest day of my life was being born. This is my second greatest day."

Irvin says he instructed Johnson to order Super Bowl rings with "diamonds bigger than headlights. I want to be able to turn off my Mercedes lights, stick my hand out the window and still be able to see where I'm going."

Haley does not wear the two Super Bowl rings he earned in San Francisco. He says he will wear this one. "It's very symbolic of the emotional struggle I've gone through," Haley says. "The Cowboys gave me unconditional acceptance, even after a lot of negative things were said about me. I kind of expected the guys to think, 'Here's a guy who will come unglued at any second.' But they let me be myself. ... I feel like a newborn child."

Immediately after the Super Bowl, Aikman said, "A tremendous weight has been lifted off my shoulders."

He looks at the quote now and, reading between his own lines, realizes why teams don't repeat.

1. *Oxford English Dictionary*

"Without question, some people get satisfied after accomplishing something they've spent their whole lives striving for," Aikman says. "You combine that with situations where players start to think they're worth more money, and they start to resent each other, and then jealousy creeps in.

"I try to do my best to spread around the attention that a quarterback naturally gets. That's how I'll try to prevent that stuff from creeping in here. I don't think it will happen here. But honestly, what I'm saying about how we'll avoid the pitfalls is the same thing every Super Bowl champion says every year, isn't it?"

Jimmy Johnson refuses to shrink at the mention of a Cowboys dynasty. "We'll be a better team (in 1993) than we were when we were the Super Bowl champions," he promises. Jerry Jones says he thinks the Cowboys will maintain their excellence because of "the great tradition of this franchise."

But are the Cowboys truly inherently special? No.

"I mean this from the bottom of my heart," says Wannstedt, now looking at the Cowboys as the coach of the Chicago Bears. "A lot of teams are as talented as we were. A lot of coaches are as good we are. The thing that got us over the hump was the relationships of the people involved. It's the people. Not tradition or mystique or that crap. Jimmy had relationships with the people on his staff. That filtered down to the players and onto the field. You hear about the nightmares on other staffs, with people attacking each other. We never had any of that, because of Jimmy."

In other words, this legendary franchise is only as special as its curators are. And it's curators' ability to keep the hatchet buried, to paraphrase Aikman, is what will determine whether the Cowboys live up to the "Team of the 1990s" tag to which they aspire. Was the Aikman-Johnson truce a one-shot deal, and will it go sour if the team does? To what extent will Dave Wannstedt, the defensive coordinator to players and confidant to the head coach, be missed? Is the Jones-Johnson pairing a long-term one, or just one that blossomed because of their shared championship experience? Will the hatchets of ego and jealously and burnout chop away at the Cowboys foundation?

"When you look at how often it's happened other places where they've had success," Wannstedt says, "it may happen in Dallas. But I'd bet Jimmy and Jerry will keep themselves in line."

Johnson sometimes dreams about escaping the pressures of his world when his contract expires after the 1999 season and moving permanently into his Galveston beach house. "Just get some cold beer and relax," he sighs. But when you ask him to seriously analyze his future, he makes it sound like he'll be with the Cowboys until death — like the almost tragic February 1993 scuba accident in the Bahamas when he went down without sufficient air in his tank — do they part.

"For fifteen years, I've been thinking the same thing at the end of the season," Johnson says. "Part of me starts immediately evaluating and looking forward to the next year, and part of me starts thinking what it would be like to spend more time on that beach. But after five days in the Bahamas, I'm ready to come back to work."

Jones sees things the same way.

"As far as burnout is concerned, I certainly couldn't have continued at the same pace I went at my first three or four years here," he says. "I never worked that hard in my life. We were doing new things when we started in 1989, and we kept doing new things seemingly every week. We did things no one had done before, and there was no book out there to teach us how to do it. It was constant pressure, like playing option quarterback every minute of every day. Now, there is less pressure. And more confidence.

"The Jimmy-Jerry thing is overplayed, especially now. There was a time, before we became accustomed to working together every day, when it wasn't as comfortable as we needed it to be. Sometimes, what I was doing I felt was in the best interests of the team and him. But it wasn't necessarily apparent to him that that's what I was doing. And sometimes he was doing things in my best interests that on first blush, I didn't perceive that way. Now we give each other the benefit of the doubt.

"Jimmy will be here for a long, long time. We'll end up extending his contract. I feel that, because I think we're just settling in. There will always be enough challenges to keep Jimmy and me motivated, and there will always been enough success for it to be fun for us."

As the Cowboys completed their Super Bowl rout with an Elliott field goal and touchdowns from Smith, Norton and Alvin Harper (who grabbed a 45-yard heave from Aikman then spiked the ball over the crossbar), Newton, Maryland and others orchestrated a sideline plot to cover Johnson in something besides glory.

"When there's two minutes left, let's get him," Maryland said.

Newton and Haley hoisted a cooler full of ice water above Johnson and spilled it on their coach. Haley screamed into Johnson's ear, "That's what we've been waiting for all year, coach!" Then Emmitt Smith jumped into the fray to rearrange the Johnson hairdo.

The Dallas Cowboys had visited their sixth Super Bowl and had won their third. The new regime had needed just four years to return "America's Team" to its former luster.

Jones and Johnson, the two men who'd spent four years of their lives repairing the Cowboys and building a dream, suddenly had nothing left to do. There were no trades to be made, no rookies to be drafted, no egos to massage, no contracts to negotiate, no butts to kiss, no topics to be argued, no skeptics to convince. Nothing to fix. Except for Johnson's hair.

As they were walking away from their 52-17 victory in Super Bowl XXVII, Jones produced a comb, and meticulously guided Johnson's brown-gray mane back into place.

Jerry Jones positions himself near the television in the bar and enjoys a cool drink, a cool breeze and a cool reception from the bartender when he requests the TV be switched to ESPN.

"Let's listen to this for a minute," says Jones, who then watches intently an ESPN report on. ... Jerry Jones.

Actually, the story unfolds into a "Building of the Cowboys" piece, a retrospective look at the franchise's evolution starting with February 1989, when Jones bought the franchise. It recounts the time when he drew chortles with the statement that might have been Johnson's epitaph: "What Jimmy will bring to us is worth more than if we had five first-round draft choices or four Heisman Trophy winners."

The report skims all the headlines. The hiring of Johnson. The firing of Tom Landry and Tex Schramm. The drafting of Troy Aikman and Emmitt Smith. The trading of Herschel Walker. The turnaround of a 1-15 laughingstock into a Super Bowl champion once again worthy of the "America's Team" tag.

Jones knows the story by heart. Hell, he helped write the story, and it's his face up on the screen talking about the story. Still, he cannot resist its living-color lure.

"Excuse me," Jones says, bugging the bartender again. "Can you turn it up a little louder?"